Foreign Policy Speeches of Obama

Edited by John Davis
Trinity Washington University

cognella™
San Diego, CA

Bassim Hamadeh, Publisher
Michael Simpson, Vice President of Acquisitions
Christopher Foster, Vice President of Marketing
Jessica Knott, Managing Editor
Stephen Milano, Creative Director
Kevin Fahey, Cognella Marketing Program Manager
Melissa Barcomb, Acquisitions Editor
Luiz Ferreira, Licensing Associate

First published in the United States of America in 2012 by University Readers, Inc.

15 14 13 12 11 1 2 3 4 5

Printed in the United States of America

ISBN: 978-1-60927-106-0

www.cognella.com 800.200.3908

Contents

Preface

In commenting on President Barack Obama and his stewardship of U.S. foreign policy, Henry N. Nau remarked in *Policy Review* that "Obama takes on problems as he inherits them. He reacts to what history serves up and sees the world as a complex system in which everything is interconnected. Problems have to be addressed comprehensively, or, like squeezing a balloon, progress in one area will only distort progress in others. He thinks and acts systematically, puzzling about how things fit together; he does not think and act strategically, identifying key problems that cause or unlock other problems. His style is oriented toward 'fixing' the world, rather than 'shaping' it."

Nau's statement is consistent with the prevailing view that after his historic election President Barack Obama assumed the stewardship of U.S. foreign policy during a period when the United States finds itself in an on-going struggle with Osama bin Laden's transnational terrorist network, two major wars (Afghanistan and Iraq), the rise of China, declining relations with Russia, an uneven and often frustrating relationship with Pakistan, a battered American image abroad, among a plethora of issues that continue to dominate his administration.

Over the course of his presidency, one question symbolizes a major dilemma concerning President Obama's management of American foreign policy: Does the president have a strategy and a vision in place to implement his goals? The answer is no. Additionally, within the foreign policy establishment there are those that observe that with no overarching framework, Obama's speeches have been the most prevalent source of information about the direction of the administration's foreign policy agenda.

It is these speeches and remarks by President Obama on the subject of foreign policy that forms the basis for compiling this volume. Similarly, this volume represents an effort to provide a comprehensive representation of President Barack Obama's stewardship of U.S. foreign policy through the prism of critical speeches and statements on numerous issues that could ultimately provide invaluable information that will assist in determining Obama's presidential legacy.

In a note to the reader, a host of Obama's speeches have been eliminated for a variety of reasons. First, numerous foreign policy speeches that offered insight into President Obama's position on a host of countries and subjects were omitted or deleted from this volume. For example, Japan, Somalia and the subject of piracy were omitted. The central reason associated with the decision to omit Japan and much of South East Asia, Somalia and other countries along with the subject of piracy and other significant issues is that space represented the critical operational variable in the calculus of what would be included and excluded.

A second variable concerned the issue of redundancy or repetition. Specifically, many of Obama's speeches that dealt with Middle East Peace were ultimately excluded from the volume. Though there was much substance to those speeches, however, in the absence of definitive progress on the always dysfunctional Israeli-Palestinian dispute they were deleted from this volume. Similarly, since many of Obama's speeches on this subject have been incessantly mentioned across presidential administrations, particularly remarks that outline the presidents "position on peace in the region," the editor decided to showcase speeches and remarks that elevated two new areas in the most volatile region in the world: President Obama's speeches "Establishing Relations with the Muslim World" and those that concern his response to the "Arab Awakening."

The decision to determine what would be included involved the following. Initially, a host of questions were posed to professors and scholars: During the 2008 presidential campaign what were the issues that represented the themes that identified the direction and represented core issues that were addressed during that period? Thereafter, the editor assessed the extent to which President Obama employed speeches or remarks as a vehicle for introducing those subjects that would form the core of the president's foreign policy agenda.

Second, another issue emerged as a significant factor in what would be considered for this volume involved a host of new issues that developed during the Obama presidency which occupied the attention of the new administration or forced the president and senior foreign policy advisors into reactive mode. A major example of an "emergent issue" that occupied the attention of President Obama and his team of senior advisors is the Arab Awakening (a quest for democratic reform sweeping the Middle East).

A third decision that determined which speeches would appear in this volume concerned those issues that represented the "unfinished business" of the administration of George W. Bush that became immediate priorities of the Obama administration. Some of the obvious issues include the continuation of the war on terror against al Qaeda, the Iraq and Afghanistan Wars, Iran's acquisition of nuclear weapons, the threat posed by North Korea's continuing acquisition and possible use of nuclear weapons represent a few notable examples.

Finally, the specific speeches included in this volume include the following: Senator Obama's speech to the Chicago Council on Global Affairs which defined his foreign policy priorities (the reader will learn the bulk of these issues would indeed form the basis of President Obama's agenda) both during and after the 2008 presidential campaign include climate change, Obama and the United Nations, regional coverage of Africa, Latin America, and Europe; democratic change sweeping the Middle East, bilateral relations with China, India, and Russia, Obama and the Nobel Peace Prize, nuclear proliferation—Iran and North Korea, the president's response to transnational terrorism, and Barack Obama: the War Time President.

Introduction

G ood morning. We all know that these are not the best of times for America's reputation in the world. We know what the war in Iraq has cost us in lives and treasure, in influence and respect. We have seen the consequences of a foreign policy based on a flawed ideology, and a belief that tough talk can replace real strength and vision.

Many around the world are disappointed with our actions. And many in our own country have come to doubt either our wisdom or our capacity to shape events beyond our borders. Some have even suggested that America's time has passed. But while we know what we have lost as a consequence of this tragic war, I also know what I have found in my travels over the past two years. In an old building in Ukraine, I saw test tubes filled with anthrax and the plague lying virtually unlocked and unguarded—dangers we were told could only be secured with America's help.

On a trip to the Middle East, I met Israelis and Palestinians who told me that peace remains a distant hope without the promise of American leadership. At a camp along the border of Chad and Darfur, refugees begged for America to step in and help stop the genocide that has taken their mothers and fathers, sons and daughters. And along the crowded streets of Kenya, I met throngs of children who asked if they'd ever get the chance to visit that magical place called America.

So I reject the notion that the American moment has passed. I dismiss the cynics who say that this new century cannot be another when, in the words of President Franklin Roosevelt, we lead the world in battling immediate evils and promoting the ultimate good.

I still believe that America is the last, best hope of Earth. We just have to show the world why this is so. This President may occupy the White House, but for the last six years the position of leader of the free world has remained open. And it's time to fill that role once more.

Remarks of Senator Barack Obama to the Chicago Council on Global Affairs, April 24, 2007. http:// www.realclearpolitics.com/articles/2007/04/remarks _ of_senator _barack _obama .html.

I believe that the single most important job of any President is to protect the American people. And I am equally convinced that doing that job effectively in the 21st century will require a new vision of American leadership and a new conception of our national security—a vision that draws from the lessons of the past, but is not bound by outdated thinking.

In today's globalized world, the security of the American people is inextricably linked to the security of all people. When Narco-trafficking and corruption threaten democracy in Latin America, it's America's problem too. When poor villagers in Indonesia have no choice but to send chickens to market infected with avian flu, it cannot be seen as a distant concern. When religious schools in Pakistan teach hatred to young children, our children are threatened as well.

Whether it's global terrorism or pandemic disease, dramatic climate change or the proliferation of weapons of mass annihilation, the threats we face at the dawn of the 21st century can no longer be contained by borders and boundaries.

The horrific attacks on that clear September day awakened us to this new reality. And after 9/11, millions around the world were ready to stand with us. They were willing to rally to our cause because it was their cause too—because they knew that if America led the world toward a new era of global cooperation, it would advance the security of people in our nation and all nations.

We now know how badly this Administration squandered that opportunity. In 2002, I stated my opposition to the war in Iraq, not only because it was an unnecessary diversion from the struggle against the terrorists who attacked us on September 11th, but also because it was based on a fundamental misunderstanding of the threats that 9/11 brought to light. I believed then, and believe now, that it was based on old ideologies and outdated strategies—a determination to fight a 21st century struggle with a 20th century mindset.

There is no doubt that the mistakes of the past six years have made our current task more difficult. World opinion has turned against us. And after all the lives lost and the billions of dollars spent, many Americans may find it tempting to turn inward, and cede our claim of leadership in world affairs.

I insist, however, that such an abandonment of our leadership is a mistake we must not make. America cannot meet the threats of this century alone, but the world cannot meet them without America. We must neither retreat from the world nor try to bully it into submission—we must lead the world, by deed and example.

We must lead by building a 21st century military to ensure the security of our people and advance the security of all people. We must lead by marshalling a global effort to stop the spread of the world's most dangerous weapons. We must lead by building and strengthening the partnerships and alliances necessary to meet our common challenges and defeat our common threats.

And America must lead by reaching out to all those living disconnected lives of despair in the world's forgotten corners—because while there will always be those who succumb to hate and strap bombs to their bodies, there are millions more who want to take another path—who want our beacon of hope to shine its light their way.

This election offers us the chance to turn the page and open a new chapter in American leadership. The disappointment that so many around the world feel toward America right now is only a testament to the high expectations they hold for us. We must meet those expectations again, not because being respected is an end in itself, but because the security of America and the wider world demands it.

This will require a new spirit—not of bluster and bombast, but of quiet confidence and sober intelligence, a spirit of care and renewed competence. It will also require a new leader. And as a candidate for President of the United States, I am asking you to entrust me with that responsibility. There are five ways America will begin to lead again when I'm President. Five ways to let the world know that we are committed to our common security, invested in our common humanity, and still a beacon of freedom and justice for the world.

The first way America will lead is by bringing a responsible end to this war in Iraq and refocusing on the critical challenges in the broader region. In a speech five months ago, I argued that there can be no military solution to what has become a political conflict between Sunni and Shi'a factions. And I laid out a plan that I still believe offers the best chance of pressuring these warring factions toward a political settlement—a phased withdrawal of American forces with the goal of removing all combat brigades from Iraq by March 31st, 2008.

I acknowledged at the time that there are risks involved in such an approach. That is why my plan provides for an over-the-horizon force that could prevent chaos in the wider region, and allows for a limited number of troops to remain in Iraq to fight al Qaeda and other terrorists.

But my plan also makes clear that continued U.S. commitment to Iraq depends on the Iraqi government meeting a series of well-defined benchmarks necessary to reach a political settlement. Thus far, the Iraqi government has made very little progress in meeting any of the benchmarks, in part because the President has refused time and again to tell the Iraqi government that we will not be there forever. The President's escalation of U.S. forces may bring a temporary reduction in the violence in Baghdad, at the price of increased U.S. casualties—though the experience so far is not encouraging. But it cannot change the political dynamic in Iraq. A phased withdrawal can.

Moreover, until we change our approach in Iraq, it will be increasingly difficult to refocus our efforts on the challenges in the wider region—on the conflict in the Middle East, where Hamas and Hezbollah feel emboldened and Israel's prospects for a secure peace seem uncertain; on Iran, which has been strengthened by the war in Iraq;

and on Afghanistan, where more American forces are needed to battle al Qaeda, track down Osama bin Laden, and stop that country from backsliding toward instability.

Burdened by Iraq, our lackluster diplomatic efforts leave a huge void. Our interests are best served when people and governments from Jerusalem and Amman to Damascus and Tehran understand that America will stand with our friends, work hard to build a peaceful Middle East, and refuse to cede the future of the region to those who seek perpetual conflict and instability. Such effective diplomacy cannot be done on the cheap, nor can it be warped by an ongoing occupation of Iraq. Instead, it will require patient, sustained effort, and the personal commitment of the President of the United States. That is a commitment I intend to make. The second way America will lead again is by building the first truly 21st century military and showing wisdom in how we deploy it.

We must maintain the strongest, best-equipped military in the world in order to defeat and deter conventional threats. But while sustaining our technological edge will always be central to our national security, the ability to put boots on the ground will be critical in eliminating the shadowy terrorist networks we now face. This is why our country's greatest military asset is the men and women who wear the uniform of the United States.

This administration's first Secretary of Defense proudly acknowledged that he had inherited the greatest fighting force in the nation's history. Six years later, he handed over a force that has been stretched to the breaking point, understaffed, and struggling to repair its equipment.

Two-thirds of the Army is now rated "not ready" for combat; 88% of the National Guard is not ready to deploy overseas, and many units cannot respond to a domestic emergency.

Our men and women in uniform are performing heroically around the world in some of the most difficult conditions imaginable. But the war in Afghanistan and the ill-advised invasion of Iraq have clearly demonstrated the consequences of underestimating the number of troops required to fight two wars and defend our homeland. That's why I strongly support the expansion of our ground forces by adding 65,000 soldiers to the Army and 27,000 Marines.

But adding troops isn't just about meeting a quota. It's about recruiting the best and brightest to service, and it's about keeping them in service by providing them with the first-rate equipment, armor, training, and incentives they deserve. It's about providing funding to enable the National Guard to achieve an adequate state of readiness again. And it's about honoring our veterans by giving them the respect and dignity they deserve and the care and benefits they have earned.

A 21st century military will also require us to invest in our men and women's ability to succeed in today's complicated conflicts. We know that on the streets of Baghdad, a little bit of Arabic can actually provide security to our soldiers. Yet, just a year ago, less than 1% of the American military could speak a language such as Arabic, Mandarin, Hindi, Urdu, or Korean. It's time we recognize these as critical skills for our military, and it's time we recruit and train for them.

Former Secretary Rumsfeld said, "You go to war with the Army you have, not the one you want." I say that if the need arises when I'm President, the Army we have will be the Army we need.

Of course, how we use our armed forces matters just as much as how they are prepared.

No President should ever hesitate to use force—unilaterally if necessary—to protect ourselves and our vital interests when we are attacked or imminently threatened. But when we use force in situations other than self-defense, we should make every effort to garner the clear support and participation of others—the kind of burden-sharing and support President George H.W. Bush mustered before he launched Operation Desert Storm.

And when we do send our men and women into harm's way, we must also clearly define the mission, prescribe concrete political and military objectives, seek out advice of our military commanders, evaluate the intelligence, plan accordingly, and ensure that our troops have the resources, support, and equipment they need to protect themselves and fulfill their mission.

We must take these steps with the knowledge that while sometimes necessary, force is the costliest weapon in the arsenal of American power in terms of lives and treasure. And it's far from the only measure of our strength.

In order to advance our national security and our common security, we must call on the full arsenal of American power and ingenuity. To constrain rogue nations, we must use effective diplomacy and muscular alliances. To penetrate terrorist networks, we need a nimble intelligence community—with strong leadership that forces agencies to share information, and invests in the tools, technologies and human intelligence that can get the job done. To maintain our influence in the world economy, we need to get our fiscal house in order. And to weaken the hand of hostile dictators, we must free ourselves from our oil addiction. None of these expressions of power can supplant the need for a strong military. Instead, they complement our military, and help ensure that the use of force is not our sole available option.

The third way America must lead again is by marshalling a global effort to meet a threat that rises above all others in urgency—securing, destroying, and stopping the spread of weapons of mass destruction.

As leaders from Henry Kissinger to George Shultz to Bill Perry to Sam Nunn have all warned, the actions we are taking today on this issue are simply not adequate to the danger. There is still about 50 tons of highly enriched uranium—some of it poorly secured—at civilian nuclear facilities in over forty countries around the world. In the former Soviet Union, there are still about 15,000 to 16,000 nuclear weapons and stockpiles of uranium and plutonium capable of making another 40,000 weapons scattered across 11 time zones. And people have already been caught trying to smuggle nuclear materials to sell them on the black market. We can do something about this. As President, I will lead a global effort to secure all nuclear weapons and material at vulnerable sites within four years—the most effective way to prevent terrorists from acquiring a bomb.

We know that Russia is neither our enemy nor close ally right now, and we shouldn't shy away from pushing for more democracy, transparency, and accountability in that country. But we also know that we can and must work with Russia to make sure every one of its nuclear weapons and every cache of nuclear material is secured. And we should fully implement the law I passed with Senator Dick Lugar that would help the United States and our allies detect and stop the smuggling of weapons of mass destruction throughout the world. While we work to secure existing stockpiles of nuclear material, we should also negotiate a verifiable global ban on the production of new nuclear weapons material.

As starting points, the world must prevent Iran from acquiring nuclear weapons and work to eliminate North Korea's nuclear weapons program. If America does not lead, these two nations could trigger regional arms races that could accelerate nuclear proliferation on a global scale and create dangerous nuclear flashpoints. In pursuit of this goal, we must never take the military option off the table. But our first line of offense here must be sustained, direct and aggressive diplomacy. For North Korea, that means ensuring the full implementation of the recent agreement. For Iran, it means getting the UN Security Council, Europe, and the Gulf States to join with us in ratcheting up the economic pressure.

We must also dissuade other countries from joining the nuclear club. Just the other day, it was reported that nearly a dozen countries in and around the Middle East—including Syria and Saudi Arabia—are interested in pursuing nuclear power.

Countries should not be able to build a weapons program under the auspices of developing peaceful nuclear power. That's why we should create an international fuel bank to back up commercial fuel supplies so there's an assured supply and no more excuses for nations like Iran to build their own enrichment plants. It's encouraging that the Nuclear Threat Initiative, backed by Warren Buffett, has already offered funding for this fuel bank, if matched two to one. But on an issue of this importance, the United States should not leave the solution to private philanthropies. It should be a central component of our national security, and that's why we should provide $50 million to get this fuel bank started and urge other nations, starting with Russia, to join us.

Finally, if we want the world to deemphasize the role of nuclear weapons, the United States and Russia must lead by example. President Bush once said, "The United States should remove as many weapons as possible from high-alert, hair-trigger status—another unnecessary vestige of Cold War confrontation." Six years later, President Bush has not acted on this promise. I will. We cannot and should not accept the threat of accidental or unauthorized nuclear launch. We can maintain a strong nuclear deterrent to protect our security without rushing to produce a new generation of warheads.

The danger of nuclear proliferation reminds us of how critical global cooperation will be in the 21st century. That's why the fourth way America must lead is to rebuild and construct the alliances and partnerships necessary to meet common challenges and confront common threats.

In the wake of the Second World War, it was America that largely built a system of international institutions that carried us through the Cold War. Leaders like Harry Truman and George Marshall knew that instead of constraining our power, these institutions magnified it.

Today it's become fashionable to disparage the United Nations, the World Bank, and other international organizations. In fact, reform of these bodies is urgently needed if they are to keep pace with the fast-moving threats we face. Such real reform will not come, however, by dismissing the value of these institutions, or by bullying other countries to ratify changes we have drafted in isolation. Real reform will come because we convince others that they too have a stake in change—that such reforms will make their world, and not just ours, more secure.

Our alliances also require constant management and revision if they are to remain effective and relevant. For example, over the last 15 years, NATO has made tremendous strides in transforming from a Cold War security structure to a dynamic partnership for peace.

Today, NATO's challenge in Afghanistan has become a test case, in the words of Dick Lugar, of whether the alliance can "overcome the growing discrepancy between NATO's expanding missions and its lagging capabilities."

We must close this gap, rallying members to contribute troops to collective security operations, urging them to invest more in reconstruction and stabilization, streamlining decision-making processes, and giving commanders in the field more flexibility.

And as we strengthen NATO, we should also seek to build new alliances and relationships in other regions important to our interests in the 21st century. In Asia, the emergence of an economically vibrant, more politically active China offers new opportunities for prosperity and cooperation, but also poses new challenges for the United States and our partners in the region. It is time for the United States to take a more active role here—to build on our strong bilateral relations and informal arrangements like the Six Party talks. As President, I intend to forge a more effective regional framework in Asia that will promote stability, prosperity and help us confront common transnational threats such as tracking down terrorists and responding to global health problems like avian flu.

In this way, the security alliances and relationships we build in the 21st century will serve a broader purpose than preventing the invasion of one country by another. They can help us meet challenges that the world can only confront together, like the unprecedented threat of global climate change.

This is a crisis that cannot be contained to one corner of the globe. Studies show that with each degree of warming, rice yields—the world's most significant crop—fall by 10%. By 2050 famine could displace more than 250 million people worldwide. That means people competing for food and water in the next fifty years in the very places that have known horrific violence in the last fifty: Africa, the Middle East, South Asia.

As the world's largest producers of greenhouse gases, America has the greatest responsibility to lead here. We must enact a cap and trade system that will dramatically reduce our carbon emissions. And we must finally free ourselves from our dependence on foreign oil by raising our fuel standards and harnessing the power of biofuels.

Such steps are not just environmental priorities, they are critical to our security. America must take decisive action in order to more plausibly demand the same effort from others. We should push for binding and enforceable commitments to reduce emissions by the nations which pollute the most—the United States, the European Union, Russia, China, and India together account for nearly two-thirds of current emissions. And we should help ensure that growth in developing countries is fueled by low-carbon energy—the market for which could grow to $500 billion by 2050 and spur the next wave of American entrepreneurship.

The fifth way America will lead again is to invest in our common humanity—to ensure that those who live in fear and want today can live with dignity and opportunity tomorrow. A recent report detailed al Qaeda's progress in recruiting a new generation of leaders to replace the ones we have captured or killed. The new recruits come from a broader range of countries than the old leadership—from Afghanistan to Chechnya, from Britain to Germany, from Algeria to Pakistan. Most of these recruits are in their early thirties.

They operate freely in the disaffected communities and disconnected corners of our interconnected world—the impoverished, weak and ungoverned states that have become the most fertile breeding grounds for transnational threats like terror and pandemic disease and the smuggling of deadly weapons.

Some of these terrorist recruits may have always been destined to take the path they did—accepting a tragically warped view of their religion in which God rewards the killing of innocents. But millions of young men and women have not.

Last summer I visited the Horn of Africa's Combined Joint Task Force, which was headquartered at Camp Lemonier in Djibouti. It's a U.S. base that was set up four years ago, originally as a place to launch counterterrorism operations. But recently, a major focus of the Task Force has been working with our diplomats and aid workers on operations to win hearts and minds. While I was there, I also took a helicopter ride with Admiral Hunt, the commander of the Task Force, to Dire Dawa, where the U.S. was helping provide food and water to Ethiopians who had been devastated by flooding.

One of the Navy captains who helps run the base recently told a reporter, "Our mission is at least 95 percent civil affairs. It's trying to get at the root causes of why people want to take on the U.S." The Admiral now in charge of the Task Force suggested that if they can provide dignity and opportunity to the people in that region, then, "the chance of extremism being welcomed greatly, if not completely, diminishes."

We have heard much over the last six years about how America's larger purpose in the world is to promote the spread of freedom—that it is the yearning of all who live in the shadow of tyranny and despair.

I agree. But this yearning is not satisfied by simply deposing a dictator and setting up a ballot box. The true desire of all mankind is not only to live free lives, but lives marked by dignity and opportunity; by security and simple justice.

Delivering on these universal aspirations requires basic sustenance like food and clean water; medicine and shelter. It also requires a society that is supported by the pillars of a sustainable democracy—a strong legislature, an independent judiciary, the rule of law, a vibrant civil society, a free press, and an honest police force. It requires building the capacity of the world's weakest states and providing them what they need to reduce poverty, build healthy and educated communities, develop markets, and generate wealth. And it requires states that have the capacity to fight terrorism, halt the proliferation of deadly weapons, and build the health care infrastructure needed to prevent and treat such deadly diseases as HIV/AIDS and malaria.

As President, I will double our annual investments in meeting these challenges to $50 billion by 2012 and ensure that those new resources are directed towards these strategic goals.

For the last twenty years, U.S. foreign aid funding has done little more than keep pace with inflation. Doubling our foreign assistance spending by 2012 will help meet the challenge laid out by Tony Blair at the 2005 G-8 conference at Gleneagles, and it will help push the rest of the developed world to invest in security and opportunity. As we have seen recently with large increases in funding for our AIDS programs, we have the capacity to make sure this funding makes a real difference.

Part of this new funding will also establish a two billion dollar Global Education Fund that calls on the world to join together in eliminating the global education deficit, similar to what the 9/11 commission proposed. Because we cannot hope to shape a world where opportunity outweighs danger unless we ensure that every child everywhere is taught to build and not to destroy.

I know that many Americans are skeptical about the value of foreign aid today. But as the U.S. military made clear in Camp Lemonier, a relatively small investment in these fragile states up front can be one of the most effective ways to prevent the terror and strife that is far more costly—both in lives and treasure—down the road. In this way, $50 billion a year in foreign aid—which is less than one-half of one percent of our GDP—doesn't sound as costly when you consider that last year, the Pentagon spent nearly double that amount in Iraq alone.

Finally, while America can help others build more secure societies, we must never forget that only the citizens of these nations can sustain them. The corruption I heard about while visiting parts of Africa has been around for decades, but the hunger to eliminate such corruption is a growing and powerful force among people there. And so in these places where fear and want still thrive, we must couple our aid with an insistent call for reform.

We must do so not in the spirit of a patron, but the spirit of a partner—a partner that is mindful of its own imperfections. Extending an outstretched hand to these states must ultimately be more than just a matter of expedience or even charity. It must be about recognizing the inherent equality and worth of all people. And it's about showing the world that America stands for something—that we can still lead.

These are the ways we will answer the challenge that arrived on our shores that September morning more than five years ago. A 21st century military to stay on the offense, from Djibouti to Kandahar. Global efforts to keep the world's deadliest weapons out of the world's most dangerous hands. Stronger alliances to share information, pool resources, and break up terrorist networks that operate in more than eighty countries. And a stronger push to defeat the terrorists' message of hate with an agenda for hope around the world.

It's time we had a President who can do this again—who can speak directly to the world, and send a message to all those men and women beyond our shores who long for lives of dignity and security that says "You matter to us. Your future is our future. And our moment is now."

It's time, as well, for a President who can build a consensus at home for this ambitious but necessary course. For in the end, no foreign policy can succeed unless the American people understand it and feel a stake in its success—and unless they trust that their government hears their more immediate concerns as well. After all, we will not be able to increase foreign aid if we fail to invest in security and opportunity for our own people. We cannot negotiate trade agreements to help spur development in poor countries so long as we provide no meaningful help to working Americans burdened by the dislocations of a global economy. We cannot expect Americans to support placing our men and women in harm's way if we cannot prove that we will use force wisely and judiciously.

But if the next President can restore the American people's trust—if they know that he or she is acting with their best interests at heart, with prudence and wisdom and some measure of humility—then I believe the American people will be ready to see America lead again.

They will be ready to show the world that we are not a country that ships prisoners in the dead of night to be tortured in far off countries. That we are not a country that runs prisons which lock people away without ever telling them why they are there or what they are charged with. That we are not a country which preaches compassion and justice to others while we allow bodies to float down the streets of a major American city. That is not who we are.

America is the country that helped liberate a continent from the march of a madman. We are the country that told the brave people of a divided city that we were Berliners too. We sent generations of young people to serve as ambassadors for peace in countries all over the world. And we're the country that rushed aid throughout Asia for the victims of a devastating tsunami.

Now it's our moment to lead—our generation's time to tell another great American story. So someday we can tell our children that this was the time when we helped forge peace in the Middle East. That this was the time when we confronted climate change and secured the weapons that could destroy the human race. This was the time when we brought opportunity to those forgotten corners of the world. And this was the time when we renewed the America that has led generations of weary travelers from all over the world to find opportunity, and liberty, and hope on our doorstep.

One of these travelers was my father. I barely knew him, but when, after his death, I finally took my first trip to his tiny village in Kenya and asked my grandmother if there was anything left from him, she opened a trunk and took out a stack of letters, which she handed to me. There were more than thirty of them, all handwritten by my father, all addressed to colleges and universities across America, all filled with the hope of a young man who dreamed of more for his life.

It is because someone in this country answered that prayer that I stand before you today with faith in our future, confidence in our story, and a determination to do my part in writing our country's next great chapter. The American moment has not passed. The American moment is here. And like generations before us, we will seize that moment, and begin the world anew. Thank you.

Chapter 1

Barack Obama and Climate Change

P RESIDENT OBAMA: **Thank you very much.** Good morning. I want to thank the Secretary General for organizing this summit, and all the leaders who are participating. That so many of us are here today is a recognition that the threat from climate change is serious, it is urgent, and it is growing. Our generation's response to this challenge will be judged by history, for if we fail to meet it—boldly, swiftly, and together—we risk consigning future generations to an irreversible catastrophe.

No nation, however large or small, wealthy or poor, can escape the impact of climate change. Rising sea levels threaten every coastline. More powerful storms and floods threaten every continent. More frequent droughts and crop failures breed hunger and conflict in places where hunger and conflict already thrive. On shrinking islands, families are already being forced to flee their homes as climate refugees. The security and stability of each nation and all peoples—our prosperity, our health, and our safety—are in jeopardy. And the time we have to reverse this tide is running out.

And yet, we can reverse it. John F. Kennedy once observed that "Our problems are man-made, therefore they may be solved by man." It is true that for too many years, mankind has been slow to respond or even recognize the magnitude of the climate threat. It is true of my own country, as well. We recognize that. But this is a new day. It is a new era. And I am proud to say that the United States has done more to promote clean energy and reduce carbon pollution in the last eight months than at any other time in our history.

We are making our government's largest ever investment in renewable energy—an investment aimed at doubling the generating capacity from wind and other renewable resources in three years. Across America, entrepreneurs are constructing wind turbines and solar panels and batteries for hybrid cars with the help of loan guarantees and

Remarks by the President at United Nations Secretary, General Ban Ki-Moon's Climate Change Summit, United Nations Headquarters, New York, New York, The White House, Office of the Press Secretary, For Immediate Release, September 22, 2009.

http://www.whitehouse.gov/the_press_office/Remarks-by-the-President-at-UN-Secretary-/

tax credits—projects that are creating new jobs and new industries. We're investing billions to cut energy waste in our homes, our buildings, and appliances—helping American families save money on energy bills in the process.

We've proposed the very first national policy aimed at both increasing fuel economy and reducing greenhouse gas pollution for all new cars and trucks—a standard that will also save consumers money and our nation oil. We're moving forward with our nation's first offshore wind energy projects. We're investing billions to capture carbon pollution so that we can clean up our coal plants. And just this week, we announced that for the first time ever, we'll begin tracking how much greenhouse gas pollution is being emitted throughout the country.

Later this week, I will work with my colleagues at the G20 to phase out fossil fuel subsidies so that we can better address our climate challenge. And already, we know that the recent drop in overall U.S. emissions is due in part to steps that promote greater efficiency and greater use of renewable energy.

Most importantly, the House of Representatives passed an energy and climate bill in June that would finally make clean energy the profitable kind of energy for American businesses and dramatically reduce greenhouse gas emissions. One committee has already acted on this bill in the Senate and I look forward to engaging with others as we move forward.

Because no one nation can meet this challenge alone, the United States has also engaged more allies and partners in finding a solution than ever before. In April, we convened the first of what have now been six meetings of the Major Economies Forum on Energy and Climate here in the United States. In Trinidad, I proposed an Energy and Climate Partnership for the Americas. We've worked through the World Bank to promote renewable energy projects and technologies in the developing world. And we have put climate at the top of our diplomatic agenda when it comes to our relationships with countries as varied as China and Brazil; India and Mexico; from the continent of Africa to the continent of Europe.

Taken together, these steps represent a historic recognition on behalf of the American people and their government. We understand the gravity of the climate threat. We are determined to act. And we will meet our responsibility to future generations.

But though many of our nations have taken bold action and share in this determination, we did not come here to celebrate progress today. We came because there's so much more progress to be made. We came because there's so much more work to be done.

It is work that will not be easy. As we head towards Copenhagen, there should be no illusions that the hardest part of our journey is in front of us. We seek sweeping but necessary change in the midst of a global recession, where every nation's most immediate priority is reviving their economy and putting their people back to work;

and so all of us will face doubts and difficulties in our own capitals as we try to reach a lasting solution to the climate challenge.

But I'm here today to say that difficulty is no excuse for complacency. Unease is no excuse for inaction. And we must not allow the perfect to become the enemy of progress. Each of us must do what we can when we can to grow our economies without endangering our planet—and we must all do it together. We must seize the opportunity to make Copenhagen a significant step forward in the global fight against climate change.

We also cannot allow the old divisions that have characterized the climate debate for so many years to block our progress. Yes, the developed nations that caused much of the damage to our climate over the last century still have a responsibility to lead—and that includes the United States. And we will continue to do so—by investing in renewable energy and promoting greater efficiency and slashing our emissions to reach the targets we set for 2020 and our long-term goal for 2050.

But those rapidly growing developing nations that will produce nearly all the growth in global carbon emissions in the decades ahead must do their part, as well. Some of these nations have already made great strides with the development and deployment of clean energy. Still, they need to commit to strong measures at home and agree to stand behind those commitments just as the developed nations must stand behind their own. We cannot meet this challenge unless all the largest emitters of greenhouse gas pollution act together. There's no other way.

We must also energize our efforts to put other developing nations—especially the poorest and most vulnerable—on a path to sustained growth. These nations do not have the same resources to combat climate change as countries like the United States or China do, but they have the most immediate stake in a solution. For these are the nations that are already living with the unfolding effects of a warming planet—famine, drought, disappearing coastal villages, and the conflicts that arise from scarce resources. Their future is no longer a choice between a growing economy and a cleaner planet, because their survival depends on both. It will do little good to alleviate poverty if you can no longer harvest your crops or find drinkable water. And that is why we have a responsibility to provide the financial and technical assistance needed to help these nations adapt to the impacts of climate change and pursue low-carbon development.

What we are seeking, after all, is not simply an agreement to limit greenhouse gas emissions. We seek an agreement that will allow all nations to grow and raise living standards without endangering the planet. By developing and disseminating clean technology and sharing our know-how, we can help developing nation's leap-frog dirty energy technologies and reduce dangerous emissions.

Mr. Secretary, as we meet here today, the good news is that after too many years of inaction and denial, there's finally widespread recognition of the urgency of the challenge before us. We know what needs to be done. We know that our planet's future depends on a global commitment to permanently reduce greenhouse gas pollution. We know that if we put the right rules and incentives in place, we will unleash the creative power of our best scientists and engineers and entrepreneurs to build a better world. And so many nations have already taken the first step on the journey towards that goal.

But the journey is long and the journey is hard. And we don't have much time left to make that journey. It's a journey that will require each of us to persevere through setbacks, and fight for every inch of progress, even when it comes in fits and starts. So let us begin. For if we are flexible and pragmatic, if we can resolve to work tirelessly in common effort, then we will achieve our common purpose: a world that is safer, cleaner, and healthier than the one we found; and a future that is worthy of our children. Thank you very much.

THE PRESIDENT: Good morning. It is an honor for me to join this distinguished group of leaders from nations around the world. We come here in Copenhagen because climate change poses a grave and growing danger to our people. All of you would not be here unless you—like me—were convinced that this danger is real. This is not fiction, it is science. Unchecked, climate change will pose unacceptable risks to our security, our economies, and our planet. This much we know.

The question, then, before us is no longer the nature of the challenge—the question is our capacity to meet it. For while the reality of climate change is not in doubt, I have to be honest, as the world watches us today, I think our ability to take collective action is in doubt right now, and it hangs in the balance.

I believe we can act boldly, and decisively, in the face of a common threat. That's why I come here today—not to talk, but to act. Now, as the world's largest economy and as the world's second largest emitter, America bears our responsibility to address climate change, and we intend to meet that responsibility. That's why we've renewed our leadership within international climate change negotiations. That's why we've worked with other nations to phase out fossil fuel subsidies. That's why we've taken bold action at home—by making historic investments in renewable energy; by putting our people to work increasing efficiency in our homes and buildings; and by pursuing comprehensive legislation to transform to a clean energy economy.

These mitigation actions are ambitious, and we are taking them not simply to meet global responsibilities. We are convinced, as some of you may be convinced, that changing the way we produce and use energy is essential to America's economic future—that it will create millions of new jobs, power new industries, keep us competitive, and

Remarks by the President at the Morning Plenary Session of the United Nations Climate Change Conference, Bella Center Copenhagen, Denmark, The White House, Office of the Press Secretary, For Immediate Release, April 13, 2010. http://www.whitehouse.gov/the-press-office/ remarks-president-opening-plenary-session-nuclear-security-summit.

spark new innovation. We're convinced, for our own self-interest, that the way we use energy, changing it to a more efficient fashion, is essential to our national security, because it helps to reduce our dependence on foreign oil, and helps us deal with some of the dangers posed by climate change.

So I want this plenary session to understand, America is going to continue on this course of action to mitigate our emissions and to move towards a clean energy economy, no matter what happens here in Copenhagen. We think it is good for us, as well as good for the world. But we also believe that we will all be stronger, all be safer, all be more secure if we act together. That's why it is in our mutual interest to achieve a global accord in which we agree to certain steps, and to hold each other accountable to certain commitments.

After months of talk, after two weeks of negotiations, after innumerable side meetings, bilateral meetings, endless hours of discussion among negotiators, I believe that the pieces of that accord should now be clear.

First, all major economies must put forward decisive national actions that will reduce their emissions, and begin to turn the corner on climate change. I'm pleased that many of us have already done so. Almost all the major economies have put forward legitimate targets, significant targets, ambitious targets. And I'm confident that America will fulfill the commitments that we have made: cutting our emissions in the range of 17 percent by 2020, and by more than 80 percent by 2050 in line with final legislation.

Second, we must have a mechanism to review whether we are keeping our commitments, and exchange this information in a transparent manner. These measures need not be intrusive, or infringe upon sovereignty. They must, however, ensure that an accord is credible, and that we're living up to our obligations. Without such accountability, any agreement would be empty words on a page.

I don't know how you have an international agreement where we all are not sharing information and ensuring that we are meeting our commitments. That doesn't make sense. It would be a hollow victory.

Number three, we must have financing that helps developing countries adapt, particularly the least developed and most vulnerable countries to climate change. America will be a part of fast-start funding that will ramp up to $10 billion by 2012. And yesterday, Secretary Hillary Clinton, my Secretary of State, made it clear that we will engage in a global effort to mobilize $100 billion in financing by 2020, if—and only if—it is part of a broader accord that I have just described.

Mitigation. Transparency. Financing. It's a clear formula—one that embraces the principle of common but differentiated responses and respective capabilities. And it adds up to a significant accord—one that takes us farther than we have ever gone before as an international community.

I just want to say to this plenary session that we are running short on time. And at this point, the question is whether we will move forward together or split apart, whether we prefer posturing to action. I'm sure that many consider this an imperfect framework that I just described. No country will get everything that it wants. There are those developing countries that want aid with no strings attached, and no obligations with respect to transparency. They think that the most advanced nations should pay a higher price; I understand that. There are those advanced nations who think that developing countries either cannot absorb this assistance, or that will not be held accountable effectively, and that the world's fastest-growing emitters should bear a greater share of the burden.

We know the fault lines because we've been imprisoned by them for years. These international discussions have essentially taken place now for almost two decades, and we have very little to show for it other than an increased acceleration of the climate change phenomenon. The time for talk is over. This is the bottom line: We can embrace this accord, take a substantial step forward, continue to refine it and build upon its foundation. We can do that, and everyone who is in this room will be part of a historic endeavor—one that makes life better for our children and our grandchildren.

Or we can choose delay, falling back into the same divisions that have stood in the way of action for years. And we will be back having the same stale arguments month after month, year after year, perhaps decade after decade, all while the danger of climate change grows until it is irreversible.

Ladies and gentlemen, there is no time to waste. America has made our choice. We have charted our course. We have made our commitments. We will do what we say. Now I believe it's the time for the nations and the people of the world to come together behind a common purpose.

We are ready to get this done today—but there has to be movement on all sides to recognize that it is better for us to act than to talk; it's better for us to choose action over inaction; the future over the past—and with courage and faith, I believe that we can meet our responsibility to our people, and the future of our planet. Thank you very much.

Chapter 2

Barack Obama and the Future of United Nations

M r. President, Mr. Secretary-General, fellow delegates, ladies and gentlemen: it is my honor to address you for the first time as the forty-fourth president of the United States. I come before you humbled by the responsibility that the American people have placed upon me; mindful of the enormous challenges of our moment in history; and determined to act boldly and collectively on behalf of justice and prosperity at home and abroad.

I have been in office for just nine months, though some days it seems a lot longer. I am well aware of the expectations that accompany my presidency around the world. These expectations are not about me.

Rather, they are rooted—I believe—in a discontent with a status quo that has allowed us to be increasingly defined by our differences, and outpaced by our problems. But they are also rooted in hope—the hope that real change is possible, and the hope that America will be a leader in bringing about such change.

I took office at a time when many around the world had come to view America with skepticism and distrust. Part of this was due to misperceptions and misinformation about my country. Part of this was due to opposition to specific policies, and a belief that on certain critical issues, America has acted unilaterally, without regard for the interests of others. This has fed an almost reflexive anti-Americanism, which too often has served as an excuse for our collective inaction.

Like all of you, my responsibility is to act in the interest of my nation and my people, and I will never apologize for defending those interests. But it is my deeply held belief that in the year 2009—more than at any point in human history—the interests of nations and peoples are shared.

Remarks by the President to the United Nations General Assembly, The White House, Office of the Press Secretary, For Immediate Release, September 23, 2009, United Nations Headquarters, New York, New York.[1]

The religious convictions that we hold in our hearts can forge new bonds among people, or tear us apart. The technology we harness can light the path to peace, or forever darken it. The energy we use can sustain our planet, or destroy it. What happens to the hope of a single child—anywhere—can enrich our world, or impoverish it.

In this hall, we come from many places, but we share a common future. No longer do we have the luxury of indulging our differences to the exclusion of the work that we must do together. I have carried this message from London to Ankara; from Port of Spain to Moscow; from Accra to Cairo; and it's what I will speak about today; because the time has come for the world to move in a new direction. We must embrace a new era of engagement based on mutual interests and mutual respect, and our work must begin now.

We know the future will be forged by deeds and not simply words. Speeches alone will not solve our problems—it will take persistent action. So for those who question the character and cause of my nation, I ask you to look at the concrete actions that we have taken in just nine months.

On my first day in office, I prohibited—without exception or equivocation—the use of torture by the United States of America. I ordered the prison at Guantánamo Bay closed, and we are doing the hard work of forging a framework to combat extremism within the rule of law. Every nation must know: America will live its values, and we will lead by example.

We have set a clear and focused goal: to work with all members of this body to disrupt, dismantle, and defeat al Qaeda and its extremist allies—a network that has killed thousands of people of many faiths and nations, and that plotted to blow up this very building. In Afghanistan and Pakistan, we—and many nations here—are helping those governments develop the capacity to take the lead in this effort, while working to advance opportunity and security for their people.

In Iraq, we are responsibly ending a war. We have removed American combat brigades from Iraqi cities, and set a deadline of next August to remove all of our combat brigades from Iraqi territory. And I have made clear that we will help Iraqis transition to full responsibility for their future, and keep our commitment to remove all American troops by the end of 2011.

I have outlined a comprehensive agenda to seek the goal of a world without nuclear weapons. In Moscow, the United States and Russia announced that we would pursue substantial reductions in our strategic warheads and launchers. At the conference on disarmament, we agreed on a work plan to negotiate an end to the production of fissile materials for nuclear weapons. And this week, my Secretary of State will become the first senior American representative to the annual members conference of the comprehensive test ban treaty.

Upon taking office, I appointed a special envoy for Middle East peace, and America has worked steadily and aggressively to advance the cause of two states—Israel and

Palestine—in which peace and security take root, and the rights of both Israelis and Palestinians are respected.

To confront climate change, we have invested $80 billion in clean energy. We have substantially increased our fuel-efficiency standards. We have provided new incentives for conservation, launched an energy partnership across the Americas, and moved from a bystander to a leader in international climate negotiations.

To overcome an economic crisis that touches every corner of the world, we worked with the G20 nations to forge a coordinated international response of over two trillion dollars in stimulus to bring the global economy back from the brink. We mobilized resources that helped prevent the crisis from spreading further to developing countries. And we joined with others to launch a $20bn global food security initiative that will lend a hand to those who need it most, and help them build their own capacity.

We have also reengaged the United Nations, We have paid our bills. We have joined the Human Rights Council. We have signed the convention on the rights of persons with disabilities. We have fully embraced the millennium development goals. And we address our priorities here, in this institution—for instance, through the Security Council meeting that I will chair tomorrow on nuclear non proliferation and disarmament, and through the issues that I will discuss today.

This is what we have done. But this is just a beginning. Some of our actions have yielded progress. Some have laid the groundwork for progress in the future. But make no mistake: this cannot be solely America's endeavor. Those who used to chastise America for acting alone in the world cannot now stand by and wait for America to solve the world's problems alone. We have sought—in word and deed—a new era of engagement with the world. Now is the time for all of us to take our share of responsibility for a global response to global challenges.

If we are honest with ourselves, we need to admit that we are not living up to that responsibility. Consider the course that we are on if we fail to confront the status quo. Extremists sowing terror in pockets of the world. Protracted conflicts that grind on and on.

Genocide and mass atrocities. More and more nations with nuclear weapons. Melting ice caps and ravaged populations. Persistent poverty and pandemic disease. I say this not to sow fear, but to state a fact: the magnitude of our challenges has yet to be met by the measure of our action.

This body was founded on the belief that the nations of the world could solve their problems together. Franklin Roosevelt, who died before he could see his vision for this institution become a reality, put it this way—and I quote: "The structure of world peace cannot be the work of one man, or one party, or one nation. It cannot be a peace of large nations—or of small nations. It must be a peace which rests on the cooperative effort of the whole world."

The cooperative effort of the whole world. Those words ring even more true today, when it is not simply peace—but our very health and prosperity that we hold in common. Yet I also know that this body is made up of sovereign states. And sadly, but not surprisingly, this body has often become a forum for sowing discord instead of forging common ground; a venue for playing politics and exploiting grievances rather than solving problems. After all, it is easy to walk up to this podium and to point fingers and stoke division. Nothing is easier than blaming others for our troubles, and absolving ourselves of responsibility for our choices and our actions. Anyone can do that.

Responsibility and leadership in the 21st century demand more. In an era when our destiny is shared, power is no longer a zero sum game. No one nation can or should try to dominate another nation. No world order that elevates one nation or group of people over another will succeed. No balance of power among nations will hold. The traditional division between nations of the south and north makes no sense in an interconnected world. Nor do alignments of nations rooted in the cleavages of a long gone cold war.

The time has come to realize that the old habits and arguments are irrelevant to the challenges faced by our people. They lead nations to act in opposition to the very goals that they claim to pursue, and to vote—often in this body—against the interests of their own people.

They build up walls between us and the future that our people seek, and the time has come for those walls to come down. Together, we must build new coalitions that bridge old divides—coalitions of different faiths and creeds; of north and south, east and west; black, white, and brown.

The choice is ours. We can be remembered as a generation that chose to drag the arguments of the 20th century into the 21st; that put off hard choices, refused to look ahead, and failed to keep pace because we defined ourselves by what we were against instead of what we were for. Or, we can be a generation that chooses to see the shoreline beyond the rough waters ahead; that comes together to serve the common interests of human beings, and finally gives meaning to the promise embedded in the name given to this institution: the United Nations.

That is the future America wants—a future of peace and prosperity that we can only reach if we recognize that all nations have rights, but all nations have responsibilities as well. That is the bargain that makes this work. That must be the guiding principle of international cooperation.

Today, I put forward four pillars that are fundamental to the future that we want for our children: non-proliferation and disarmament; the promotion of peace and security; the preservation of our planet; and a global economy that advances opportunity for all people.

First, we must stop the spread of nuclear weapons, and seek the goal of a world without them. This institution was founded at the dawn of the atomic age, in part because man's capacity to kill had to be contained. For decades, we averted disaster, even under the shadow of a superpower stand-off. But today, the threat of proliferation is growing in scope and complexity. If we fail to act, we will invite nuclear arms races in every region, and the prospect of wars and acts of terror on a scale that we can hardly imagine.

A fragile consensus stands in the way of this frightening outcome—the basic bargain that shapes the nuclear non proliferation treaty. It says that all nations have the right to peaceful nuclear energy; that nations with nuclear weapons have the responsibility to move toward disarmament; and those without them have the responsibility to forsake them. The next twelve months could be pivotal in determining whether this compact will be strengthened or will slowly dissolve.

America will keep our end of the bargain. We will pursue a new agreement with Russia to substantially reduce our strategic warheads and launchers. We will move forward with ratification of the test ban treaty, and work with others to bring the Treaty into force so that nuclear testing is permanently prohibited. We will complete a nuclear posture review that opens the door to deeper cuts, and reduces the role of nuclear weapons. And we will call upon countries to begin negotiations in January on a treaty to end the production of fissile material for weapons.

I will also host a summit next April that reaffirms each nation's responsibility to secure nuclear material on its territory, and to help those who can't—because we must never allow a single nuclear device to fall into the hands of a violent extremist. And we will work to strengthen the institutions and initiatives that combat nuclear smuggling and theft.

All of this must support efforts to strengthen the NPT. Those nations that refuse to live up to their obligations must face consequences. This is not about singling out individual nations—it is about standing up for the rights of all nations that do live up to their responsibilities. Because a world in which IAEA inspections are avoided and the United Nation's demands are ignored will leave all people less safe, and all nations less secure.

In their actions to date, the governments of North Korea and Iran threaten to take us down this dangerous slope. We respect their rights as members of the community of nations. I am committed to diplomacy that opens a path to greater prosperity and a more secure peace for both nations if they live up to their obligations.

But if the governments of Iran and North Korea choose to ignore international standards; if they put the pursuit of nuclear weapons ahead of regional stability and the security and opportunity of their own people; if they are oblivious to the dangers of escalating nuclear arms races in both East Asia and the Middle East—then they must be held accountable. The world must stand together to demonstrate that international law is not an empty promise, and that Treaties will be enforced. We must insist that the future not belong to fear.

That brings me to the second pillar for our future: the pursuit of peace. The United Nations was born of the belief that the people of the world can live their lives, raise their families, and resolve their differences peacefully. And yet we know that in too many parts of the world, this ideal remains an abstraction. We can either accept that outcome as inevitable and tolerate constant and crippling conflict.

Or we can recognize that the yearning for peace is universal, and reassert our resolve to end conflicts around the world. That effort must begin with an unshakeable determination that the murder of innocent men, women and children will never be tolerated. On this, there can be no dispute. The violent extremists who promote conflict by distorting faith have discredited and isolated themselves. They offer nothing but hatred and destruction. In confronting them, America will forge lasting partnerships to target terrorists, share intelligence, coordinate law enforcement, and protect our people. We will permit no safe-haven for al-Qaeda to launch attacks from Afghanistan or any other nation. We will stand by our friends on the front lines, as we and many nations will do in pledging support for the Pakistani people tomorrow. And we will pursue positive engagement that builds bridges among faiths, and new partnerships for opportunity.

But our efforts to promote peace cannot be limited to defeating violent extremists. For the most powerful weapon in our arsenal is the hope of human beings—the belief that the future belongs to those who build, not destroy; the confidence that conflicts can end, and a new day begin.

That is why we will strengthen our support for effective peacekeeping, while energizing our efforts to prevent conflicts before they take hold. We will pursue a lasting peace in Sudan through support for the people of Darfur, and the implementation of the comprehensive peace agreement, so that we secure the peace that the Sudanese people deserve. And in countries ravaged by violence—from Haiti to Congo to East Timor—we will work with the UN and other partners to support an enduring peace.

I will also continue to seek a just and lasting peace between Israel, Palestine, and the Arab world. Yesterday, I had a constructive meeting with Prime Minister Netanyahu and President Abbas. We have made some progress. Palestinians have strengthened their efforts on security. Israelis have facilitated greater freedom of movement for the Palestinians. As a result of these efforts by both sides, the economy in the West Bank has begun to grow. But more progress is needed. We continue to call on Palestinians to end incitement against Israel, and we continue to emphasize that America does not accept the legitimacy of continued Israeli settlements.

The time has come to relaunch negotiations—without preconditions—that address the permanent-status issues: security for Israelis and Palestinians; borders, refugees and Jerusalem. The goal is clear: two states living side by side in peace and security—a Jewish state of Israel, with true security for all Israelis; and a viable, independent Palestinian state with contiguous territory that ends the occupation that began in

1967, and realizes the potential of the Palestinian people. As we pursue this goal, we will also pursue peace between Israel and Lebanon, Israel and Syria, and a broader peace between Israel and its many neighbors. In pursuit of that goal, we will develop regional initiatives with multilateral participation, alongside bilateral negotiations.

I am not naive. I know this will be difficult. But all of us must decide whether we are serious about peace, or whether we only lend it lip-service. To break the old patterns—to break the cycle of insecurity and despair—all of us must say publicly what we would acknowledge in private. The United States does Israel no favors when we fail to couple an unwavering commitment to its security with an insistence that Israel respect the legitimate claims and rights of the Palestinians. And nations within this body do the Palestinians no favors when they choose vitriolic attacks over a constructive willingness to recognize Israel's legitimacy, and its right to exist in peace and security.

We must remember that the greatest price of this conflict is not paid by us. It is paid by the Israeli girl in Sderot who closes her eyes in fear that a rocket will take her life in the night. It is paid by the Palestinian boy in Gaza who has no clean water and no country to call his own. These are God's children. And after all of the politics and all of the posturing, this is about the right of every human being to live with dignity and security. That is a lesson embedded in the three great faiths that call one small slice of Earth the Holy Land. And that is why—even though there will be setbacks, and false starts, and tough days—I will not waiver in my pursuit of peace.

Third, we must recognize that in the 21st century, there will be no peace unless we take responsibility for the preservation of our planet. The danger posed by climate change cannot be denied, and our responsibility to meet it must not be deferred. If we continue down our current course, every member of this assembly will see irreversible changes within their borders. Our efforts to end conflicts will be eclipsed by wars over refugees and resources.

Development will be devastated by drought and famine. Land that human beings have lived on for millennia will disappear. Future generations will look back and wonder why we refused to act—why we failed to pass on intact the environment that was our inheritance.

That is why the days when America dragged its feet on this issue are over. We will move forward with investments to transform our energy economy, while providing incentives to make clean energy the profitable kind of energy. We will press ahead with deep cuts in emissions to reach the goals that we set for 2020, and eventually 2050. We will continue to promote renewable energy and efficiency—and share new technologies—with countries around the world. And we will seize every opportunity for progress to address this threat in a cooperative effort with the whole world.

Those wealthy nations that did so much to damage the environment in the 20th century must accept our obligation to lead. But responsibility does not end there. While we must acknowledge the need for differentiated responses, any effort to curb carbon emissions must include the fast-growing carbon emitters who can do more to reduce their air pollution without inhibiting growth. And any effort that fails to help the poorest nations both adapt to the problems that climate change has already wrought—and travel a path of clean development—will not work.

It is hard to change something as fundamental as how we use energy. It's even harder to do so in the midst of a global recession. Certainly, it will be tempting to sit back and wait for others to move first. But we cannot make this journey unless we all move forward together. As we head into Copenhagen, let us resolve to focus on what each of us can do for the sake of our common future.

This leads me to the final pillar that must fortify our future: a global economy that advances opportunity for all people. The world is still recovering from the worst economic crisis since the Great Depression. In America, we see the engine of growth beginning to churn, yet many still struggle to find a job or pay their bills. Across the globe, we find promising signs, yet little certainty about what lies ahead. And far too many people in far too many places live through the daily crises that challenge our common humanity—the despair of an empty stomach; the thirst brought on by dwindling water; the injustice of a child dying from a treatable disease, or a mother losing her life as she gives birth.

In Pittsburgh, we will work with the world's largest economies to chart a course for growth that is balanced and sustained. That means vigilance to ensure that we do not let up until our people are back to work. That means taking steps to rekindle demand, so that a global recovery can be sustained. And that means setting new rules of the road and strengthening regulation for all financial centers, so that we put an end to the greed, excess and abuse that led us into disaster, and prevent a crisis like this from ever happening again.

At a time of such interdependence, we have a moral and pragmatic interest in broader questions of development. And so we will continue our historic effort to help people feed themselves. We have set aside $63 billion to carry forward the fight against HIV/AIDS; to end deaths from tuberculosis and malaria; to eradicate polio; and to strengthen public health systems. We are joining with other countries to contribute H1N1 vaccines to the World Health Organization. We will integrate more economies into a system of global trade. We will support the Millennium Development Goals, and approach next year's summit with a global plan to make them a reality. And we will set our sights on the eradication of extreme poverty in our time.

Now is the time for all of us to do our part. Growth will not be sustained or shared unless all nations embrace their responsibility. Wealthy nations must open their markets to more goods and extend a hand to those with less, while reforming international institutions to give more nations a greater voice. Developing nations must root out the corruption that is an obstacle to progress—for opportunity cannot thrive where individuals are oppressed and business have to pay bribes. That's why we will support honest police and independent judges; civil society and a vibrant private sector. Our goal is simple: a global economy in which growth is sustained, and opportunity is available to all.

The changes that I have spoken about today will not be easy to make. And they will not be realized simply by leaders like us coming together in forums like this. For as in any assembly of members, real change can only come through the people we represent. That is why we must do the hard work to lay the groundwork for progress in our own capitals. That is where we will build the consensus to end conflicts and to harness technology for peaceful purposes; to change the way we use energy, and to promote growth that can be sustained and shared.

I believe that the people of the world want this future for their children. And that is why we must champion those principles which ensure that governments reflect the will of the people. These principles cannot be afterthoughts—democracy and human rights are essential to achieving each of the goals that I have discussed today.

Because governments of the people and by the people are more likely to act in the broader interests of their own people, rather than the narrow interest of those in power.

The test of our leadership will not be the degree to which we feed the fears and old hatreds of our people. True leadership will not be measured by the ability to muzzle dissent, or to intimidate and harass political opponents at home. The people of the world want change. They will not long tolerate those who are on the wrong side of history.

This assembly's Charter commits each of us, and I quote—"to reaffirm faith in fundamental human rights, in the dignity and worth of the human person, in the equal rights of men and women."

Among those rights is the freedom to speak your mind and worship as you please; the promise of equality of the races, and the opportunity for women and girls to pursue their own potential; the ability of citizens to have a say in how you are governed, and to have confidence in the administration of justice. For just as no nation should be forced to accept the tyranny of another nation, no individual should be forced to accept the tyranny of their own government.

As an African-American, I will never forget that I would not be here today without the steady pursuit of a more perfect union in my country. That guides my belief that no matter how dark the day may seem, transformative change can be forged by those who choose the side of justice. And I pledge that America will always stand with those who stand up for their dignity and their rights—for the student who seeks to learn; the voter who demands to be heard; the innocent who longs to be free; and the oppressed who yearns to be equal.

Democracy cannot be imposed on any nation from the outside. Each society must search for its own path, and no path is perfect. Each country will pursue a path rooted in the culture of its people, and—in the past—America has too often been selective in its promotion of democracy. But that does not weaken our commitment, it only reinforces it. There are basic principles that are universal; there are certain truths which are self-evident—and the United States of America will never waiver in our efforts to stand up for the right of people everywhere to determine their own destiny.

Sixty-five years ago, a weary Franklin Roosevelt spoke to the American people in his fourth and final inaugural address. After years of war, he sought to sum up the lessons that could be drawn from the terrible suffering and enormous sacrifice that had taken place. "We have learned," he said, "to be citizens of the world, members of the human community."

The United Nations was built by men and women like Roosevelt from every corner of the world—from Africa and Asia; form Europe to the Americas. These architects of international cooperation had an idealism that was anything but naïve—it was rooted in the hard-earned lessons of war, and the wisdom that nations could advance their interests by acting together instead of splitting apart.

Now it falls to us—for this institution will be what we make of it. The United Nations does extraordinary good around the world in feeding the hungry, caring for the sick, and mending places that have been broken. But it also struggles to enforce its will, and to live up to the ideals of its founding.

I believe that those imperfections are not a reason to walk away from this institution—they are a calling to redouble our efforts. The United Nations can either be a place where we bicker about outdated grievances, or forge common ground; a place where we focus on what drives us apart, or what brings us together; a place where we indulge tyranny, or a source of moral authority. In short, the United Nations can be an institution that is disconnected from what matters in the lives of our citizens, or it can be indispensable in advancing the interests of the people we serve.

THE PRESIDENT: Mr. President, Mr. Secretary-General, my fellow delegates, ladies and gentlemen. It is a great honor to address this Assembly for the second time, nearly two years after my election as President of the United States.

We know this is no ordinary time for our people. Each of us comes here with our own problems and priorities. But there are also challenges that we share in common as leaders and as nations.

We meet within an institution built from the rubble of war, designed to unite the world in pursuit of peace. And we meet within a city that for centuries has welcomed people from across the globe, demonstrating that individuals of every color, faith and

Remarks by the President to the United Nations General Assembly, Millennium Development Goals Summit, United Nations Headquarters, New York, New York, White House, Office of the Press Secretary, For Immediate Release, September 23, 2010. http://www.whitehouse.gov/the-press-office/2010/09/23/remarks-president-united-nations-general-assembly.

station can come together to pursue opportunity, build a community, and live with the blessing of human liberty.

Outside the doors of this hall, the blocks and neighborhoods of this great city tell the story of a difficult decade. Nine years ago, the destruction of the World Trade Center signaled a threat that respected no boundary of dignity or decency. Two years ago this month, a financial crisis on Wall Street devastated American families on Main Street. These separate challenges have affected people around the globe. Men and women and children have been murdered by extremists from Casablanca to London; from Jalalabad to Jakarta. The global economy suffered an enormous blow during the financial crisis, crippling markets and deferring the dreams of millions on every continent. Underneath these challenges to our security and prosperity lie deeper fears: that ancient hatreds and religious divides are once again ascendant; that a world which has grown more interconnected has somehow slipped beyond our control.

These are some of the challenges that my administration has confronted since we came into office. And today, I'd like to talk to you about what we've done over the last 20 months to meet these challenges; what our responsibility is to pursue peace in the Middle East; and what kind of world we are trying to build in this 21st century.

Let me begin with what we have done. I have had no greater focus as President than rescuing our economy from potential catastrophe. And in an age when prosperity is shared, we could not do this alone. So America has joined with nations around the world to spur growth, and the renewed demand that could restart job creation.

We are reforming our system of global finance, beginning with Wall Street reform here at home, so that a crisis like this never happens again. And we made the G20 the focal point for international coordination, because in a world where prosperity is more diffuse, we must broaden our circle of cooperation to include emerging economies— economies from every corner of the globe.

There is much to show for our efforts, even as there is much work to be done. The global economy has been pulled back from the brink of a depression, and is growing once more. We have resisted protectionism, and are exploring ways to expand trade and commerce among nations. But we cannot—and will not—rest until these seeds of progress grow into a broader prosperity, not only for all Americans, but for peoples around the globe.

As for our common security, America is waging a more effective fight against al Qaeda, while winding down the war in Iraq. Since I took office, the United States has removed nearly 100,000 troops from Iraq. We have done so responsibly, as Iraqis have transitioned to lead responsibility for the security of their country.

We are now focused on building a lasting partnership with the Iraqi people, while keeping our commitment to remove the rest of our troops by the end of next year. While drawing down in Iraq, we have refocused on defeating al Qaeda and denying its affiliates a safe haven. In Afghanistan, the United States and our allies are pursuing a strategy to break the Taliban's momentum and build the capacity of Afghanistan's government and security forces, so that a transition to Afghan responsibility can begin next July. And from South Asia to the Horn of Africa, we are moving toward a more targeted approach—one that strengthens our partners and dismantles terrorist networks without deploying large American armies.

As we pursue the world's most dangerous extremists, we're also denying them the world's most dangerous weapons, and pursuing the peace and security of a world without nuclear weapons.

Earlier this year, 47 nations embraced a work-plan to secure all vulnerable nuclear materials within four years. We have joined with Russia to sign the most comprehensive arms control treaty in decades. We have reduced the role of nuclear weapons in our security strategy. And here, at the United Nations, we came together to strengthen the Nuclear Non-Proliferation Treaty.

As part of our effort on non-proliferation, I offered the Islamic Republic of Iran an extended hand last year, and underscored that it has both rights and responsibilities as a member of the international community. I also said—in this hall—that Iran must be held accountable if it failed to meet those responsibilities. And that is what we have done.

Iran is the only party to the NPT that cannot demonstrate the peaceful intentions of its nuclear program, and those actions have consequences. Through U.N. Security Council Resolution 1929, we made it clear that international law is not an empty promise. Now let me be clear once more: The United States and the international community seek a resolution to our differences with Iran, and the door remains open to diplomacy should Iran choose to walk through it. But the Iranian government must demonstrate a clear and credible commitment and confirm to the world the peaceful intent of its nuclear program.

As we combat the spread of deadly weapons, we're also confronting the specter of climate change. After making historic investments in clean energy and efficiency at home, we helped forge an accord in Copenhagen that—for the first time—commits all major economies to reduce their emissions. We are keenly aware this is just a first step. And going forward, we will support a process in which all major economies meet our responsibilities to protect the planet while unleashing the power of clean energy to serve as an engine of growth and development.

America has also embraced unique responsibilities with come—that come with our power. Since the rains came and the floodwaters rose in Pakistan, we have pledged our assistance, and we should all support the Pakistani people as they recover and rebuild. And when the earth shook and Haiti was devastated by loss, we joined a coalition of nations in response. Today, we honor those from the U.N. family who lost their lives in the earthquake, and commit ourselves to stand with the people of Haiti until they can stand on their own two feet.

Amidst this upheaval, we have also been persistent in our pursuit of peace. Last year, I pledged my best efforts to support the goal of two states, Israel and Palestine, living side by side in peace and security, as part of a comprehensive peace between Israel and all of its neighbors. We have travelled a winding road over the last 12 months, with few peaks and many valleys. But this month, I am pleased that we have pursued direct negotiations between Israelis and Palestinians in Washington, Sharm el Sheikh and Jerusalem.

Now I recognize many are pessimistic about this process. The cynics say that Israelis and Palestinians are too distrustful of each other, and too divided internally, to forge lasting peace. Rejectionists on both sides will try to disrupt the process, with bitter words and with bombs and with gunfire. Some say that the gaps between the parties are too big; the potential for talks to break down is too great; and that after decades of failure, peace is simply not possible.

I hear those voices of skepticism. But I ask you to consider the alternative. If an agreement is not reached, Palestinians will never know the pride and dignity that comes with their own state. Israelis will never know the certainty and security that comes with sovereign and stable neighbors who are committed to coexistence. The hard realities of demography will take hold. More blood will be shed. This Holy Land will remain a symbol of our differences, instead of our common humanity.

I refuse to accept that future. And we all have a choice to make. Each of us must choose the path of peace. Of course, that responsibility begins with the parties themselves, who must answer the call of history. Earlier this month at the White House, I was struck by the words of both the Israeli and Palestinian leaders. Prime Minister Netanyahu said, "I came here today to find a historic compromise that will enable both people to live in peace, security, and dignity." And President Abbas said, "We will spare no effort and we will work diligently and tirelessly to ensure these negotiations achieve their cause."

These words must now be followed by action and I believe that both leaders have the courage to do so. But the road that they have to travel is exceedingly difficult, which is why I call upon Israelis and Palestinians—and the world—to rally behind the goal that these leaders now share. We know that there will be tests along the way and that one test is fast approaching. Israel's settlement moratorium has made a difference on the ground and improved the atmosphere for talks.

And our position on this issue is well known. We believe that the moratorium should be extended. We also believe that talks should press on until completed. Now is the time for the parties to help each other overcome this obstacle. Now is the time to build the trust—and provide the time—for substantial progress to be made. Now is the time for this opportunity to be seized, so that it does not slip away.

Now, peace must be made by Israelis and Palestinians, but each of us has a responsibility to do our part as well. Those of us who are friends of Israel must understand that true security for the Jewish state requires an independent Palestine—one that allows the Palestinian people to live with dignity and opportunity. And those of us who are friends of the Palestinians must understand that the rights of the Palestinian people will be won only through peaceful means—including genuine reconciliation with a secure Israel.

I know many in this hall count themselves as friends of the Palestinians. But these pledges of friendship must now be supported by deeds. Those who have signed on to the Arab Peace Initiative should seize this opportunity to make it real by taking tangible steps towards the normalization that it promises Israel.

And those who speak on behalf of Palestinian self-government should help the Palestinian Authority politically and financially, and in doing so help the Palestinians build the institutions of their state.

Those who long to see an independent Palestine must also stop trying to tear down Israel. After thousands of years, Jews and Arabs are not strangers in a strange land. After 60 years in the community of nations, Israel's existence must not be a subject for debate.

Israel is a sovereign state, and the historic homeland of the Jewish people. It should be clear to all that efforts to chip away at Israel's legitimacy will only be met by the unshakeable opposition of the United States. And efforts to threaten or kill Israelis will do nothing to help the Palestinian people. The slaughter of innocent Israelis is not resistance—it's injustice. And make no mistake: The courage of a man like President Abbas, who stands up for his people in front of the world under very difficult circumstances, is far greater than those who fire rockets at innocent women and children.

The conflict between Israelis and Arabs is as old as this institution. And we can come back here next year, as we have for the last 60 years, and make long speeches about it. We can read familiar lists of grievances. We can table the same resolutions. We can further empower the forces of rejectionism and hate. And we can waste more time by carrying forward an argument that will not help a single Israeli or Palestinian child achieve a better life. We can do that.

Or, we can say that this time will be different—that this time we will not let terror, or turbulence, or posturing, or petty politics stand in the way. This time, we will think not of ourselves, but of the young girl in Gaza who wants to have no ceiling on her dreams, or the young boy in Sderot who wants to sleep without the nightmare of rocket fire.

This time, we should draw upon the teachings of tolerance that lie at the heart of three great religions that see Jerusalem's soil as sacred. This time we should reach for what's best within ourselves. If we do, when we come back here next year, we can have an agreement that will lead to a new member of the United Nations—an independent, sovereign state of Palestine, living in peace with Israel.

It is our destiny to bear the burdens of the challenges that I've addressed—recession and war and conflict. And there is always a sense of urgency—even emergency—that drives most of our foreign policies. Indeed, after millennia marked by wars, this very institution reflects the desire of human beings to create a forum to deal with emergencies that will inevitably come.

But even as we confront immediate challenges, we must also summon the foresight to look beyond them, and consider what we are trying to build over the long term? What is the world that awaits us when today's battles are brought to an end? And that is what I would like to talk about with the remainder of my time today.

One of the first actions of this General Assembly was to adopt a Universal Declaration of Human Rights in 1948. That Declaration begins by stating that "recognition of the inherent dignity and of the equal and inalienable rights of all members of the human family is the foundation of freedom, justice, and peace in the world."

The idea is a simple one—that freedom, justice and peace for the world must begin with freedom, justice, and peace in the lives of individual human beings. And for the United States, this is a matter of moral and pragmatic necessity. As Robert Kennedy said, "the individual man, the child of God, is the touchstone of value, and all society, groups, the state, exist for his benefit." So we stand up for universal values because it's the right thing to do. But we also know from experience that those who defend these values for their people have been our closest friends and allies, while those who have denied those rights—whether terrorist groups or tyrannical governments—have chosen to be our adversaries.

Human rights have never gone unchallenged—not in any of our nations, and not in our world. Tyranny is still with us—whether it manifests itself in the Taliban killing girls who try to go to school, a North Korean regime that enslaves its own people, or an armed group in Congo-Kinshasa that use rape as a weapon of war.

In times of economic unease, there can also be an anxiety about human rights. Today, as in past times of economic downturn, some put human rights aside for the promise of short term stability or the false notion that economic growth can come at the expense of freedom. We see leaders abolishing term limits. We see crackdowns on civil society. We see corruption smothering entrepreneurship and good governance. We see democratic reforms deferred indefinitely.

As I said last year, each country will pursue a path rooted in the culture of its own people. Yet experience shows us that history is on the side of liberty; that the strongest foundation for human progress lies in open economies, open societies, and open governments. To put it simply, democracy, more than any other form of government, delivers for our citizens. And I believe that truth will only grow stronger in a world where the borders between nations are blurred.

America is working to shape a world that fosters this openness, for the rot of a closed or corrupt economy must never eclipse the energy and innovation of human beings. All of us want the right to educate our children, to make a decent wage, to care for the sick, and to be carried as far as our dreams and our deeds will take us. But that depends upon economies that tap the power of our people, including the potential of women and girls. That means letting entrepreneurs start a business without paying a bribe and governments that support opportunity instead of stealing from their people. And that means rewarding hard work, instead of reckless risk-taking.

Yesterday, I put forward a new development policy that will pursue these goals, recognizing that dignity is a human right and global development is in our common interest. America will partner with nations that offer their people a path out of poverty. And together, we must unleash growth that powers by individuals and emerging markets in all parts of the globe.

There is no reason why Africa should not be an exporter of agriculture, which is why our food security initiative is empowering farmers. There is no reason why entrepreneurs shouldn't be able to build new markets in every society, which is why I hosted a summit on entrepreneurship earlier this spring, because the obligation of government is to empower individuals, not to impede them.

The same holds true for civil society. The arc of human progress has been shaped by individuals with the freedom to assemble and by organizations outside of government that insisted upon democratic change and by free media that held the powerful accountable. We have seen that from the South Africans who stood up to apartheid, to the Poles of Solidarity, to the mothers of the disappeared who spoke out against the Dirty War, to Americans who marched for the rights of all races, including my own.

Civil society is the conscience of our communities and America will always extend our engagement abroad with citizens beyond the halls of government. And we will call out those who suppress ideas and serve as a voice for those who are voiceless. We will promote new tools of communication so people are empowered to connect with one another and, in repressive societies, to do so with security. We will support a free and open Internet, so individuals have the information to make up their own minds. And it is time to embrace and effectively monitor norms that advance the rights of civil society and guarantee its expansion within and across borders.

Open society supports open government, but it cannot substitute for it. There is no right more fundamental than the ability to choose your leaders and determine your destiny. Now, make no mistake: The ultimate success of democracy in the world won't come because the United States dictates it; it will come because individual citizens demand a say in how they are governed.

There is no soil where this notion cannot take root, just as every democracy reflects the uniqueness of a nation. Later this fall, I will travel to Asia. And I will visit India, which peacefully threw off colonialism and established a thriving democracy of over a billion people.

I'll continue to Indonesia, the world's largest Muslim-majority country, which binds together thousands of islands through the glue of representative government and civil society. I'll join the G20 meeting on the Korean Peninsula, which provides the world's clearest contrast between a society that is dynamic and open and free, and one that is imprisoned and closed. And I will conclude my trip in Japan, an ancient culture that found peace and extraordinary development through democracy.

Each of these countries gives life to democratic principles in their own way. And even as some governments roll back reform, we also celebrate the courage of a President in Colombia who willingly stepped aside, or the promise of a new constitution in Kenya.

The common thread of progress is the principle that government is accountable to its citizens. And the diversity in this room makes clear—no one country has all the answers, but all of us must answer to our own people.

In all parts of the world, we see the promise of innovation to make government more open and accountable. And now, we must build on that progress. And when we gather back here next year, we should bring specific commitments to promote transparency; to fight corruption; to energize civic engagement; to leverage new technologies so that we strengthen the foundations of freedom in our own countries, while living up to the ideals that can light the world.

This institution can still play an indispensable role in the advance of human rights. It's time to welcome the efforts of U.N. Women to protect the rights of women around the globe.

It's time for every member state to open its elections to international monitors and increase the U.N. Democracy Fund. It's time to reinvigorate U.N. peacekeeping, so that missions have the resources necessary to succeed, and so atrocities like sexual violence are prevented and justice is enforced—because neither dignity nor democracy can thrive without basic security.

And it's time to make this institution more accountable as well, because the challenges of a new century demand new ways of serving our common interests. The world that America seeks is not one we can build on our own. For human rights to reach those who suffer the boot of oppression, we need your voices to speak out. In particular, I appeal to those nations who emerged from tyranny and inspired the world in the second half of the last century—from South Africa to South Asia; from Eastern Europe to South America. Don't stand idly by, don't be silent, when dissidents elsewhere are imprisoned and protesters are beaten. Recall your own history; because part of the price of our own freedom is standing up for the freedom of others.

That belief will guide America's leadership in this 21st century. It is a belief that has seen us through more than two centuries of trial, and it will see us through the challenges we face today—be it war or recession; conflict or division.

So even as we have come through a difficult decade, I stand here before you confident in the future—a future where Iraq is governed by neither tyrant nor a foreign power, and Afghanistan is freed from the turmoil of war; a future where the children of Israel and Palestine can build the peace that was not possible for their parents; a world where the promise of development reaches into the prisons of poverty and disease; a future where the cloud of recession gives way to the light of renewal and the dream of opportunity is available to all.

This future will not be easy to reach. It will not come without setbacks, nor will it be quickly claimed. But the founding of the United Nations itself is a testament to human progress. Remember, in times that were far more trying than our own, our predecessors chose the hope of unity over the ease of division and made a promise to future generations that the dignity and equality of human beings would be our common cause.

It falls to us to fulfill that promise. And though we will be met by dark forces that will test our resolve, Americans have always had cause to believe that we can choose a better history; that we need only to look outside the walls around us. For through the citizens of every conceivable ancestry who make this city their own, we see living proof that opportunity can be accessed by all, that what unites us as human beings is far greater than what divides us, and that people from every part of this world can live together in peace. Thank you very much.

Notes

1. "Remarks by the President to the United Nations General Assembly," The White House, Office of the Press Secretary, For Immediate Release, September 23, 2009, United Nations Headquarters, New York, New York.
http://www.whitehouse.gov/the_press_office/
Remarks-by-the-President-to-the-United-Nations-General-Assembly/.

Chapter 3

Barack Obama and Africa

G ood morning. It is an honor for me to be in Accra, and to speak to the representatives of the people of Ghana. I am deeply grateful for the welcome that I've received, as are Michelle, Malia, and Sasha Obama. Ghana's history is rich, the ties between our two countries are strong, and I am proud that this is my first visit to sub-Saharan Africa as President of the United States.

I am speaking to you at the end of a long trip. I began in Russia, for a Summit between two great powers. I traveled to Italy, for a meeting of the world's leading economies. And I have come here, to Ghana, for a simple reason: the 21st century will be shaped by what happens not just in Rome or Moscow or Washington, but by what happens in Accra as well.

This is the simple truth of a time when the boundaries between people are overwhelmed by our connections. Your prosperity can expand America's. Your health and security can contribute to the world's. And the strength of your democracy can help advance human rights for people everywhere.

So I do not see the countries and peoples of Africa as a world apart; I see Africa as a fundamental part of our interconnected world—as partners with America on behalf of the future that we want for all our children. That partnership must be grounded in mutual responsibility, and that is what I want to speak with you about today.

We must start from the simple premise that Africa's future is up to Africans. I say this knowing full well the tragic past that has sometimes haunted this part of the world. I have the blood of Africa within me, and my family's own story encompasses both the tragedies and triumphs of the larger African story.

My grandfather was a cook for the British in Kenya, and though he was a respected elder in his village, his employers called him 'boy" for much of his life. He was on the periphery of Kenya's liberation struggles, but he was still imprisoned briefly during repressive times. In his life, colonialism wasn't simply the creation of unnatural borders

Remarks by the President to the Ghanaian Parliament, Accra International Conference Center, Accra, Ghana, The White House Office of the Press Secretary, For Immediate Release, July 11, 2009. http://www.whitehouse.gov/the-press-office/remarks-president-ghanaian-parliament.

or unfair terms of trade—it was something experienced personally, day after day, year after year.

My father grew up herding goats in a tiny village, an impossible distance away from the American universities where he would come to get an education. He came of age at an extraordinary moment of promise for Africa. The struggles of his own father's generation were giving birth to new nations, beginning right here in Ghana. Africans were educating and asserting themselves in new ways. History was on the move.

But despite the progress that has been made—and there has been considerable progress in parts of Africa—we also know that much of that promise has yet to be fulfilled. Countries like Kenya, which had a per capita economy larger than South Korea's when I was born, have been badly outpaced. Disease and conflict have ravaged parts of the African continent. In many places, the hope of my father's generation gave way to cynicism, even despair.

It is easy to point fingers, and to pin the blame for these problems on others. Yes, a colonial map that made little sense bred conflict, and the West has often approached Africa as a patron, rather than a partner. But the West is not responsible for the destruction of the Zimbabwean economy over the last decade, or wars in which children are enlisted as combatants. In my father's life, it was partly tribalism and patronage in an independent Kenya that for a long stretch derailed his career, and we know that this kind of corruption is a daily fact of life for far too many.

Of course, we also know that is not the whole story. Here in Ghana, you show us a face of Africa that is too often overlooked by a world that sees only tragedy or the need for charity. The people of Ghana have worked hard to put democracy on a firmer footing, with peaceful transfers of power even in the wake of closely contested elections. And with improved governance and an emerging civil society, Ghana's economy has shown impressive rates of growth.

This progress may lack the drama of the 20th century's liberation struggles, but make no mistake: it will ultimately be more significant. For just as it is important to emerge from the control of another nation, it is even more important to build one's own.

So I believe that this moment is just as promising for Ghana—and for Africa—as the moment when my father came of age and new nations were being born. This is a new moment of promise. Only this time, we have learned that it will not be giants like Nkrumah and Kenyatta who will determine Africa's future. Instead, it will be you—the men and women in Ghana's Parliament, and the people you represent. Above all, it will be the young people—brimming with talent and energy and hope—who can claim the future that so many in my father's generation never found.

To realize that promise, we must first recognize a fundamental truth that you have given life to in Ghana: development depends upon good governance. That is the ingredient which has been missing in far too many places, for far too long. That is the change that can unlock Africa's potential. And that is a responsibility that can only be met by Africans.

As for America and the West, our commitment must be measured by more than just the dollars we spend. I have pledged substantial increases in our foreign assistance, which is in Africa's interest and America's. But the true sign of success is not whether we are a source of aid that helps people scrape by—it is whether we are partners in building the capacity for transformational change.

This mutual responsibility must be the foundation of our partnership. And today, I will focus on four areas that are critical to the future of Africa and the entire developing world: democracy; opportunity; health; and the peaceful resolution of conflict.

First, we must support strong and sustainable democratic governments. As I said in Cairo, each nation gives life to democracy in its own way, and in line with its own traditions. But history offers a clear verdict: governments that respect the will of their own people are more prosperous, more stable, and more successful than governments that do not.

This is about more than holding elections—it's also about what happens between them. Repression takes many forms, and too many nations are plagued by problems that condemn their people to poverty. No country is going to create wealth if its leaders exploit the economy to enrich themselves, or police can be bought off by drug traffickers. No business wants to invest in a place where the government skims 20 percent off the top, or the head of the Port Authority is corrupt. No person wants to live in a society where the rule of law gives way to the rule of brutality and bribery. That is not democracy that is tyranny, and now is the time for it to end.

In the 21st century, capable, reliable and transparent institutions are the key to success—strong parliaments and honest police forces; independent judges and journalists; a vibrant private sector and civil society. Those are the things that give life to democracy, because that is what matters in people's lives.

Time and again, Ghanaians have chosen Constitutional rule over autocracy, and shown a democratic spirit that allows the energy of your people to break through. We see that in leaders who accept defeat graciously, and victors who resist calls to wield power against the opposition. We see that spirit in courageous journalists like Anas Aremeyaw Anas, who risked his life to report the truth. We see it in police like Patience Quaye, who helped prosecute the first human trafficker in Ghana. We see it in the young people who are speaking up against patronage, and participating in the political process.

Across Africa, we have seen countless examples of people taking control of their destiny, and making change from the bottom up. We saw it in Kenya, where civil society and business came together to help stop post-election violence. We saw it in South Africa, where over three quarters of the country voted in the recent election— the fourth since the end of Apartheid. We saw it in Zimbabwe, where the Election

Support Network braved brutal repression to stand up for the principle that a person's vote is their sacred right.

Make no mistake: history is on the side of these brave Africans, and not with those who use coups or change Constitutions to stay in power. Africa doesn't need strongmen, it needs strong institutions.

America will not seek to impose any system of government on any other nation—the essential truth of democracy is that each nation determines its own destiny. What we will do is increase assistance for responsible individuals and institutions, with a focus on supporting good governance—on parliaments, which check abuses of power and ensure that opposition voices are heard; on the rule of law, which ensures the equal administration of justice; on civic participation, so that young people get involved; and on concrete solutions to corruption like forensic accounting, automating services, strengthening hotlines, and protecting whistle-blowers to advance transparency and accountability.

As we provide this support, I have directed my Administration to give greater attention to corruption in our Human Rights report. People everywhere should have the right to start a business or get an education without paying a bribe. We have a responsibility to support those who act responsibly and to isolate those who don't, and that is exactly what America will do. This leads directly to our second area of partnership—supporting development that provides opportunity for more people.

With better governance, I have no doubt that Africa holds the promise of a broader base for prosperity. The continent is rich in natural resources. And from cell phone entrepreneurs to small farmers, Africans have shown the capacity and commitment to create their own opportunities. But old habits must also be broken. Dependence on commodities—or on a single export—concentrates wealth in the hands of the few, and leaves people too vulnerable to downturns.

In Ghana, for instance, oil brings great opportunities, and you have been responsible in preparing for new revenue. But as so many Ghanaians know, oil cannot simply become the new cocoa. From South Korea to Singapore, history shows that countries thrive when they invest in their people and infrastructure; when they promote multiple export industries, develop a skilled workforce, and create space for small and medium-sized businesses that create jobs.

As Africans reach for this promise, America will be more responsible in extending our hand. By cutting costs that go to Western consultants and administration, we will put more resources in the hands of those who need it, while training people to do more for themselves. That is why our $3.5 billion food security initiative is focused on new methods and technologies for farmers—not simply sending American producers or goods to Africa. Aid is not an end in itself. The purpose of foreign assistance must be creating the conditions where it is no longer needed.

America can also do more to promote trade and investment. Wealthy nations must open our doors to goods and services from Africa in a meaningful way. And where there is good governance, we can broaden prosperity through public-private partnerships that invest in better roads and electricity; capacity-building that trains people to grow a business; and financial services that reach poor and rural areas. This is also in our own interest—for if people are lifted out of poverty and wealth is created in Africa, new markets will open for our own goods.

One area that holds out both undeniable peril and extraordinary promise is energy. Africa gives off less greenhouse gas than any other part of the world, but it is the most threatened by climate change. A warming planet will spread disease, shrink water resources, and deplete crops, creating conditions that produce more famine and conflict. All of us—particularly the developed world—have a responsibility to slow these trends—through mitigation, and by changing the way that we use energy. But we can also work with Africans to turn this crisis into opportunity.

Together, we can partner on behalf of our planet and prosperity, and help countries increase access to power while skipping the dirtier phase of development. Across Africa, there is bountiful wind and solar power; geothermal energy and bio-fuels. From the Rift Valley to the North African deserts; from the Western coast to South Africa's crops—Africa's boundless natural gifts can generate its own power, while exporting profitable, clean energy abroad.

These steps are about more than growth numbers on a balance sheet. They're about whether a young person with an education can get a job that supports a family; a farmer can transfer their goods to the market; or an entrepreneur with a good idea can start a business. It's about the dignity of work. It's about the opportunity that must exist for Africans in the 21st century. Just as governance is vital to opportunity, it is also critical to the third area that I will talk about—strengthening public health.

In recent years, enormous progress has been made in parts of Africa. Far more people are living productively with HIV/AIDS, and getting the drugs they need. But too many still die from diseases that shouldn't kill them. When children are being killed because of a mosquito bite, and mothers are dying in childbirth, then we know that more progress must be made.

Yet because of incentives—often provided by donor nations—many African doctors and nurses understandably go overseas, or work for programs that focus on a single disease. This creates gaps in primary care and basic prevention. Meanwhile, individual Africans also have to make responsible choices that prevent the spread of disease, while promoting public health in their communities and countries.

Across Africa, we see examples of people tackling these problems. In Nigeria, an Interfaith effort of Christians and Muslims has set an example of cooperation to confront malaria. Here in Ghana and across Africa, we see innovative ideas for filling gaps in care—for instance, through E-Health initiatives that allow doctors in big cities to support those in small towns.

America will support these efforts through a comprehensive, global health strategy. Because in the 21st century, we are called to act by our conscience and our common interest. When a child dies of a preventable illness in Accra, that diminishes us everywhere. And when disease goes unchecked in any corner of the world, we know that it can spread across oceans and continents.

That is why my Administration has committed $63 billion to meet these challenges. Building on the strong efforts of President Bush, we will carry forward the fight against HIV/AIDS. We will pursue the goal of ending deaths from malaria and tuberculosis, and eradicating polio. We will fight neglected tropical disease. And we won't confront illnesses in isolation—we will invest in public health systems that promote wellness, and focus on the health of mothers and children.

As we partner on behalf of a healthier future, we must also stop the destruction that comes not from illness, but from human beings—and so the final area that I will address is conflict.

Now let me be clear: Africa is not the crude caricature of a continent at war. But for far too many Africans, conflict is a part of life, as constant as the sun. There are wars over land and wars over resources. And it is still far too easy for those without conscience to manipulate whole communities into fighting among faiths and tribes.

These conflicts are a millstone around Africa's neck. We all have many identities—of tribe and ethnicity; of religion and nationality. But defining oneself in opposition to someone who belongs to a different tribe, or who worships a different prophet, has no place in the 21st century. Africa's diversity should be a source of strength, not a cause for division. We are all God's children. We all share common aspirations—to live in peace and security; to access education and opportunity; to love our families, our communities, and our faith. That is our common humanity.

That is why we must stand up to inhumanity in our midst. It is never justifiable to target innocents in the name of ideology. It is the death sentence of a society to force children to kill in wars. It is the ultimate mark of criminality and cowardice to condemn women to relentless and systematic rape. We must bear witness to the value of every child in Darfur and the dignity of every woman in Congo. No faith or culture should condone the outrages against them. All of us must strive for the peace and security necessary for progress.

Africans are standing up for this future. Here, too, Ghana is helping to point the way forward. Ghanaians should take pride in your contributions to peacekeeping from Congo to Liberia to Lebanon, and in your efforts to resist the scourge of the drug trade. We welcome the steps that are being taken by organizations like the African Union and ECOWAS to better resolve conflicts, keep the peace, and support those in need. And we encourage the vision of a strong, regional security architecture that can bring effective, transnational force to bear when needed.

America has a responsibility to advance this vision, not just with words, but with support that strengthens African capacity. When there is genocide in Darfur or terrorists in Somalia, these are not simply African problems—they are global security challenges, and they demand a global response. That is why we stand ready to partner through diplomacy, technical assistance, and logistical support, and will stand behind efforts to hold war criminals accountable. And let me be clear: our Africa Command is focused not on establishing a foothold in the continent, but on confronting these common challenges to advance the security of America, Africa and the world.

In Moscow, I spoke of the need for an international system where the universal rights of human beings are respected, and violations of those rights are opposed. That must include a commitment to support those who resolve conflicts peacefully, to sanction and stop those who don't, and to help those who have suffered. But ultimately, it will be vibrant democracies like Botswana and Ghana which roll back the causes of conflict, and advance the frontiers of peace and prosperity.

As I said earlier, Africa's future is up to Africans. The people of Africa are ready to claim that future. In my country, African-Americans—including so many recent immigrants—have thrived in every sector of society. We have done so despite a difficult past, and we have drawn strength from our African heritage. With strong institutions and a strong will, I know that Africans can live their dreams in Nairobi and Lagos; in Kigali and Kinshasa; in Harare and right here in Accra.

Fifty-two years ago, the eyes of the world were on Ghana. And a young preacher named Martin Luther King traveled here, to Accra, to watch the Union Jack come down and the Ghanaian flag go up. This was before the march on Washington or the success of the civil rights movement in my country. Dr. King was asked how he felt while watching the birth of a nation. And he said: "It renews my conviction in the ultimate triumph of justice."

Now, that triumph must be won once more, and it must be won by you. And I am particularly speaking to the young people. In places like Ghana, you make up over half of the population. Here is what you must know: the world will be what you make of it.

You have the power to hold your leaders accountable, and to build institutions that serve the people. You can serve in your communities, and harness your energy and education to create new wealth and build new connections to the world. You can conquer disease, end conflicts, and make change from the bottom up. You can do that. Yes you can. Because in this moment, history is on the move.

But these things can only be done if you take responsibility for your future. It won't be easy. It will take time and effort. There will be suffering and setbacks. But I can promise you this: America will be with you. As a partner. As a friend. Opportunity won't come from any other place, though—it must come from the decisions that you make, the things that you do, and the hope that you hold in your hearts.

Freedom is your inheritance. Now, it is your responsibility to build upon freedom's foundation. And if you do, we will look back years from now to places like Accra and say that this was the time when the promise was realized—this was the moment when prosperity was forged; pain was overcome; and a new era of progress began. This can be the time when we witness the triumph of justice once more. Thank you.

Today, my Administration is releasing a comprehensive strategy to confront the serious and urgent situation in Sudan. For years, the people of Sudan have faced enormous and unacceptable hardship. The genocide in Darfur has claimed the lives of hundreds of thousands of people and left millions more displaced. Conflict in the region has wrought more suffering, posing dangers beyond Sudan's borders and blocking the potential of this important part of Africa. Sudan is now poised to fall further into chaos if swift action is not taken.

Our conscience and our interests in peace and security call upon the United States and the international community to act with a sense of urgency and purpose. First, we must seek a definitive end to conflict, gross human rights abuses and genocide in Darfur. Second, the Comprehensive Peace Agreement between the North and South in Sudan must be implemented to create the possibility of long-term peace. These two goals must both be pursued simultaneously with urgency. Achieving them requires the commitment of the United States, as well as the active participation of international partners. Concurrently, we will work aggressively to ensure that Sudan does not provide a safe-haven for international terrorists.

The United States Special Envoy has worked actively and effectively to engage all of the parties involved, and he will continue to pursue engagement that saves lives and achieves results. Later this week, I will renew the declaration of a National Emergency with respect to Sudan, which will continue tough sanctions on the Sudanese Government. If the Government of Sudan acts to improve the situation on the ground and to advance peace, there will be incentives; if it does not, then there will be increased pressure imposed by the United States and the international community. As the United States and our international partners meet our responsibility to act, the Government of Sudan must meet its responsibilities to take concrete steps in a new direction.

Over the last several years, governments, non-governmental organizations, and individuals, and from around the world have taken action to address the situation in Sudan, and to end the genocide in Darfur. Going forward, all of our efforts must be measured by the lives that are led by the people of Sudan. After so much suffering, they

Statement by President Obama on Sudan Strategy, The White House, Office of the Press Secretary, October 19, 2009. http://www.whitehouse.gov/the-press-office/statement-president-barack-obama-sudan-strategy.

deserve a future that allows them to live with greater dignity, security, and opportunity. It will not be easy, and there are no simple answers to the extraordinary challenges that confront this part of the world. But now is the time for all of us to come together, and to make a strong and sustained effort on behalf of a better future for the people of Sudan.

THE PRESIDENT: Thank you so much. Thank you. Please, everybody have a seat. Everybody have a seat. What a wonderful evening. Before I begin, let me just acknowledge some folks here in the crowd. First of all, Ms. Kerry Kennedy, for the great work that she's doing day in and day out. Mr. Philip Johnston, thank you to both of you for helping to organize this tonight.

Obviously I've got to say thanks to my favorite people—Mrs. Robert F. Kennedy, also known as Ethel Kennedy. To Representative Donald Payne, Representative Gregory Meeks, and Representative Edward Markey, who are all here—thank you for your attendance and your support of this important award.

You know, every year for 24 years, starting the year this award was established, my friend, Senator Edward Ted Kennedy, spoke at this event. And I'm told that he looked forward to it all year—that he relished the chance to shine a bright light on an injustice and on those fighting it, and to support them in that fight. He also enjoyed a family reunion. He relished the chance to pay tribute to those carrying on the unfinished work of his brother's life—work that for nearly half a century in the U.S. Senate he made his own.

He was pleased that this award honored men and women across the globe doing a wide range of urgent work—fighting to end apartheid, advance democracy, empower minorities and indigenous peoples, promote free speech and elections and more. Because Ted understood that Bobby's legacy wasn't a devotion to one particular cause or a faith in a certain ideology—but rather, it was a sensibility. A belief that in this world, there is right and there is wrong, and it is our job to build our laws and our lives around recognizing the difference.

A sensitivity to injustice so acute that it can't be relieved by the rationalizations that make life comfortable for the rest of us—that others' suffering is not our problem, that the ills of the world are somehow not our concern. A moral orientation that renders certain people constitutionally incapable of remaining a bystander in the face of evil—a sensibility that recognizes the power of all people, however humble their circumstances, to change the course of history.

Those are the traits of Bobby Kennedy that this award recognizes—the very traits that define the character and guide the life of this year's recipient. And while we feel a

Remarks by the President at the Presentation of the Robert F. Kennedy Human Rights Award, The White House, Office of the Press Secretary, November 24, 2009. http://www.zimbabwesituation. org/?p=3734.

certain sadness that Senator Kennedy is not with us to honor her, let us also take pleasure tonight in knowing just how much he would have loved and admired Magodonga Mahlangu and the organization that she helps lead—WOZA, which stands for Women of Zimbabwe Arise, and is represented tonight by one of its founders, Jenni Williams.

As a young girl raised in Matabeleland—in the Matabeleland region of Zimbabwe in the early 1980s, Magodonga witnessed the—I've got to make sure I get this right—Gukurahundi massacres—the systematic murder of many thousands of people, including her uncle and several cousins—many of whom were buried in mass graves that they'd been forced to dig themselves.

She witnessed the fearful silence that followed, as talking about these events was forbidden. Magodonga found this to be intolerable. She wanted to speak out—she wanted people to know the truth about what was happening in her country.

So it was a revelation when, years later, she discovered a group called WOZA whose mission is the very opposite of silence. WOZA was started back in 2003 to empower women to speak out about the issues affecting their families and their country—desperate hunger; crumbling health and education systems; domestic violence and rape; and government repression ranging from restrictions on free expression to abduction and murder of dissidents.

WOZA's guiding principle is "tough love"—the idea that political leaders in Zimbabwe could use a little discipline. And who better to provide that than the nation's mothers? Since its founding, the organization has grown from a handful of activists to a movement of 75,000 strong. There's even a men's branch, I understand—MOZA.

And over the past seven years, they have conducted more than a hundred protests—maids and hairdressers, vegetable sellers and seamstresses, taking to the streets; singing and dancing; banging on pots empty of food and brandishing brooms to express their wish to sweep the government clean.

They often don't get far before being confronted by President Mugabe's riot police. They have been gassed, abducted, threatened with guns, and badly beaten—forced to count out loud as each blow was administered. Three thousand WOZA members have spent time in custody or in prison, sometimes dragged with their babies into cells.

Magodonga and Jenni are due back in court on December 7th, charged with "conduct likely to cause a breach of [the] peace." They face a five year sentence if convicted. That so many women have decided to risk and endure so much is in many ways a testament to the extraordinary example of tonight's honoree.

Each time they see Magodonga beaten back—beaten black and blue during one protest, only to get right back up and lead another—singing freedom songs at the top of her lungs in full view of security forces—the threat of a policeman's baton loses some of its power.

Each time her house is searched, or her life is threatened, or she's once again arrested—more than 30 times so far—she continues to stand in public and inspire the people of Zimbabwe—the power of the state then seems a little less absolute.

Each time she has emerged from incarceration after enduring deplorable conditions and brutal abuse—and gone right back to work—the prospect of prison loses some of its capacity to deter.

By her example, Magodonga has shown the women of WOZA and the people of Zimbabwe that they can undermine their oppressors' power with their own power—that they can sap a dictator's strength with their own. Her courage has inspired others to summon theirs. And the organization's name, WOZA—which means "come forward"—has become its impact—its impact has been even more as people know of the violence that they face, and more people have come forward to join them.

More people have come to realize what Magodonga and the women of WOZA have known all along: that the only real way to teach love and non-violence is by example. Even when that means sitting down while being arrested, both as a sign that they refuse to retaliate, absorbing each blow without striking back—and a warning that, come what may, they're not going anywhere.

They even manage to show love to those who imprison them. As Jenni put it, "Many a time we have in effect conducted a 'workshop' for our jailers, acting out the role of a mother and teaching how the country can be rebuilt if we have love in our hearts."

When asked how they can endure so much violence—and what keeps them going in the face of such overwhelming odds—the women of WOZA reply, simply: "each other." And that may be Madogonga's greatest achievement—that she has given the women of Zimbabwe each other. That she has given people who long for peace and justice each other. That she has given them a voice they can only have collectively—and a strength they can only have together. They are a force to be reckoned with. Because history tells us, truth has a life of its own once it's told. Love can transform a nation once it's taught. Courage can be contagious; righteousness can spread; and there is much wisdom in the old proverb: that God could not be everywhere, so he created mothers.

In the end, history has a clear direction—and it is not the way of those who arrest women and babies for singing in the streets. It's not the way of those who starve and silence their own people, and cling to power by threat of force.

It is the way of the maid walking home in Montgomery; the young woman marching silently in the streets of Tehran; the leader imprisoned in her own home for her commitment to democracy.

It is the way of young people in Cape Town who braved the wrath of government to hear a young senator from New York speak about the ripples of hope one righteous act can create. And it is the way that Magadonga Mahlangu and Jenni Williams and the women and men who take to the streets of Harare and Bulawayo and Victoria Falls because they love their country and love their children and know that something better is possible.

Bobby Kennedy once said, "All great questions must be raised by great voices, and the greatest voice is the voice of the people—speaking out—in prose, or painting or poetry or music; speaking out—in homes and halls, streets and farms, courts and cafes—let that voice speak and the stillness you hear will be the gratitude of mankind." Magodongo and WOZA have given so many of their fellow citizens of Zimbabwe that voice—and tonight, we express our gratitude for their work.

PRESIDENT OBAMA: Good afternoon, everybody. I want to officially welcome the South African delegation to this nuclear summit and thank President Zuma for his extraordinary leadership.

So far today I've already met with Prime Minister Singh of India, as well as the President of Kazakhstan, and now we are meeting with the President of South Africa. I'll be meeting with the Prime Minister of Pakistan after this meeting.

The central focus of this nuclear summit is the fact that the single biggest threat to U.S. security, both short term, medium term and long term, would be the possibility of a terrorist organization obtaining a nuclear weapon. This is something that could change the security landscape of this country and around the world for years to come. If there was ever a detonation in New York City, or London, or Johannesburg, the ramifications economically, politically, and from a security perspective would be devastating. And we know that organizations like al Qaeda are in the process of trying to secure a nuclear weapon—a weapon of mass destruction that they have no compunction at using.

Unfortunately, we have a situation in which there is a lot of loose nuclear material around the world. And so the central focus for this summit is getting the international community on the path in which we are locking down that nuclear material in a very specific time frame with a specific work plan. And one of the things that I'm very pleased about is that countries have embraced this goal and they're coming to this summit, not just talking about general statements of support but rather very specific approaches to how we can solve this profound international problem.

I wanted to especially single out South Africa because South Africa is singular in having had a nuclear weapons program, had moved forward on it, and then decided this was not the right path; dismantled it; and has been a strong, effective leader in the international community around non-proliferation issues.

Remarks by President Obama and President Zuma of South Africa before Bilateral Meeting, Blair House, The White House, Office of the Press Secretary, For Immediate Release, April 11, 2010. http://www.white-house.gov/the-press-office/remarks-president-obama-and-president-zuma-south-africa-bilateral-meeting.

And so South Africa has special standing in being a moral leader on this issue. And I wanted to publicly compliment President Zuma and his administration for the leadership they've shown. And we are looking forward toward the possibility of them helping to guide other countries down a similar direction of non-proliferation.

But I feel very good at this stage in the degree of commitment and sense of urgency that I've seen from the world leaders so far on this issue. We think we can make enormous progress on this. And this then becomes part and parcel of the broader focus that we've had over the last several weeks, with the signing of the START treaty between the United States and Russia, reducing our nuclear stockpiles; a Nuclear Posture Review that has been released that sends a clear signal that those who abide by the non-proliferation treaties will have negative assurances, meaning that if they're abiding by their obligations, then they will not be targeted for potential nuclear weapons. And this then becomes a central part of a process that is probably the most urgent one and one that we're most concerned with in the short term. So, thank you again, Mr. President, for your participation and your leadership. Thank you.

I congratulate Kenya on the promulgation of the new constitution, which was approved by a majority of voters on August 4, 2010. This historic approval and signing of the constitution is an important step forward, and demonstrates the commitment of Kenya's leaders and people to a future of unity, democracy, and equal justice for all—even the powerful. With this Constitution, the people of Kenya have set a positive example for all of Africa and the world.

Today represents a moment of promise for Kenya, similar to the early days of independence—a new moment of promise that must be seized to usher in an era of progress for the Kenyan people. The United States looks forward to partnering with Kenya as it moves through the multi-year process of implementing the new constitution. We share the expectations of the Kenyan people that this process will usher in an era of deepened democracy and expanded economic opportunity for all Kenyans.

I am disappointed that Kenya hosted Sudanese President Omar al-Bashir in defiance of International Criminal Court arrest warrants for war crimes, crimes against humanity, and genocide. The Government of Kenya has committed itself to full cooperation with the ICC, and we consider it important that Kenya honor its commitments to the

Statement by President Obama on the Promulgation of Kenya's New Constitution, The White House, Office of the Press Secretary, For Immediate Release, August 27, 2010. http://www.whitehouse. gov/the-press-office/2010/08/27/statement-president-obama-promulgation-kenyas-new-constitution.
Statement by President Barack Obama on the Violence in Cote d'Ivoire, The White House, Office of the Press Secretary, For Immediate Release, March 9, 2011. http://www.whitehouse.gov/ the-press-office/2011/03/09/statement-president-barack-obama-violence-cote-divoire.

ICC and to international justice, along with all nations that share those responsibilities. In Kenya and beyond, justice is a critical ingredient for lasting peace.

I strongly condemn the abhorrent violence against unarmed civilians in Cote d'Ivoire. I am particularly appalled by the indiscriminate killing of unarmed civilians during peaceful rallies, many of them women, including those who were gunned down as they marched in support of the legitimately elected President Alassane Ouattara. Reports indicate that the women were shot to death by security forces loyal to former President Laurent Gbagbo. On March 8—the 100th Anniversary of International Women's Day—we saw pictures of women peacefully rallying with signs that said, "Don't shoot us"—a strong testament to the bravery of women exercising their right of peaceful assembly.

The United States remains deeply concerned about escalating violence, including the deepening humanitarian and economic crisis and its impact in Cote d'Ivoire and neighboring countries. All armed parties in Cote d'Ivoire must make every effort to protect civilians from being targeted, harmed, or killed. The United States reiterates its commitment to work with the international community to ensure that perpetrators of such atrocities be identified and held individually accountable for their actions.

As we have said since the election results in Cote d'Ivoire were certified: the people of Cote d'Ivoire elected Alassane Ouattara as their President, and Laurent Gbagbo lost the election. Former President Gbagbo's efforts to hold on to power at the expense of his own country are an assault on the universal rights of his people, and the democracy that the Cote d'Ivoire deserves. The people of Cote d'Ivoire have extraordinary talent and potential, and they deserve leadership that is responsive to their hopes and aspirations. It is time for former President Gbagbo to heed the will of his people, and to complete a peaceful transition of power to President Ouattara.

Chapter 4

Barack Obama and Latin America

These are extraordinary times for our country. We are confronting an historic economic crisis. We are fighting two wars. We face a range of challenges that will define the way that Americans will live in the 21st century. There is no shortage of work to be done, or responsibilities to bear.

And we have begun to make progress. Just this week, we have taken steps to protect American consumers and homeowners, and to reform our system of government contracting so that we better protect our people while spending our money more wisely. The engines of our economy are slowly beginning to turn, and we are working toward historic reform of health care and energy. I welcome the hard work that has been done by the Congress on these and other issues.

In the midst of all these challenges, however, my single most important responsibility as President is to keep the American people safe. That is the first thing that I think about when I wake up in the morning. It is the last thing that I think about when I go to sleep at night.

This responsibility is only magnified in an era when an extremist ideology threatens our people, and technology gives a handful of terrorists the potential to do us great harm. We are less than eight years removed from the deadliest attack on American soil in our history. We know that al Qaeda is actively planning to attack us again. We know that this threat will be with us for a long time, and that we must use all elements of our power to defeat it.

Already, we have taken several steps to achieve that goal. For the first time since 2002, we are providing the necessary resources and strategic direction to take the fight to the extremists who attacked us on 9/11 in Afghanistan and Pakistan. We are investing in the 21st century military and intelligence capabilities that will allow us to stay one

Remarks of President Barack Obama—As Prepared for Delivery Protecting Our Security and Our Values, The White House, Office of the Press Secretary, For Immediate Release, National Archives Museum, Washington, D.C., May 21, 2009.

step ahead of a nimble enemy. We have re-energized a global non-proliferation regime to deny the world's most dangerous people access to the world's deadliest weapons, and launched an effort to secure all loose nuclear materials within four years. We are better protecting our border, and increasing our preparedness for any future attack or natural disaster. We are building new partnerships around the world to disrupt, dismantle, and defeat al Qaeda and its affiliates. And we have renewed American diplomacy so that we once again have the strength and standing to truly lead the world.

These steps are all critical to keeping America secure. But I believe with every fiber of my being that in the long run we also cannot keep this country safe unless we enlist the power of our most fundamental values. The documents that we hold in this very hall—the Declaration of Independence, the Constitution, the Bill of Rights—are not simply words written into aging parchment. They are the foundation of liberty and justice in this country, and a light that shines for all who seek freedom, fairness, equality and dignity in the world.

I stand here today as someone whose own life was made possible by these documents. My father came to our shores in search of the promise that they offered. My mother made me rise before dawn to learn of their truth when I lived as a child in a foreign land. My own American journey was paved by generations of citizens who gave meaning to those simple words—"to form a more perfect union." I have studied the Constitution as a student; I have taught it as a teacher; I have been bound by it as a lawyer and legislator. I took an oath to preserve, protect and defend the Constitution as Commander-in-Chief, and as a citizen, I know that we must never-ever turn our back on its enduring principles for expedience sake.

I make this claim not simply as a matter of idealism. We uphold our most cherished values not only because doing so is right, but because it strengthens our country and keeps us safe. Time and again, our values have been our best national security asset—in war and peace; in times of ease and in eras of upheaval.

Fidelity to our values is the reason why the United States of America grew from a small string of colonies under the writ of an empire to the strongest nation in the world.

It is the reason why enemy soldiers have surrendered to us in battle, knowing they'd receive better treatment from America's armed forces than from their own government.

It is the reason why America has benefited from strong alliances that amplified our power, and drawn a sharp and moral contrast with our adversaries. It is the reason why we've been able to overpower the iron fist of fascism, outlast the iron curtain of communism, and enlist free nations and free people everywhere in common cause and common effort.

From Europe to the Pacific, we have been a nation that has shut down torture chambers and replaced tyranny with the rule of law. That is who we are. And where terrorists offer only the injustice of disorder and destruction, America must demonstrate that our values and institutions are more resilient than a hateful ideology.

After 9/11, we knew that we had entered a new era—that enemies who did not abide by any law of war would present new challenges to our application of the law; that our government would need new tools to protect the American people, and that these tools would have to allow us to prevent attacks instead of simply prosecuting those who try to carry them out.

Unfortunately, faced with an uncertain threat, our government made a series of hasty decisions. And I believe that those decisions were motivated by a sincere desire to protect the American people. But I also believe that—too often—our government made decisions based upon fear rather than foresight, and all too often trimmed facts and evidence to fit ideological predispositions. Instead of strategically applying our power and our principles, we too often set those principles aside as luxuries that we could no longer afford. And in this season of fear, too many of us—Democrats and Republicans; politicians, journalists and citizens—fell silent.

In other words, we went off course. And this is not my assessment alone. It was an assessment that was shared by the American people, who nominated candidates for President from both major parties who, despite our many differences, called for a new approach—one that rejected torture, and recognized the imperative of closing the prison at Guantanamo Bay.

Now let me be clear: we are indeed at war with al Qaeda and its affiliates. We do need to update our institutions to deal with this threat. But we must do so with an abiding confidence in the rule of law and due process; in checks and balances and accountability. For reasons that I will explain, the decisions that were made over the last eight years established an ad hoc legal approach for fighting terrorism that was neither effective nor sustainable—a framework that failed to rely on our legal traditions and time-tested institutions; that failed to use our values as a compass. And that is why I took several steps upon taking office to better protect the American people.

First, I banned the use of so-called enhanced interrogation techniques by the United States of America. I know some have argued that brutal methods like water-boarding were necessary to keep us safe. I could not disagree more. As Commander-in-Chief, I see the intelligence, I bear responsibility for keeping this country safe, and I reject the assertion that these are the most effective means of interrogation. What's more, they undermine the rule of law. They alienate us in the world. They serve as a recruitment tool for terrorists, and increase the will of our enemies to fight us, while decreasing the will of others to work with America. They risk the lives of our troops by making it less likely that others will surrender to them in battle, and more likely that Americans will be mistreated if they are captured. In short, they did not advance our war and counter-terrorism efforts—they undermined them, and that is why I ended them once and for all.

The arguments against these techniques did not originate from my Administration. As Senator McCain once said, torture "serves as a great propaganda tool for those who recruit people to fight against us." And even under President Bush, there was recognition among members of his Administration—including a Secretary of State, other senior officials, and many in the military and intelligence community—that those who argued for these tactics were on the wrong side of the debate, and the wrong side of history. We must leave these methods where they belong—in the past. They are not who we are. They are not America.

The second decision that I made was to order the closing of the prison camp at Guantanamo Bay. For over seven years, we have detained hundreds of people at Guantanamo. During that time, the system of Military Commissions at Guantanamo succeeded in convicting a grand total of three suspected terrorists. Let me repeat that: three convictions in over seven years. Instead of bringing terrorists to justice, efforts at prosecution met setbacks, cases lingered on, and in 2006 the Supreme Court invalidated the entire system. Meanwhile, over five hundred and twenty-five detainees were released from Guantanamo under the Bush Administration. Let me repeat that: two-thirds of the detainees were released before I took office and ordered the closure of Guantanamo.

There is also no question that Guantanamo set back the moral authority that is America's strongest currency in the world. Instead of building a durable framework for the struggle against al Qaeda that drew upon our deeply held values and traditions, our government was defending positions that undermined the rule of law. Indeed, part of the rationale for establishing Guantanamo in the first place was the misplaced notion that a prison there would be beyond the law—a proposition that the Supreme Court soundly rejected. Meanwhile, instead of serving as a tool to counter-terrorism, Guantanamo became a symbol that helped al Qaeda recruit terrorists to its cause. Indeed, the existence of Guantanamo likely created more terrorists around the world than it ever detained.

So the record is clear: rather than keep us safer, the prison at Guantanamo has weakened American national security. It is a rallying cry for our enemies. It sets back the willingness of our allies to work with us in fighting an enemy that operates in scores of countries. By any measure, the costs of keeping it open far exceed the complications involved in closing it. That is why I argued that it should be closed throughout my campaign. And that is why I ordered it closed within one year.

The third decision that I made was to order a review of all the pending cases at Guantanamo. I knew when I ordered Guantanamo closed that it would be difficult and complex. There are 240 people there who have now spent years in legal limbo. In dealing with this situation, we do not have the luxury of starting from scratch. We are cleaning up something that is—quite simply—a mess; a misguided experiment that has left in its wake a flood of legal challenges that my Administration is forced to deal with on a constant basis, and that consumes the time of government officials whose time should be spent on better protecting our country.

Indeed, the legal challenges that have sparked so much debate in recent weeks in Washington would be taking place whether or not I decided to close Guantanamo. For example, the court order to release seventeen Uighur detainees took place last fall—when George Bush was President. The Supreme Court that invalidated the system of prosecution at Guantanamo in 2006 was overwhelmingly appointed by Republican Presidents. In other words, the problem of what to do with Guantanamo detainees was not caused by my decision to close the facility; the problem exists because of the decision to open Guantanamo in the first place.

There are no neat or easy answers here. But I can tell you that the wrong answer is to pretend like this problem will go away if we maintain an unsustainable status quo. As President, I refuse to allow this problem to fester. Our security interests won't permit it. Our courts won't allow it. And neither should our conscience.

Now, over the last several weeks, we have seen a return of the politicization of these issues that have characterized the last several years. I understand that these problems arouse passions and concerns. They should. We are confronting some of the most complicated questions that a democracy can face. But I have no interest in spending our time re-litigating the policies of the last eight years. I want to solve these problems, and I want to solve them together as Americans.

And we will be ill-served by some of the fear-mongering that emerges whenever we discuss this issue. Listening to the recent debate, I've heard words that are calculated to scare people rather than educate them; words that have more to do with politics than protecting our country. So I want to take this opportunity to lay out what we are doing, and how we intend to resolve these outstanding issues. I will explain how each action that we are taking will help build a framework that protects both the American people and the values that we hold dear. And I will focus on two broad areas: first, issues relating to Guantanamo and our detention policy; second, issues relating to security and transparency.

Let me begin by disposing of one argument as plainly as I can: we are not going to release anyone if it would endanger our national security, nor will we release detainees within the United States who endanger the American people. Where demanded by justice and national security, we will seek to transfer some detainees to the same type of facilities in which we hold all manner of dangerous and violent criminals within our borders—highly secure prisons that ensure the public safety. As we make these decisions, bear in mind the following fact: nobody has ever escaped from one of our federal "supermax" prisons, which hold hundreds of convicted terrorists. As Senator Lindsey Graham said: "The idea that we cannot find a place to securely house 250-plus detainees within the United States is not rational."

We are currently in the process of reviewing each of the detainee cases at Guantanamo to determine the appropriate policy for dealing with them. As we do so, we are acutely aware that under the last Administration, detainees were released only to return to the battlefield. That is why we are doing away with the poorly planned, haphazard approach that let those detainees go in the past. Instead, we are treating these cases with the care and attention that the law requires and our security demands. Going forward, these cases will fall into five distinct categories.

First, when feasible, we will try those who have violated American criminal laws in federal courts—courts provided for by the United States Constitution. Some have derided our federal courts as incapable of handling the trials of terrorists. They are wrong. Our courts and juries of our citizens are tough enough to convict terrorists, and the record makes that clear. Ramzi Yousef tried to blow up the World Trade Center—he was convicted in our courts, and is serving a life sentence in U.S. prison. Zaccarias Moussaoui has been identified as the 20th 9/11 hijacker—he was convicted in our courts, and he too is serving a life sentence in prison. If we can try those terrorists in our courts and hold them in our prisons, then we can do the same with detainees from Guantanamo.

Recently, we prosecuted and received a guilty plea from a detainee—al-Marri—in federal court after years of legal confusion. We are preparing to transfer another detainee to the Southern District of New York, where he will face trial on charges related to the 1998 bombings of our embassies in Kenya and Tanzania—bombings that killed over 200 people. Preventing this detainee from coming to our shores would prevent his trial and conviction. And after over a decade, it is time to finally see that justice is served, and that is what we intend to do.

The second category of cases involves detainees who violate the laws of war and are best tried through Military Commissions. Military commissions have a history in the United States dating back to George Washington and the Revolutionary War. They are an appropriate venue for trying detainees for violations of the laws of war. They allow for the protection of sensitive sources and methods of intelligence-gathering; for the safety and security of participants; and for the presentation of evidence gathered from the battlefield that cannot be effectively presented in federal Courts.

Now, some have suggested that this represents a reversal on my part. They are wrong. In 2006, I did strongly oppose legislation proposed by the Bush Administration and passed by the Congress because it failed to establish a legitimate legal framework, with the kind of meaningful due process and rights for the accused that could stand up on appeal. I did, however, support the use of military commissions to try detainees, provided there were several reforms. And those are the reforms that we are making.

Instead of using the flawed Commissions of the last seven years, my Administration is bringing our Commissions in line with the rule of law. The rule will no longer permit us to use as evidence statements that have been obtained using cruel, inhuman, or degrading interrogation methods. We will no longer place the burden to prove that hearsay is unreliable on the opponent of the hearsay. And we will give detainees greater latitude in selecting their own counsel, and more protections if they refuse to testify. These reforms—among others—will make our Military Commissions a more credible and effective means of administering justice, and I will work with Congress and legal authorities across the political spectrum on legislation to ensure that these Commissions are fair, legitimate, and effective.

The third category of detainees includes those who we have been ordered released by the courts. Let me repeat what I said earlier: this has absolutely nothing to do with my decision to close Guantanamo. It has to do with the rule of law. The courts have found that there is no legitimate reason to hold twenty-one of the people currently held at Guantanamo. Twenty of these findings took place before I came into office. The United States is a nation of laws, and we must abide by these rulings.

The fourth category of cases involves detainees who we have determined can be transferred safely to another country. So far, our review team has approved fifty detainees for transfer. And my Administration is in ongoing discussions with a number of other countries about the transfer of detainees to their soil for detention and rehabilitation.

Finally, there remains the question of detainees at Guantanamo who cannot be prosecuted yet who pose a clear danger to the American people. I want to be honest: this is the toughest issue we will face. We are going to exhaust every avenue that we have to prosecute those at Guantanamo who pose a danger to our country. But even when this process is complete, there may be a number of people who cannot be prosecuted for past crimes, but who nonetheless pose a threat to the security of the United States. Examples of that threat include people who have received extensive explosives training at al Qaeda training camps, commanded Taliban troops in battle, expressed their allegiance to Osama bin Laden, or otherwise made it clear that they want to kill Americans. These are people who, in effect, remain at war with the United States.

As I said, I am not going to release individuals who endanger the American people. Al Qaeda terrorists and their affiliates are at war with the United States, and those that we capture—like other prisoners of war—must be prevented from attacking us again. However, we must recognize that these detention policies cannot be unbounded. That is why my Administration has begun to reshape these standards to ensure they are in line with the rule of law. We must have clear, defensible and lawful standards for those who fall in this category. We must have fair procedures so that we don't make mistakes. We must have a thorough process of periodic review, so that any prolonged detention is carefully evaluated and justified.

I know that creating such a system poses unique challenges. Other countries have grappled with this question, and so must we. But I want to be very clear that our goal is to construct a legitimate legal framework for Guantanamo detainees—not to avoid one. In our constitutional system, prolonged detention should not be the decision of any one man. If and when we determine that the United States must hold individuals to keep them from carrying out an act of war, we will do so within a system that involves judicial and congressional oversight. And so going forward, my Administration will work with Congress to develop an appropriate legal regime so that our efforts are consistent with our values and our Constitution.

As our efforts to close Guantanamo move forward, I know that the politics in Congress will be difficult. These issues are fodder for 30-second commercials and direct mail pieces that are designed to frighten. I get it. But if we continue to make decisions from within a climate of fear, we will make more mistakes. And if we refuse to deal with these issues today, then I guarantee you that they will be an albatross around our efforts to combat terrorism in the future. I have confidence that the American people are more interested in doing what is right to protect this country than in political posturing. I am not the only person in this city who swore an oath to uphold the Constitution—so did each and every member of Congress. Together we have a responsibility to enlist our values in the effort to secure our people, and to leave behind the legacy that makes it easier for future Presidents to keep this country safe.

The second set of issues that I want to discuss relates to security and transparency. National security requires a delicate balance. Our democracy depends upon transparency, but some information must be protected from public disclosure for the sake of our security—for instance, the movements of our troops; our intelligence-gathering; or the information we have about a terrorist organization and its affiliates. In these and other cases, lives are at stake.

Several weeks ago, as part of an ongoing court case, I released memos issued by the previous Administration's Office of Legal Counsel. I did not do this because I disagreed with the enhanced interrogation techniques that those memos authorized, or because I reject their legal rationale—although I do on both counts. I released the memos because the existence of that approach to interrogation was already widely known, the Bush Administration had acknowledged its existence, and I had already banned those methods. The argument that somehow by releasing those memos, we are providing terrorists with information about how they will be interrogated is unfounded—we will not be interrogating terrorists using that approach, because that approach is now prohibited.

In short, I released these memos because there was no overriding reason to protect them. And the ensuing debate has helped the American people better understand how these interrogation methods came to be authorized and used.

On the other hand, I recently opposed the release of certain photographs that were taken of detainees by U.S. personnel between 2002 and 2004. Individuals who violated standards of behavior in these photos have been investigated and held accountable. There is no debate as to whether what is reflected in those photos is wrong, and nothing has been concealed to absolve perpetrators of crimes. However, it was my judgment—informed by my national security team—that releasing these photos would inflame anti-American opinion, and allow our enemies to paint U.S. troops with a broad, damning and inaccurate brush, endangering them in theaters of war.

In short, there is a clear and compelling reason to not release these particular photos. There are nearly 200,000 Americans who are serving in harm's way, and I have a solemn responsibility for their safety as Commander-in-Chief. Nothing would be gained by the release of these photos that matters more than the lives of our young men and women serving in harm's way.

In each of these cases, I had to strike the right balance between transparency and national security. This balance brings with it a precious responsibility. And there is no doubt that the American people have seen this balance tested. In the images from Abu Ghraib and the brutal interrogation techniques made public long before I was President, the American people learned of actions taken in their name that bear no resemblance to the ideals that generations of Americans have fought for. And whether it was the run-up to the Iraq War or the revelation of secret programs, Americans often felt like part of the story had been unnecessarily withheld from them. That causes suspicion to build up. That leads to a thirst for accountability.

I ran for President promising transparency, and I meant what I said. That is why, whenever possible, we will make information available to the American people so that they can make informed judgments and hold us accountable. But I have never argued—and never will—that our most sensitive national security matters should be an open book. I will never abandon—and I will vigorously defend—the necessity of classification to defend our troops at war; to protect sources and methods; and to safeguard confidential actions that keep the American people safe. And so, whenever we cannot release certain information to the public for valid national security reasons, I will insist that there is oversight of my actions—by Congress or by the courts.

We are launching a review of current policies by all of those agencies responsible for the classification of documents to determine where reforms are possible, and to assure that the other branches of government will be in a position to review executive branch decisions on these matters. Because in our system of checks and balances, someone must always watch over the watchers—especially when it comes to sensitive information.

Along those same lines, my Administration is also confronting challenges to what is known as the "State Secrets" privilege. This is a doctrine that allows the government to challenge legal cases involving secret programs. It has been used by many past Presidents—Republican and Democrat—for many decades. And while this principle is absolutely necessary to protect national security, I am concerned that it has been over-used. We must not protect information merely because it reveals the violation of a law or embarrasses the government. That is why my Administration is nearing completion of a thorough review of this practice.

We plan to embrace several principles for reform. We will apply a stricter legal test to material that can be protected under the State Secrets privilege. We will not assert the privilege in court without first following a formal process, including review by a Justice Department committee and the personal approval of the Attorney General. Finally, each year we will voluntarily report to Congress when we have invoked the privilege and why, because there must be proper oversight of our actions.

On all of these matters related to the disclosure of sensitive information, I wish I could say that there is a simple formula. But there is not. These are tough calls involving competing concerns, and they require a surgical approach. But the common thread that runs through all of my decisions is simple: we will safeguard what we must to protect the American people, but we will also ensure the accountability and oversight that is the hallmark of our constitutional system. I will never hide the truth because it is uncomfortable. I will deal with Congress and the courts as co-equal branches of government. I will tell the American people what I know and don't know, and when I release something publicly or keep something secret, I will tell you why.

In all of the areas that I have discussed today, the policies that I have proposed represent a new direction from the last eight years. To protect the American people and our values, we have banned enhanced interrogation techniques. We are closing the prison at Guantanamo. We are reforming Military Commissions, and we will pursue a new legal regime to detain terrorists. We are declassifying more information and embracing more oversight of our actions, and narrowing our use of the State Secrets privilege. These are dramatic changes that will put our approach to national security on a surer, safer and more sustainable footing, and their implementation will take time.

There is a core principle that we will apply to all of our actions: even as we clean up the mess at Guantanamo, we will constantly re-evaluate our approach, subject our decisions to review from the other branches of government, and seek the strongest and most sustainable legal framework for addressing these issues in the long-term. By doing that, we can leave behind a legacy that outlasts my Administration, and that endures for the next President and the President after that; a legacy that protects the American people, and enjoys broad legitimacy at home and abroad.

That is what I mean when I say that we need to focus on the future. I recognize that many still have a strong desire to focus on the past. When it comes to the actions of the last eight years, some Americans are angry; others want to re-fight debates that have been settled, most clearly at the ballot box in November. And I know that these debates lead directly to a call for a fuller accounting, perhaps through an Independent Commission.

I have opposed the creation of such a Commission because I believe that our existing democratic institutions are strong enough to deliver accountability. The Congress can review abuses of our values, and there are ongoing inquiries by the Congress into matters like enhanced interrogation techniques. The Department of Justice and our courts can work through and punish any violations of our laws.

I understand that it is no secret that there is a tendency in Washington to spend our time pointing fingers at one another. And our media culture feeds the impulses that lead to a good fight. Nothing will contribute more to that than an extended re-litigation of the last eight years. Already, we have seen how that kind of effort only leads those in Washington to different sides laying blame, and can distract us from focusing our time, our effort, and our politics on the challenges of the future.

We see that, above all, in how the recent debate has been obscured by two opposite and absolutist ends. On one side of the spectrum, there are those who make little allowance for the unique challenges posed by terrorism, and who would almost never put national security over transparency. On the other end of the spectrum, there are those who embrace a view that can be summarized in two words: "anything goes." Their arguments suggest that the ends of fighting terrorism can be used to justify any means, and that the President should have blanket authority to do whatever he wants—provided that it is a President with whom they agree.

Both sides may be sincere in their views, but neither side is right. The American people are not absolutist, and they don't elect us to impose a rigid ideology on our problems. They know that we need not sacrifice our security for our values, nor sacrifice our values for our security, so long as we approach difficult questions with honesty, and care, and a dose of common sense. That, after all, is the unique genius of America. That is the challenge laid down by our Constitution. That has been the source of our strength through the ages. That is what makes the United States of America different as a nation.

I can stand here today, as President of the United States, and say without exception or equivocation that we do not torture, and that we will vigorously protect our people while forging a strong and durable framework that allows us to fight terrorism while abiding by the rule of law. Make no mistake: if we fail to turn the page on the approach that was taken over the past several years, then I will not be able to say that as President. And if we cannot stand for those core values, then we are not keeping faith with the documents that are enshrined in this hall.

The Framers who drafted the Constitution could not have foreseen the challenges that have unfolded over the last two hundred and twenty two years. But our Constitution has endured through secession and civil rights—through World War and Cold War—because it provides a foundation of principles that can be applied pragmatically; it provides a compass that can help us find our way. It hasn't always been easy. We are an imperfect people. Every now and then, there are those who think that America's safety and success requires us to walk away from the sacred principles enshrined in this building. We hear such voices today. But the American people have resisted that temptation. And though we have made our share of mistakes and course corrections, we have held fast to the principles that have been the source of our strength, and a beacon to the world.

Now, this generation faces a great test in the specter of terrorism. Unlike the Civil War or World War II, we cannot count on a surrender ceremony to bring this journey to an end. Right now, in distant training camps and in crowded cities, there are people plotting to take American lives. That will be the case a year from now, five years from now, and—in all probability—ten years from now. Neither I nor anyone else can stand here today and say that there will not be another terrorist attack that takes American lives. But I can say with certainty that my Administration—along with our extraordinary troops and the patriotic men and women who defend our national security—will do everything in our power to keep the American people safe. And I do know with certainty that we can defeat al Qaeda. Because the terrorists can only succeed if they swell their ranks and alienate America from our allies, and they will never be able to do that if we stay true to who we are; if we forge tough and durable approaches to fighting terrorism that are anchored in our timeless ideals.

This must be our common purpose. I ran for President because I believe that we cannot solve the challenges of our time unless we solve them together. We will not be safe if we see national security as a wedge that divides America—it can and must be a cause that unites us as one people, as one nation. We have done so before in times that were more perilous than ours. We will do so once again. Thank you, God Bless you, and God bless the United States of America.

WASHINGTON—In his weekly address, President Obama discussed his trip to Latin America and the importance of strengthening our economic partnership with the region to create good jobs at home. He expressed a need to open more global markets and increase exports as a way of expanding the U.S. economy.

In recent days, we've seen turmoil and tragedy around the world, from change in the Middle East and North Africa to the earthquake and tsunami in Japan. As I said on Friday, we will work with our partners in the region to protect innocent civilians in Libya and hold the Gaddafi regime accountable. And we will continue to stand with the people of Japan in their greatest hour of need.

As we respond to these immediate crises abroad, we also will not let up in our efforts to tackle the pressing, ongoing challenges facing our country, including accelerating economic growth. That's why, over the weekend, I'll be in Latin America. One of the main reasons for my trip is to strengthen economic partnerships abroad so that we create good jobs at home.

President Obama on Economic Lessons from Latin American Nations, The White House, Office of the Press Secretary, March 19, 2011. Distributed by the Bureau of International Information Programs, U.S. Department of State. Web site: http://www.whitehouse.gov/the-press-office/2011/03/19/president-announces-economic-lessons-be-learned-countries-latin-america-.

Latin America is a part of the world where the economy is growing very quickly. And as these markets grow, so does their demand for goods and services. The question is, where are those goods and services going to come from? As President, I want to make sure these products are made in America. I want to open more markets around the world so that American companies can do more business and hire more of our people.

Here's a statistic to explain why this is important. Every $1 billion of goods and services we export supports more than 5,000 jobs in the United States. So, the more we sell overseas, the more jobs we create on our shores. That's why, last year, I set a goal for this country: to double our exports by 2014. And it's a goal we're on track to meet.

Part of the reason why is the rapid growth of Latin America, and their openness to American business. We now export more than three times as much to Latin America as we do to China, and our exports to the region will soon support more than two million jobs here in the United States. Brazil, the first stop on our trip, is a great example.

In 2010, America's exports to Brazil supported more than 250,000 American jobs. These are jobs at places like Capstone Turbine in California, which recently sold $2 million worth of high-tech energy equipment to Brazil. Another company is Rhino Assembly, a small business in Charlotte, North Carolina that sells and repairs tools for building cars and planes. A deal with a distributor in Brazil has resulted in new sales and new employees at that firm. And we can point to large companies like Sikorsky, whose helicopter sales to Brazil help sustain a large, skilled workforce in Connecticut, Alabama, and Pennsylvania.

Today, Brazil imports more goods from the United States than from any other nation. And I'll be meeting with business leaders from both countries to talk about how we can create even more jobs by deepening these economic ties. After Brazil, I'll also visit Chile, a country with a growing economy, and increasing demand for American goods. In fact, since 2004, our exports there are up 300 percent, and now support about 70,000 jobs in the United States. Finally, we'll head to El Salvador, a nation with so much promise for growth with the potential to benefit both of our nations.

We've always had a special bond with our neighbors to the south. It's a bond born of shared history and values, and strengthened by the millions of Americans who proudly trace their roots to Latin America. But what is clear is that in an increasingly global economy, our partnership with these nations is only going to become more vital. For it's a source of growth and prosperity—and not just for the people of Latin America, but for the American people as well.

Thank you.

THE PRESIDENT: Alo! Cidade! Maravilhoso! Boa tarde, todo o povo brasileiro.

Since the moment we arrived, the people of this nation have graciously shown my family the warmth and generosity of the Brazilian spirit. Obrigado. Thank you. And I want to give a special thanks to all of you for being here, because I've been told that there's a Vasco football game coming. Botafogo. So I know that—I realize Brazilians don't give up their soccer very easily.

Now, one of my earliest impressions of Brazil was a movie I saw with my mother as a very young child, a movie called Black Orpheus, that is set in the favelas of Rio during Carnival. And my mother loved that movie, with its singing and dancing against the backdrop of the beautiful green hills. And it first premiered as a play right here in Teatro Municipal. That's my understanding.

And my mother is gone now, but she would have never imagined that her son's first trip to Brazil would be as President of the United States. She would have never imagined that. And I never imagined that this country would be even more beautiful than it was in the movie. You are, as Jorge Ben-Jor sang, "A tropical country, blessed by God, and beautiful by nature." I've seen that beauty in the cascading hillsides, in your endless miles of sand and ocean, and in the vibrant, diverse gatherings of brasileiros who have come here today.

And we have a wonderfully mixed group. We have Cariocas and Paulistas, Baianas, Mineiros. We've got men and women from the cities to the interior, and so many young people here who are the great future of this great nation. Now, yesterday, I met with your wonderful new President, Dilma Rousseff, and talked about how we can strengthen the partnership between our governments. But today, I want to speak directly to the Brazilian people about how we can strengthen the friendship between our nations. I've come here to share some ideas because I want to speak of the values that we share, the hopes that we have in common, and the difference that we can make together.

When you think about it, the journeys of the United States of America and Brazil began in similar ways. Our lands are rich with God's creation, home to ancient and indigenous peoples. From overseas, the Americas were discovered by men who sought a New World, and settled by pioneers who pushed westward, across vast frontiers. We became colonies claimed by distant crowns, but soon declared our independence. We then welcomed waves of immigrants to our shores, and eventually after a long struggle, we cleansed the stain of slavery from our land.

The United States was the first nation to recognize Brazil's independence, and set up a diplomatic outpost in this country. The first head of state to visit the United States was the leader of Brazil, Dom Pedro II. In the Second World War, our brave men

Remarks by the President to the People of Brazil in Rio de Janeiro, Brazil Teatro Municipal Rio de Janeiro, The White House, Office of the Press Secretary, For Immediate Release, March 20, 2011. http://www.whitehouse.gov/the-press-office/2011/03/20/remarks-president-people-brazil-rio-de-janeiro-brazil.

and women fought side-by-side for freedom. And after the war, both of our nations struggled to achieve the full blessings of liberty.

On the streets of the United States, men and women marched and bled and some died so that every citizen could enjoy the same freedoms and opportunities—no matter what you looked like, no matter where you came from. In Brazil, you fought against two decades of dictatorships for the same right to be heard—the right to be free from fear, free from want. And yet, for years, democracy and development were slow to take hold, and millions suffered as a result.

But I come here today because those days have passed. Brazil today is a flourishing democracy—a place where people are free to speak their mind and choose their leaders; where a poor kid from Pernambuco can rise from the floors of a copper factory to the highest office in Brazil.

Over the last decade, the progress made by the Brazilian people has inspired the world. More than half of this nation is now considered middle class. Millions have been lifted from poverty. For the first time, hope is returning to places where fear had long prevailed. I saw this today when I visited Cidade de Deus—the City of God.

It isn't just the new security efforts and social programs—and I want to congratulate the mayor and the governor for the excellent work that they're doing. But it's also a change in attitudes. As one young resident said, "People have to look at favelas not with pity, but as a source of presidents and lawyers and doctors, artists, [and] people with solutions."

With each passing day, Brazil is a country with more solutions. In the global community, you've gone from relying on the help of other nations, to now helping fight poverty and disease wherever they exist. You play an important role in the global institutions that protect our common security and promote our common prosperity. And you will welcome the world to your shores when the World Cup and the Olympic games come to Rio de Janeiro.

Now, you may be aware that this city was not my first choice for the Summer Olympics. But if the games could not be held in Chicago, then there's no place I'd rather see them than right here in Rio. And I intend to come back in 2016 to watch what happens. For so long, Brazil was a nation brimming with potential but held back by politics, both at home and abroad. For so long, you were called a country of the future, told to wait for a better day that was always just around the corner.

Meus amigos, that day has finally come. And this is a country of the future no more. The people of Brazil should know that the future has arrived. It is here now. And it's time to seize it.

Now, our countries have not always agreed on everything. And just like many nations, we're going to have our differences of opinion going forward. But I'm here to tell you that the American people don't just recognize Brazil's success—we root for Brazil's success. As you confront the many challenges you still face at home as well as abroad, let us stand together—not as senior and junior partners, but as equal partners, joined in a spirit of mutual interest and mutual respect, committed to the progress that I know that we can make together. I'm confident we can do it.

Together we can advance our common prosperity. As two of the world's largest economies, we worked side by side during the financial crisis to restore growth and confidence. And to keep our economies growing, we know what's necessary in both of our nations. We need a skilled, educated workforce—which is why American and Brazilian companies have pledged to help increase student exchanges between our two nations.

We need a commitment to innovation and technology—which is why we've agreed to expand cooperation between our scientists, researchers, and engineers. We need world-class infrastructure—which is why American companies want to help you build and prepare this city for Olympic success.

In a global economy, the United States and Brazil should expand trade, expand investment, so that we create new jobs and new opportunities in both of our nations. And that's why we're working to break down barriers to doing business. That's why we're building closer relationships between our workers and our entrepreneurs.

Together we can also promote energy security and protect our beautiful planet. As two nations that are committed to greener economies, we know that the ultimate solution to our energy challenges lies in clean and renewable power. And that's why half the vehicles in this country can run on bio-fuels, and most of your electricity comes from hydropower. That's also why, in the United States, we've jumpstarted a new clean energy industry. And that's why the United States and Brazil are creating new energy partnerships—to share technologies, create new jobs, and leave our children a world that is cleaner and safer than we found it.

Together, our two nations can also help defend our citizens' security. We're working together to stop narco-trafficking that has destroyed too many lives in this hemisphere. We seek the goal of a world without nuclear weapons. We're working together to enhance nuclear security across our hemisphere. From Africa to Haiti, we are working side by side to combat the hunger, disease, and corruption that can rot a society and rob human beings of dignity and opportunity.

And as two countries that have been greatly enriched by our African heritage, it's absolutely vital that we are working with the continent of Africa to help lift it up. That is something that we should be committed to doing together. Today, we're both also delivering assistance and support to the Japanese people at their greatest hour of need. The ties that bind our nations to Japan are strong. In Brazil, you are home to the largest Japanese population outside of Japan. In the United States, we forged an alliance of more than 60 years. The people of Japan are some of our closest friends, and we will pray with them, and stand with them, and rebuild with them until this crisis has passed.

In these and other efforts to promote peace and prosperity throughout the world, the United States and Brazil are partners not just because we share history, not just because we're in the same hemisphere; not just because we share ties of commerce and culture, but also because we share certain enduring values and ideals.

We both believe in the power and promise of democracy. We believe that no other form of government is more effective at promoting growth and prosperity that reaches every human being—not just some but all. And those who argue otherwise, those who argue that democracy stands in the way of economic progress, they must contend with the example of Brazil.

The millions in this country who have climbed from poverty into the middle class, they could not do so in a closed economy controlled by the state. You're prospering as a free people with open markets and a government that answers to its citizens. You're proving that the goal of social justice and social inclusion can be best achieved through freedom—that democracy is the greatest partner of human progress.

We also believe that in nations as big and diverse as ours, shaped by generations of immigrants from every race and faith and background, democracy offers the best hope that every citizen is treated with dignity and respect, and that we can resolve our differences peacefully, that we find strength in our diversity.

We know that experience in the United States. We know how important it is to be able to work together—even when we often disagree. I understand that our chosen form of government can be slow and messy. We understand that democracy must be constantly strengthened and perfected over time. We know that different nations take different paths to realize the promise of democracy. And we understand that no one nation should impose its will on another.

But we also know that there's certain aspirations shared by every human being: We all seek to be free. We all seek to be heard. We all yearn to live without fear or discrimination. We all yearn to choose how we are governed. And we all want to shape our own destiny. These are not American ideals or Brazilian ideals. These are not Western ideals. These are universal rights, and we must support them everywhere.

Today, we are seeing the struggle for these rights unfold across the Middle East and North Africa. We've seen a revolution born out of a yearning for basic human dignity in Tunisia. We've seen peaceful protestors pour into Tahrir Square—men and women, young and old, Christian and Muslim. We've seen the people of Libya take a courageous stand against a regime determined to brutalize its own citizens. Across the region, we've seen young people rise up—a new generation demanding the right to determine their own future.

From the beginning, we have made clear that the change they seek must be driven by their own people. But for our two nations, for the United States and Brazil, two nations who have struggled over many generations to perfect our own democracies, the

United States and Brazil know that the future of the Arab World will be determined by its people.

No one can say for certain how this change will end, but I do know that change is not something that we should fear. When young people insist that the currents of history are on the move, the burdens of the past can be washed away. When men and women peacefully claim their human rights, our own common humanity is enhanced. Wherever the light of freedom is lit, the world becomes a brighter place.

That is the example of Brazil. That is the example of Brazil. Brazil—a country that shows that a dictatorship can become a thriving democracy. Brazil—a country that shows democracy delivers both freedom and opportunity to its people. Brazil—a country that shows how a call for change that starts in the streets can transform a city, transform a country, transform a world.

Decades ago, it was directly outside of this theater, in Cinelandia Square, where the call for change was heard in Brazil. Students and artists and political leaders of all stripes would gather with banners that said, "Down with the dictatorship. The people in power." Their democratic aspirations would not be fulfilled until years later, but one of the young Brazilians in that generation's movement would go on to forever change the history of this country. A child of an immigrant, her participation in the movement led to her arrest and her imprisonment, her torture at the hands of her own government. And so she knows what it's like to live without the most basic human rights that so many are fighting for today. But she also knows what it is to persevere. She knows what it is to overcome—because today that woman is your nation's president, Dilma Rousseff.

Our two nations face many challenges. On the road ahead, we will certainly encounter many obstacles. But in the end, it is our history that gives us hope for a better tomorrow. It is the knowledge that the men and women who came before us have triumphed over greater trials than these—that we live in places where ordinary people have done extraordinary things.

It's that sense of possibility, that sense of optimism that first drew pioneers to this New World. It's what binds our nations together as partners in this new century. It's why we believe, in the words of Paul Coelho, one of your most famous writers, "With the strength of our love and our will, we can change our destiny, as well as the destiny of many others." Muito obrigado. Thank you.

PRESIDENT OBAMA: It is my great pleasure to welcome President Santos and the rest of the delegation from Colombia here to the White House. I had the

Remarks by President Obama and President Santos of Colombia After Bilateral Meeting, Oval Office, The White House, Office of the Press Secretary, For Immediate Release, April 07, 2011. http://www.whitehouse.gov/the-press-office/2011/04/07/remarks-president-obama-and-president-santos-colombia-after-bilateral-me.

pleasure of meeting President Santos shortly after he was elected, on the sidelines of meetings at the United Nations, and we are now continuing our conversation.

The United States has an enormous interest in the development of Latin America and an enormous interest in progress in Colombia. We have been a partner there as Colombia dealt with some very difficult times and has now blossomed into a strong democracy that is respectful of human rights and is moving forward vigorously to provide economic opportunity for all of its people.

President Santos I think is at the forefront of a progressive and thoughtful agenda within Colombia. He's obviously initiating a whole range of reforms. Colombia is also a leader when it comes to security in the region, and we are glad that we've been able to partner with Colombia not only to deal with security situations inside Colombia, but now increasingly Colombia can be a role model for the rest of the region. And I just realized I was going to have translation, so let me stop there, and then we can continue.

In short, Colombia is one of our strongest partners not only in the region but around the world. And when we met in September, I suggested to President Santos that we should do even more to deepen and strengthen our relationship. And in pursuit of that deepening relationship, I dispatched my team to Colombia to discuss how we can finally move forward on trade agreements between our two countries.

So today, I am very pleased to announce that we have developed an action plan for labor rights in Colombia, consistent with our values and interests, but more importantly, consistent with President Santos' vision of a just and equitable society inside of Colombia. And we believe that this serves as a basis for us moving forward on a U.S.-Colombia free trade agreement.

Now, there's obviously a lot of work to do to translate this action plan into reality. And we are going to continue to engage with President Santos and his administration in an active process to ensure good working conditions, to make sure that trade unionists are protected, to make sure that we're creating a level of playing field for business and workers here and around the world. And so I very much appreciate President Santos' efforts. He emphasized to me how important this is to him personally and the fact that Colombia sees a vision for its country in which all workers are treated fairly. And I have great confidence in his ability to be able to execute on this plan, and we look forward to working with him on it.

Now, obviously, the United States represents an important market for Colombian businesses, and so this is going to be a win for Colombia. It's also a win for the United States. This represents a potential $1 billion of exports and it could mean thousands of jobs for workers here in the United States. And so I believe that we can structure a trade agreement that is a win-win for both our countries, and I'm looking forward to working with President Santos to ensure that both countries benefit. And this will help me meet my goal of making sure the United States has doubled exports over the coming years and that we're as competitive as we can be in a global marketplace in the 21st century.

Finally, let me just say that President Santos obviously has strong connections with the United States and particularly with the Kansas Jayhawks. We were both disappointed that Kansas did not go all the way, but President Santos assures me that there's always next year.

And so I appreciate President Santos not only for having faith in my bracket, but also having faith in the strong relationship and friendship between the United States and Colombia. And I am looking forward to visiting Colombia next year for the Summit of the Americas, in which I think, under President Santos' leadership, I'm confident we'll be able to do a lot of work to strengthen relations with all the countries in the hemisphere.

Chapter 5

Establishing New Relations with the Muslim World

PRESIDENT OBAMA: Mr. Speaker, Madam Deputy Speaker, distinguished members, I am honored to speak in this chamber, and I am committed to renewing the alliance between our nations and the friendship between our people.

This is my first trip overseas as President of the United States. I've been to the G20 summit in London, and the NATO summit in Strasbourg, and the European Union summit in Prague. Some people have asked me if I chose to continue my travels to Ankara and Istanbul to send a message to the world. And my answer is simple: Evet—yes. Turkey is a critical ally. Turkey is an important part of Europe. And Turkey and the United States must stand together—and work together—to overcome the challenges of our time.

This morning I had the great privilege of visiting the tomb of your extraordinary founder of your republic. And I was deeply impressed by this beautiful memorial to a man who did so much to shape the course of history. But it is also clear that the greatest monument to Ataturk's life is not something that can be cast in stone and marble. His greatest legacy is Turkey's strong, vibrant, secular democracy, and that is the work that this assembly carries on today.

This future was not easily assured, it was not guaranteed. At the end of World War I, Turkey could have succumbed to the foreign powers that were trying to claim its territory, or sought to restore an ancient empire. But Turkey chose a different future. You freed yourself from foreign control, and you founded a republic that commands the respect of the United States and the wider world.

And there is a simple truth to this story: Turkey's democracy is your own achievement. It was not forced upon you by any outside power, nor did it come without

Remarks by President Obama to the Turkish Parliament, Turkish Grand National Assembly Complex, Ankara, Turkey, The White House, Office of the Press Secretary, For Immediate Release, April 6, 2009. http://www.whitehouse.gov/the_press_office/Remarks-By-President-Obama-To-The-Turkish-Parliament/.

struggle and sacrifice. Turkey draws strength from both the successes of the past, and from the efforts of each generation of Turks that makes new progress for your people.

Now, my country's democracy has its own story. The general who led America in revolution and governed as our first President was, as many of you know, George Washington. And like you, we built a grand monument to honor our founding father—a towering obelisk that stands in the heart of the capital city that bears Washington's name. I can see the Washington Monument from the window of the White House every day.

It took decades to build. There were frequent delays. Over time, more and more people contributed to help make this monument the inspiring structure that still stands tall today. Among those who came to our aid were friends from all across the world who offered their own tributes to Washington and the country he helped to found.

And one of those tributes came from Istanbul. Ottoman Sultan Abdulmecid sent a marble plaque that helped to build the Washington Monument. Inscribed in the plaque was a poem that began with a few simple words: "So as to strengthen the friendship between the two countries."

Over 150 years have passed since those words were carved into marble. Our nations have changed in many ways. But our friendship is strong, and our alliance endures. It is a friendship that flourished in the years after World War II, when President Truman committed our nation to the defense of Turkey's freedom and sovereignty, and Turkey committed itself into the NATO Alliance. Turkish troops have served by our side from Korea to Kosovo to Kabul. Together, we withstood the great test of the Cold War. Trade between our nations has steadily advanced. So has cooperation in science and research.

The ties among our people have deepened, as well, and more and more Americans of Turkish origin live and work and succeed within our borders. And as a basketball fan, I've even noticed that Hedo Turkoglu and Mehmet Okur have got some pretty good basketball games.

The United States and Turkey have not always agreed on every issue, and that's to be expected—no two nations do. But we have stood together through many challenges over the last 60 years. And because of the strength of our alliance and the endurance of our friendship, both America and Turkey are stronger and the world is more secure.

Now, our two democracies are confronted by an unprecedented set of challenges: An economic crisis that recognizes no borders; extremism that leads to the killing of innocent men and women and children; strains on our energy supply and a changing climate; the proliferation of the world's deadliest weapons; and the persistence of tragic conflict.

These are the great tests of our young century. And the choices that we make in the coming years will determine whether the future will be shaped by fear or by freedom; by poverty or by prosperity; by strife or by a just, secure and lasting peace.

This much is certain: No one nation can confront these challenges alone, and all nations have a stake in overcoming them. That is why we must listen to one another, and seek common ground. That is why we must build on our mutual interests, and rise above our differences. We are stronger when we act together. That is the message that I've carried with me throughout this trip to Europe. That is the message that I delivered when I had the privilege of meeting with your President and with your Prime Minister. That will be the approach of the United States of America going forward.

Already, America and Turkey are working with the G20 on an unprecedented response to an unprecedented economic crisis. Now, this past week, we came together to ensure that the world's largest economies take strong and coordinated action to stimulate growth and restore the flow of credit; to reject the pressures of protectionism, and to extend a hand to developing countries and the people hit hardest by this downturn; and to dramatically reform our regulatory system so that the world never faces a crisis like this again.

As we go forward, the United States and Turkey can pursue many opportunities to serve prosperity for our people. The President and I this morning talked about expanding the ties of commerce and trade. There's enormous opportunity when it comes to energy to create jobs. And we can increase new sources to not only free ourselves from dependence of other energies—other countries' energy sources, but also to combat climate change. We should build on our Clean Technology Fund to leverage efficiency and renewable energy investments in Turkey. And to power markets in Turkey and Europe, the United States will continue to support your central role as an East-West corridor for oil and natural gas.

This economic cooperation only reinforces the common security that Europe and the United States share with Turkey as a NATO ally, and the common values that we share as democracies. So in meeting the challenges of the 21st century, we must seek the strength of a Europe that is truly united, peaceful and free.

So let me be clear: The United States strongly supports Turkey's bid to become a member of the European Union. We speak not as members of the EU, but as close friends of both Turkey and Europe. Turkey has been a resolute ally and a responsible partner in transatlantic and European institutions. Turkey is bound to Europe by more than the bridges over the Bosphorous. Centuries of shared history, culture, and commerce bring you together. Europe gains by the diversity of ethnicity, tradition and faith—it is not diminished by it. And Turkish membership would broaden and strengthen Europe's foundation once more.

Now, of course, Turkey has its own responsibilities. And you've made important progress towards membership. But I also know that Turkey has pursued difficult political reforms not simply because it's good for EU membership, but because it's right for Turkey.

In the last several years, you've abolished state security courts, you've expanded the right to counsel. You've reformed the penal code and strengthened laws that govern the freedom of the press and assembly. You've lifted bans on teaching and broadcasting Kurdish, and the world noted with respect the important signal sent through a new state Kurdish television station.

These achievements have created new laws that must be implemented, and a momentum that should be sustained. For democracies cannot be static—they must move forward. Freedom of religion and expression lead to a strong and vibrant civil society that only strengthens the state, which is why steps like reopening Halki Seminary will send such an important signal inside Turkey and beyond. An enduring commitment to the rule of law is the only way to achieve the security that comes from justice for all people. Robust minority rights let societies benefit from the full measure of contributions from all citizens.

I say this as the President of a country that not very long ago made it hard for somebody who looks like me to vote, much less be President of the United States. But it is precisely that capacity to change that enriches our countries. Every challenge that we face is more easily met if we tend to our own democratic foundation. This work is never over. That's why, in the United States, we recently ordered the prison at Guantanamo Bay closed. That's why we prohibited—without exception or equivocation—the use of torture. All of us have to change. And sometimes change is hard.

Another issue that confronts all democracies as they move to the future is how we deal with the past. The United States is still working through some of our own darker periods in our history. Facing the Washington Monument that I spoke of is a memorial of Abraham Lincoln, the man who freed those who were enslaved even after Washington led our Revolution. Our country still struggles with the legacies of slavery and segregation, the past treatment of Native Americans.

Human endeavor is by its nature imperfect. History is often tragic, but unresolved it can be a heavy weight. Each country must work through its past. And reckoning with the past can help us seize a better future. I know there's strong views in this chamber about the terrible events of 1915. And while there's been a good deal of commentary about my views, it's really about how the Turkish and Armenian people deal with the past. And the best way forward for the Turkish and Armenian people is a process that works through the past in a way that is honest, open and constructive.

We've already seen historic and courageous steps taken by Turkish and Armenian leaders. These contacts hold out the promise of a new day. An open border would return the Turkish and Armenian people to a peaceful and prosperous coexistence that would serve both of your nations. So I want you to know that the United States strongly supports the full normalization of relations between Turkey and Armenia. It is a cause worth working towards.

It speaks to Turkey's leadership that you are poised to be the only country in the region to have normal and peaceful relations with all the South Caucasus nations. And to advance that peace, you can play a constructive role in helping to resolve the Nagorno-Karabakh conflict, which has continued for far too long.

Advancing peace also includes the disputes that persist in the Eastern Mediterranean. And here there's a cause for hope. The two Cypriot leaders have an opportunity through their commitment to negotiations under the United Nations Good Offices Mission. The United States is willing to offer all the help sought by the parties as they work towards a just and lasting settlement that reunifies Cyprus into a bizonal and bicommunal federation.

These efforts speak to one part of the critical region that surrounds Turkey. And when we consider the challenges before us, on issue after issue, we share common goals. In the Middle East, we share the goal of a lasting peace between Israel and its neighbors. Let me be clear: The United States strongly supports the goal of two states, Israel and Palestine, living side by side in peace and security. That is a goal shared by Palestinians, Israelis, and people of goodwill around the world. That is a goal that the parties agreed to in the road map and at Annapolis. That is a goal that I will actively pursue as President of the United States.

We know the road ahead will be difficult. Both Israelis and Palestinians must take steps that are necessary to build confidence and trust. Both Israelis and Palestinians, both must live up to the commitments they have made. Both must overcome long-standing passions and the politics of the moment to make progress towards a secure and lasting peace.

The United States and Turkey can help the Palestinians and Israelis make this journey. Like the United States, Turkey has been a friend and partner in Israel's quest for security. And like the United States, you seek a future of opportunity and statehood for the Palestinians. So now, working together, we must not give into pessimism and mistrust. We must pursue every opportunity for progress, as you've done by supporting negotiations between Syria and Israel. We must extend a hand to those Palestinians who are in need, while helping them strengthen their own institutions. We must reject the use of terror, and recognize that Israel's security concerns are legitimate.

The peace of the region will also be advanced if Iran forgoes any nuclear weapons ambitions. Now, as I made clear in Prague yesterday, no one is served by the spread of nuclear weapons, least of all Turkey. You live in a difficult region and a nuclear arm race would not serve the security of this nation well. This part of the world has known enough violence. It has known enough hatred. It does not need a race for an ever-more powerful tool of destruction.

Now, I have made it clear to the people and leaders of the Islamic Republic of Iran that the United States seeks engagement based on mutual interest and mutual respect. We want Iran to play its rightful role in the community of nations. Iran is a great civilization. We want them to engage in the economic and political integration that brings prosperity and security. But Iran's leaders must choose whether they will try to build a weapon or build a better future for their people.

So both Turkey and the United States support a secure and united Iraq that does not serve as a safe haven for terrorists. I know there were differences about whether to go to war. There were differences within my own country, as well. But now we must come together as we end this war responsibly, because the future of Iraq is inseparable from the future of the broader region. As I've already announced, and many of you are aware, the United States will remove our combat brigades by the end of next August, while working with the Iraqi government as they take responsibility for security. And we will work with Iraq, Turkey, and all Iraq's neighbors, to forge a new dialogue that reconciles differences and advances our common security.

Make no mistake, though: Iraq, Turkey, and the United States face a common threat from terrorism. That includes the al Qaeda terrorists who have sought to drive Iraqis apart and destroy their country. That includes the PKK. There is no excuse for terror against any nation.

As President, and as a NATO ally, I pledge that you will have our support against the terrorist activities of the PKK or anyone else. These efforts will be strengthened by the continued work to build ties of cooperation between Turkey, the Iraqi government, and Iraq's Kurdish leaders, and by your continued efforts to promote education and opportunity and democracy for the Kurdish population here inside Turkey.

Finally, we share the common goal of denying al Qaeda a safe haven in Pakistan or Afghanistan. The world has come too far to let this region backslide, and to let al Qaeda terrorists plot further attacks. That's why we are committed to a more focused effort to disrupt, dismantle, and defeat al Qaeda. That is why we are increasing our efforts to train Afghans to sustain their own security, and to reconcile former adversaries. That's why we are increasing our support for the people of Afghanistan and Pakistan, so that we stand on the side not only of security, but also of opportunity and the promise of a better life.

Turkey has been a true partner. Your troops were among the first in the International Security Assistance Force. You have sacrificed much in this endeavor. Now we must achieve our goals together. I appreciate that you've offered to help us train and support Afghan security forces, and expand opportunity across the region. Together, we can rise to meet this challenge like we have so many before.

I know there have been difficulties these last few years. I know that the trust that binds the United States and Turkey has been strained, and I know that strain is shared in many places where the Muslim faith is practiced. So let me say this as clearly as I can: The United States is not, and will never be, at war with Islam. In fact, our partnership with the Muslim world is critical not just in rolling back the violent ideologies that people of all faiths reject, but also to strengthen opportunity for all its people.

I also want to be clear that America's relationship with the Muslim community, the Muslim world, cannot, and will not, just be based upon opposition to terrorism. We seek broader engagement based on mutual interest and mutual respect. We will listen carefully, we will bridge misunderstandings, and we will seek common ground. We will be respectful, even when we do not agree. We will convey our deep appreciation for the Islamic faith, which has done so much over the centuries to shape the world—including in my own country. The United States has been enriched by Muslim Americans. Many other Americans have Muslims in their families or have lived in a Muslim-majority country—I know, because I am one of them.

Above all, above all we will demonstrate through actions our commitment to a better future. I want to help more children get the education that they need to succeed. We want to promote health care in places where people are vulnerable. We want to expand the trade and investment that can bring prosperity for all people. In the months ahead, I will present specific programs to advance these goals. Our focus will be on what we can do, in partnership with people across the Muslim world, to advance our common hopes and our common dreams. And when people look back on this time, let it be said of America that we extended the hand of friendship to all people.

There's an old Turkish proverb: "You cannot put out fire with flames." America knows this. Turkey knows this. There's some who must be met by force, they will not compromise. But force alone cannot solve our problems, and it is no alternative to extremism. The future must belong to those who create, not those who destroy. That is the future we must work for, and we must work for it together.

I know there are those who like to debate Turkey's future. They see your country at the crossroads of continents, and touched by the currents of history. They know that this has been a place where civilizations meet, and different peoples come together. They wonder whether you will be pulled in one direction or another.

But I believe here is what they don't understand: Turkey's greatness lies in your ability to be at the center of things. This is not where East and West divide—this is where they come together. In the beauty of your culture. In the richness of your history. In the strength of your democracy. In your hopes for tomorrow. I am honored to stand here with you—to look forward to the future that we must reach for together—and to reaffirm America's commitment to our strong and enduring friendship. Thank you very much.

PRESIDENT OBAMA: Thank you very much. Good afternoon. I am honored to be in the timeless city of Cairo, and to be hosted by two remarkable institutions. For over a thousand years, Al-Azhar has stood as a beacon of Islamic learning; and for over a

Remarks by the President on a New Beginning, Cairo University, Cairo, Egypt, The White House, Office of the Press Secretary, For Immediate Release, June 4, 2009. http://www.whitehouse.gov/the-press-office/remarks-president-cairo-university-6-04-09.

century, Cairo University has been a source of Egypt's advancement. And together, you represent the harmony between tradition and progress. I'm grateful for your hospitality, and the hospitality of the people of Egypt. And I'm also proud to carry with me the goodwill of the American people, and a greeting of peace from Muslim communities in my country: Assalaamu alaykum.

We meet at a time of great tension between the United States and Muslims around the world—tension rooted in historical forces that go beyond any current policy debate. The relationship between Islam and the West includes centuries of coexistence and cooperation, but also conflict and religious wars. More recently, tension has been fed by colonialism that denied rights and opportunities to many Muslims, and a Cold War in which Muslim-majority countries were too often treated as proxies without regard to their own aspirations. Moreover, the sweeping change brought by modernity and globalization led many Muslims to view the West as hostile to the traditions of Islam.

Violent extremists have exploited these tensions in a small but potent minority of Muslims. The attacks of September 11, 2001 and the continued efforts of these extremists to engage in violence against civilians has led some in my country to view Islam as inevitably hostile not only to America and Western countries, but also to human rights. All this has bred more fear and more mistrust.

So long as our relationship is defined by our differences, we will empower those who sow hatred rather than peace, those who promote conflict rather than the cooperation that can help all of our people achieve justice and prosperity. And this cycle of suspicion and discord must end.

I've come here to Cairo to seek a new beginning between the United States and Muslims around the world, one based on mutual interest and mutual respect, and one based upon the truth that America and Islam are not exclusive and need not be in competition. Instead, they overlap, and share common principles—principles of justice and progress; tolerance and the dignity of all human beings.

I do so recognizing that change cannot happen overnight. I know there's been a lot of publicity about this speech, but no single speech can eradicate years of mistrust, nor can I answer in the time that I have this afternoon all the complex questions that brought us to this point. But I am convinced that in order to move forward, we must say openly to each other the things we hold in our hearts and that too often are said only behind closed doors. There must be a sustained effort to listen to each other; to learn from each other; to respect one another; and to seek common ground. As the Holy Koran tells us, "Be conscious of God and speak always the truth." That is what I will try to do today—to speak the truth as best I can, humbled by the task before us, and firm in my belief that the interests we share as human beings are far more powerful than the forces that drive us apart.

Now part of this conviction is rooted in my own experience. I'm a Christian, but my father came from a Kenyan family that includes generations of Muslims. As a boy, I spent several years in Indonesia and heard the call of the azaan at the break of dawn and at the fall of dusk. As a young man, I worked in Chicago communities where many found dignity and peace in their Muslim faith.

As a student of history, I also know civilization's debt to Islam. It was Islam—at places like Al-Azhar—that carried the light of learning through so many centuries, paving the way for Europe's Renaissance and Enlightenment. It was innovation in Muslim communities, it was innovation in Muslim communities that developed the order of algebra; our magnetic compass and tools of navigation; our mastery of pens and printing; our understanding of how disease spreads and how it can be healed. Islamic culture has given us majestic arches and soaring spires; timeless poetry and cherished music; elegant calligraphy and places of peaceful contemplation. And throughout history, Islam has demonstrated through words and deeds the possibilities of religious tolerance and racial equality.

I also know that Islam has always been a part of America's story. The first nation to recognize my country was Morocco. In signing the Treaty of Tripoli in 1796, our second President, John Adams, wrote, "The United States has in itself no character of enmity against the laws, religion or tranquility of Muslims." And since our founding, American Muslims have enriched the United States. They have fought in our wars, they have served in our government, they have stood for civil rights, they have started businesses, they have taught at our universities, they've excelled in our sports arenas, they've won Nobel Prizes, built our tallest building, and lit the Olympic Torch. And when the first Muslim American was recently elected to Congress, he took the oath to defend our Constitution using the same Holy Koran that one of our Founding Fathers—Thomas Jefferson—kept in his personal library.

So I have known Islam on three continents before coming to the region where it was first revealed. That experience guides my conviction that partnership between America and Islam must be based on what Islam is, not what it isn't. And I consider it part of my responsibility as President of the United States to fight against negative stereotypes of Islam wherever they appear.

But that same principle must apply to Muslim perceptions of America. Just as Muslims do not fit a crude stereotype, America is not the crude stereotype of a self-interested empire. The United States has been one of the greatest sources of progress that the world has ever known. We were born out of revolution against an empire. We were founded upon the ideal that all are created equal, and we have shed blood and struggled for centuries to give meaning to those words—within our borders, and around the world. We are shaped by every culture, drawn from every end of the Earth, and dedicated to a simple concept: *E pluribus unum*—"Out of many, one."

Now, much has been made of the fact that an African American with the name Barack Hussein Obama could be elected President. But my personal story is not so unique. The dream of opportunity for all people has not come true for everyone in America, but its promise exists for all who come to our shores—and that includes nearly 7 million American Muslims in our country today who, by the way, enjoy incomes and educational levels that are higher than the American average.

Moreover, freedom in America is indivisible from the freedom to practice one's religion. That is why there is a mosque in every state in our union, and over 1,200 mosques within our borders. That's why the United States government has gone to court to protect the right of women and girls to wear the hijab and to punish those who would deny it.

So let there be no doubt: Islam is a part of America. And I believe that America holds within her the truth that regardless of race, religion, or station in life, all of us share common aspirations—to live in peace and security; to get an education and to work with dignity; to love our families, our communities, and our God. These things we share. This is the hope of all humanity.

Of course, recognizing our common humanity is only the beginning of our task. Words alone cannot meet the needs of our people. These needs will be met only if we act boldly in the years ahead; and if we understand that the challenges we face are shared, and our failure to meet them will hurt us all.

For we have learned from recent experience that when a financial system weakens in one country, prosperity is hurt everywhere. When a new flu infects one human being, all are at risk. When one nation pursues a nuclear weapon, the risk of nuclear attack rises for all nations. When violent extremists operate in one stretch of mountains, people are endangered across an ocean. When innocents in Bosnia and Darfur are slaughtered, that is a stain on our collective conscience. That is what it means to share this world in the 21st century. That is the responsibility we have to one another as human beings.

And this is a difficult responsibility to embrace. For human history has often been a record of nations and tribes—and, yes, religions—subjugating one another in pursuit of their own interests. Yet in this new age, such attitudes are self-defeating. Given our interdependence, any world order that elevates one nation or group of people over another will inevitably fail. So whatever we think of the past, we must not be prisoners to it. Our problems must be dealt with through partnership; our progress must be shared. Now, that does not mean we should ignore sources of tension. Indeed, it suggests the opposite: We must face these tensions squarely. And so in that spirit, let me speak as clearly and as plainly as I can about some specific issues that I believe we must finally confront together.

The first issue that we have to confront is violent extremism in all of its forms. In Ankara, I made clear that America is not—and never will be—at war with Islam. We will, however, relentlessly confront violent extremists who pose a grave threat to our security—because we reject the same thing that people of all faiths reject: the killing of innocent men, women, and children. And it is my first duty as President to protect the American people.

The situation in Afghanistan demonstrates America's goals, and our need to work together. Over seven years ago, the United States pursued al Qaeda and the Taliban with broad international support. We did not go by choice; we went because of necessity. I'm aware that there's still some who would question or even justify the events of 9/11. But let us be clear: Al Qaeda killed nearly 3,000 people on that day. The victims were innocent men, women and children from America and many other nations who had done nothing to harm anybody. And yet al Qaeda chose to ruthlessly murder these people, claimed credit for the attack, and even now states their determination to kill on a massive scale. They have affiliates in many countries and are trying to expand their reach. These are not opinions to be debated; these are facts to be dealt with.

Now, make no mistake: We do not want to keep our troops in Afghanistan. We see no military—we seek no military bases there. It is agonizing for America to lose our young men and women. It is costly and politically difficult to continue this conflict. We would gladly bring every single one of our troops home if we could be confident that there were not violent extremists in Afghanistan and now Pakistan determined to kill as many Americans as they possibly can. But that is not yet the case.

And that's why we're partnering with a coalition of 46 countries. And despite the costs involved, America's commitment will not weaken. Indeed, none of us should tolerate these extremists. They have killed in many countries. They have killed people of different faiths—but more than any other, they have killed Muslims. Their actions are irreconcilable with the rights of human beings, the progress of nations, and with Islam. The Holy Koran teaches that whoever kills an innocent is as—it is as if he has killed all mankind. And the Holy Koran also says whoever saves a person, it is as if he has saved all mankind. The enduring faith of over a billion people is so much bigger than the narrow hatred of a few. Islam is not part of the problem in combating violent extremism—it is an important part of promoting peace.

Now, we also know that military power alone is not going to solve the problems in Afghanistan and Pakistan. That's why we plan to invest $1.5 billion each year over the next five years to partner with Pakistanis to build schools and hospitals, roads and businesses, and hundreds of millions to help those who've been displaced. That's why we are providing more than $2.8 billion to help Afghans develop their economy and deliver services that people depend on.

Let me also address the issue of Iraq. Unlike Afghanistan, Iraq was a war of choice that provoked strong differences in my country and around the world. Although I believe that the Iraqi people are ultimately better off without the tyranny of Saddam Hussein, I also believe that events in Iraq have reminded America of the need to use diplomacy and build international consensus to resolve our problems whenever possible. Indeed, we can recall the words of Thomas Jefferson, who said: "I hope that our wisdom will grow with our power, and teach us that the less we use our power the greater it will be."

Today, America has a dual responsibility: to help Iraq forge a better future—and to leave Iraq to Iraqis. And I have made it clear to the Iraqi people I have made it clear to the Iraqi people that we pursue no bases, and no claim on their territory or resources. Iraq's sovereignty is its own. And that's why I ordered the removal of our combat brigades by next August. That is why we will honor our agreement with Iraq's democratically elected government to remove combat troops from Iraqi cities by July, and to remove all of our troops from Iraq by 2012. We will help Iraq train its security forces and develop its economy. But we will support a secure and united Iraq as a partner, and never as a patron.

And finally, just as America can never tolerate violence by extremists, we must never alter or forget our principles. Nine-eleven was an enormous trauma to our country. The fear and anger that it provoked was understandable, but in some cases, it led us to act contrary to our traditions and our ideals. We are taking concrete actions to change course. I have unequivocally prohibited the use of torture by the United States, and I have ordered the prison at Guantanamo Bay closed by early next year.

America will defend itself, respectful of the sovereignty of nations and the rule of law. And we will do so in partnership with Muslim communities which are also threatened. The sooner the extremists are isolated and unwelcome in Muslim communities, the sooner we will all be safer.

The second major source of tension that we need to discuss is the situation between Israelis, Palestinians and the Arab world. America's strong bonds with Israel are well known. This bond is unbreakable. It is based upon cultural and historical ties, and the recognition that the aspiration for a Jewish homeland is rooted in a tragic history that cannot be denied.

Around the world, the Jewish people were persecuted for centuries, and anti-Semitism in Europe culminated in an unprecedented Holocaust. Tomorrow, I will visit Buchenwald, which was part of a network of camps where Jews were enslaved, tortured, shot and gassed to death by the Third Reich. Six million Jews were killed—more than the entire Jewish population of Israel today. Denying that fact is baseless, it is ignorant, and it is hateful. Threatening Israel with destruction—or repeating vile stereotypes about Jews—is deeply wrong, and only serves to evoke in the minds of Israelis this most painful of memories while preventing the peace that the people of this region deserve.

On the other hand, it is also undeniable that the Palestinian people—Muslims and Christians—have suffered in pursuit of a homeland. For more than 60 years they've endured the pain of dislocation. Many wait in refugee camps in the West Bank, Gaza, and neighboring lands for a life of peace and security that they have never been able to lead. They endure the daily humiliations—large and small—that come with occupation. So let there be no doubt: The situation for the Palestinian people is intolerable. And America will not turn our backs on the legitimate Palestinian aspiration for dignity, opportunity, and a state of their own.

For decades then, there has been a stalemate: two peoples with legitimate aspirations, each with a painful history that makes compromise elusive. It's easy to point fingers—for Palestinians to point to the displacement brought about by Israel's founding, and for Israelis to point to the constant hostility and attacks throughout its history from within its borders as well as beyond. But if we see this conflict only from one side or the other, then we will be blind to the truth: The only resolution is for the aspirations of both sides to be met through two states, where Israelis and Palestinians each live in peace and security.

That is in Israel's interest, Palestine's interest, America's interest, and the world's interest. And that is why I intend to personally pursue this outcome with all the patience and dedication that the task requires. The obligations—the obligations that the parties have agreed to under the road map are clear. For peace to come, it is time for them—and all of us—to live up to our responsibilities.

Palestinians must abandon violence. Resistance through violence and killing is wrong and it does not succeed. For centuries, black people in America suffered the lash of the whip as slaves and the humiliation of segregation. But it was not violence that won full and equal rights. It was a peaceful and determined insistence upon the ideals at the center of America's founding. This same story can be told by people from South Africa to South Asia; from Eastern Europe to Indonesia. It's a story with a simple truth: that violence is a dead end. It is a sign neither of courage nor power to shoot rockets at sleeping children, or to blow up old women on a bus. That's not how moral authority is claimed; that's how it is surrendered.

Now is the time for Palestinians to focus on what they can build. The Palestinian Authority must develop its capacity to govern, with institutions that serve the needs of its people. Hamas does have support among some Palestinians, but they also have to recognize they have responsibilities. To play a role in fulfilling Palestinian aspirations, to unify the Palestinian people, Hamas must put an end to violence, recognize past agreements, recognize Israel's right to exist.

At the same time, Israelis must acknowledge that just as Israel's right to exist cannot be denied, neither can Palestine's. The United States does not accept the legitimacy of continued Israeli settlements. This construction violates previous agreements and undermines efforts to achieve peace. It is time for these settlements to stop.

And Israel must also live up to its obligation to ensure that Palestinians can live and work and develop their society. Just as it devastates Palestinian families, the continuing humanitarian crisis in Gaza does not serve Israel's security; neither does the continuing lack of opportunity in the West Bank. Progress in the daily lives of the Palestinian people must be a critical part of a road to peace, and Israel must take concrete steps to enable such progress.

And finally, the Arab states must recognize that the Arab Peace Initiative was an important beginning, but not the end of their responsibilities. The Arab-Israeli conflict should no longer be used to distract the people of Arab nations from other problems. Instead, it must be a cause for action to help the Palestinian people develop the institutions that will sustain their state, to recognize Israel's legitimacy, and to choose progress over a self-defeating focus on the past.

America will align our policies with those who pursue peace, and we will say in public what we say in private to Israelis and Palestinians and Arabs. We cannot impose peace. But privately, many Muslims recognize that Israel will not go away. Likewise, many Israelis recognize the need for a Palestinian state. It is time for us to act on what everyone knows to be true.

Too many tears have been shed. Too much blood has been shed. All of us have a responsibility to work for the day when the mothers of Israelis and Palestinians can see their children grow up without fear; when the Holy Land of the three great faiths is the place of peace that God intended it to be; when Jerusalem is a secure and lasting home for Jews and Christians and Muslims, and a place for all of the children of Abraham to mingle peacefully together as in the story of Isra, as in the story of Isra, when Moses, Jesus, and Mohammed, peace be upon them, joined in prayer.

The third source of tension is our shared interest in the rights and responsibilities of nations on nuclear weapons. This issue has been a source of tension between the United States and the Islamic Republic of Iran. For many years, Iran has defined itself in part by its opposition to my country, and there is in fact a tumultuous history between us. In the middle of the Cold War, the United States played a role in the overthrow of a democratically elected Iranian government. Since the Islamic Revolution, Iran has played a role in acts of hostage-taking and violence against U.S. troops and civilians. This history is well known. Rather than remain trapped in the past, I've made it clear to Iran's leaders and people that my country is prepared to move forward. The question now is not what Iran is against, but rather what future it wants to build.

I recognize it will be hard to overcome decades of mistrust, but we will proceed with courage, rectitude, and resolve. There will be many issues to discuss between our two countries, and we are willing to move forward without preconditions on the basis of mutual respect. But it is clear to all concerned that when it comes to nuclear weapons, we have reached a decisive point. This is not simply about America's interests. It's about preventing a nuclear arms race in the Middle East that could lead this region and the world down a hugely dangerous path.

I understand those who protest that some countries have weapons that others do not. No single nation should pick and choose which nation holds nuclear weapons.

And that's why I strongly reaffirmed America's commitment to seek a world in which no nations hold nuclear weapons. And any nation—including Iran—should have the right to access peaceful nuclear power if it complies with its responsibilities under the nuclear Non-Proliferation Treaty. That commitment is at the core of the treaty, and it must be kept for all who fully abide by it. And I'm hopeful that all countries in the region can share in this goal.

The fourth issue that I will address is democracy. I know—I know there has been controversy about the promotion of democracy in recent years, and much of this controversy is connected to the war in Iraq. So let me be clear: No system of government can or should be imposed by one nation by any other.

That does not lessen my commitment, however, to governments that reflect the will of the people. Each nation gives life to this principle in its own way, grounded in the traditions of its own people. America does not presume to know what is best for everyone, just as we would not presume to pick the outcome of a peaceful election. But I do have an unyielding belief that all people yearn for certain things: the ability to speak your mind and have a say in how you are governed; confidence in the rule of law and the equal administration of justice; government that is transparent and doesn't steal from the people; the freedom to live as you choose. These are not just American ideas; they are human rights. And that is why we will support them everywhere.

Now, there is no straight line to realize this promise. But this much is clear: Governments that protect these rights are ultimately more stable, successful and secure. Suppressing ideas never succeeds in making them go away. America respects the right of all peaceful and law-abiding voices to be heard around the world, even if we disagree with them. And we will welcome all elected, peaceful governments—provided they govern with respect for all their people.

This last point is important because there are some who advocate for democracy only when they're out of power; once in power, they are ruthless in suppressing the rights of others. So no matter where it takes hold, government of the people and by the people sets a single standard for all who would hold power: You must maintain your power through consent, not coercion; you must respect the rights of minorities, and participate with a spirit of tolerance and compromise; you must place the interests of your people and the legitimate workings of the political process above your party. Without these ingredients, elections alone do not make true democracy.

The fifth issue that we must address together is religious freedom. Islam has a proud tradition of tolerance. We see it in the history of Andalusia and Cordoba during the Inquisition. I saw it firsthand as a child in Indonesia, where devout Christians worshiped freely in an overwhelmingly Muslim country. That is the spirit we need today. People in every country should be free to choose and live their faith based upon the persuasion of the mind and the heart and the soul. This tolerance is essential for religion to thrive, but it's being challenged in many different ways.

Among some Muslims, there's a disturbing tendency to measure one's own faith by the rejection of somebody else's faith. The richness of religious diversity must be upheld—whether it is for Maronites in Lebanon or the Copts in Egypt. And if we are being honest, fault lines must be closed among Muslims, as well, as the divisions between Sunni and Shia have led to tragic violence, particularly in Iraq.

Freedom of religion is central to the ability of peoples to live together. We must always examine the ways in which we protect it. For instance, in the United States, rules on charitable giving have made it harder for Muslims to fulfill their religious obligation. That's why I'm committed to working with American Muslims to ensure that they can fulfill zakat.

Likewise, it is important for Western countries to avoid impeding Muslim citizens from practicing religion as they see fit—for instance, by dictating what clothes a Muslim woman should wear. We can't disguise hostility towards any religion behind the pretence of liberalism.

In fact, faith should bring us together. And that's why we're forging service projects in America to bring together Christians, Muslims, and Jews. That's why we welcome efforts like Saudi Arabian King Abdullah's interfaith dialogue and Turkey's leadership in the Alliance of Civilizations. Around the world, we can turn dialogue into interfaith service, so bridges between peoples lead to action—whether it is combating malaria in Africa, or providing relief after a natural disaster.

The sixth issue—the sixth issue that I want to address is women's rights. I know—I know—and you can tell from this audience, that there is a healthy debate about this issue. I reject the view of some in the West that a woman who chooses to cover her hair is somehow less equal, but I do believe that a woman who is denied an education is denied equality. And it is no coincidence that countries where women are well educated are far more likely to be prosperous.

Now, let me be clear: Issues of women's equality are by no means simply an issue for Islam. In Turkey, Pakistan, Bangladesh, Indonesia, we've seen Muslim-majority countries elect a woman to lead. Meanwhile, the struggle for women's equality continues in many aspects of American life, and in countries around the world.

I am convinced that our daughters can contribute just as much to society as our sons. Our common prosperity will be advanced by allowing all humanity—men and women—to reach their full potential. I do not believe that women must make the same choices as men in order to be equal, and I respect those women who choose to live their lives in traditional roles. But it should be their choice. And that is why the United States will partner with any Muslim-majority country to support expanded literacy for girls, and to help young women pursue employment through micro-financing that helps people live their dreams.

Finally, I want to discuss economic development and opportunity. I know that for many, the face of globalization is contradictory. The Internet and television can bring knowledge and information, but also offensive sexuality and mindless violence into the home. Trade can bring new wealth and opportunities, but also huge disruptions and change in communities. In all nations—including America—this change can bring fear. Fear that because of modernity we lose control over our economic choices, our politics, and most importantly our identities—those things we most cherish about our communities, our families, our traditions, and our faith.

But I also know that human progress cannot be denied. There need not be contradictions between development and tradition. Countries like Japan and South Korea grew their economies enormously while maintaining distinct cultures. The same is true for the astonishing progress within Muslim-majority countries from Kuala Lumpur to Dubai. In ancient times and in our times, Muslim communities have been at the forefront of innovation and education.

And this is important because no development strategy can be based only upon what comes out of the ground, nor can it be sustained while young people are out of work. Many Gulf states have enjoyed great wealth as a consequence of oil, and some are beginning to focus it on broader development. But all of us must recognize that education and innovation will be the currency of the 21st century and in too many Muslim communities, there remains underinvestment in these areas. I'm emphasizing such investment within my own country. And while America in the past has focused on oil and gas when it comes to this part of the world, we now seek a broader engagement.

On education, we will expand exchange programs, and increase scholarships, like the one that brought my father to America. At the same time, we will encourage more Americans to study in Muslim communities. And we will match promising Muslim students with internships in America; invest in online learning for teachers and children around the world; and create a new online network, so a young person in Kansas can communicate instantly with a young person in Cairo.

On economic development, we will create a new corps of business volunteers to partner with counterparts in Muslim-majority countries. And I will host a Summit on Entrepreneurship this year to identify how we can deepen ties between business leaders, foundations and social entrepreneurs in the United States and Muslim communities around the world.

On science and technology, we will launch a new fund to support technological development in Muslim-majority countries, and to help transfer ideas to the marketplace so they can create more jobs. We'll open centers of scientific excellence in Africa, the Middle East and Southeast Asia, and appoint new science envoys to collaborate on programs that develop new sources of energy, create green jobs, digitize records, clean water, grow new crops. Today I'm announcing a new global effort with the Organization of the Islamic Conference to eradicate polio. And we will also expand partnerships with Muslim communities to promote child and maternal health.

All these things must be done in partnership. Americans are ready to join with citizens and governments; community organizations, religious leaders, and businesses in Muslim communities around the world to help our people pursue a better life.

The issues that I have described will not be easy to address. But we have a responsibility to join together on behalf of the world that we seek—a world where extremists no longer threaten our people, and American troops have come home; a world where Israelis and Palestinians are each secure in a state of their own, and nuclear energy is used for peaceful purposes; a world where governments serve their citizens, and the rights of all God's children are respected. Those are mutual interests. That is the world we seek. But we can only achieve it together.

I know there are many—Muslim and non-Muslim—who question whether we can forge this new beginning. Some are eager to stoke the flames of division, and to stand in the way of progress. Some suggest that it isn't worth the effort—that we are fated to disagree, and civilizations are doomed to clash. Many more are simply skeptical that real change can occur. There's so much fear, so much mistrust that has built up over the years. But if we choose to be bound by the past, we will never move forward. And I want to particularly say this to young people of every faith, in every country—you, more than anyone, have the ability to reimagine the world, to remake this world.

All of us share this world for but a brief moment in time. The question is whether we spend that time focused on what pushes us apart, or whether we commit ourselves to an effort—a sustained effort—to find common ground, to focus on the future we seek for our children, and to respect the dignity of all human beings.

It's easier to start wars than to end them. It's easier to blame others than to look inward. It's easier to see what is different about someone than to find the things we share. But we should choose the right path, not just the easy path. There's one rule that lies at the heart of every religion—that we do unto others as we would have them do unto us. This truth transcends nations and peoples—a belief that isn't new; that isn't black or white or brown; that isn't Christian or Muslim or Jew. It's a belief that pulsed in the cradle of civilization, and that still beats in the hearts of billions around the world. It's a faith in other people, and it's what brought me here today.

We have the power to make the world we seek, but only if we have the courage to make a new beginning, keeping in mind what has been written. The Holy Koran tells us: "O mankind! We have created you male and a female; and we have made you into nations and tribes so that you may know one another."

The Talmud tells us: "The whole of the Torah is for the purpose of promoting peace."

The Holy Bible tells us: "Blessed are the peacemakers, for they shall be called sons of God." The people of the world can live together in peace. We know that is God's vision. Now that must be our work here on Earth. Thank you. And may God's peace be upon you.

Today, I want to extend my best wishes to all who are celebrating Nowruz in the United States and around the world. Each year of my presidency, I have marked this holiday by speaking directly to the people of Iran. That is what I would like to do once more.

This is a holiday for the Iranian people to spend time with friends and family; to reflect on the extraordinary blessings that you enjoy; and to look forward to the promise of a new day. After all, this is a season of hope and renewal. And today, we know that this is also a season of promise across the Middle East and North Africa, even as there are also enormous challenges.

I believe that there are certain values that are universal—the freedom of peaceful assembly and association; the ability to speak your mind and choose your leaders. And what we are seeing across the region is the insistence on governments that are accountable to the people.

But we also know that these movements for change are not unique to these last few months. The same forces of hope that swept across Tahrir Square were seen in Azadi Square in June of 2009. And just as the people of the region have insisted that they have a choice in how they are governed, so do the governments of the region have a choice in their response. So far, the Iranian government has responded by demonstrating that it cares far more about preserving its own power than respecting the rights of the Iranian people.

For nearly two years, there has been a campaign of intimidation and abuse. Young and old; men and women; rich and poor—the Iranian people have been persecuted. Hundreds of prisoners of conscience are in jail. The innocent have gone missing. Journalists have been silenced. Women tortured. Children sentenced to death.

The world has watched these unjust actions with alarm. We have seen Nasrin Sotoudeh jailed for defending human rights; Jaffar Panahi imprisoned and unable to make his films; Abdolreza Tajik thrown in jail for being a journalist. The Bahai community and Sufi Muslims punished for their faith; Mohammad Valian, a young student, sentenced to death for throwing three stones.

These choices do not demonstrate strength, they show fear. For it is telling when a government is so afraid of its own citizens that it won't even allow them the freedom to access information or to communicate with each other. But the future of Iran will not be shaped by fear. The future of Iran belongs to the young people—the youth who will determine their own destiny. Over 60 percent of the Iranian people were born after 1979. You are not bound by the chains of the past—the distracting hatred of America that will create no jobs or opportunity; the rigid and unaccountable government; the

President Obama's Message to all People Celebrating Nowruz, The White House, Office of the Press Secretary, Nowruz Message, March 20, 2010, Washington, D.C. http://www.whitehouse.gov/the-press-office/remarks-president-obama-marking-nowruz.

refusal to let the Iranian people realize their full potential for fear of undermining the authority of the state.

Instead, you—the young people of Iran—carry within you both the ancient greatness of Persian civilization, and the power to forge a country that is responsive to your aspirations. Your talent, your hopes, and your choices will shape the future of Iran, and help light the world. And though times may seem dark, I want you to know that I am with you.

On this day—a celebration that serves as a bridge from the past to the future—I would like to close with a quote from the poet Simin Behbahani—a woman who has been banned from travelling beyond Iran, even though her words have moved the world: "Old, I may be, but, given the chance, I will learn. I will begin a second youth alongside my progeny. I will recite the Hadith of love of country with such fervor as to make each word bear life." Let this be a season of second youth for all Iranians—a time in which a new season bears new life once more. Thank you. And Aid-e-Shoma Mobarak.

Chapter 6

Barack Obama's Response to the Arab Awakening

I condemn and deplore the use of violence against citizens peacefully voicing their opinion in Tunisia, and I applaud the courage and dignity of the Tunisian people. The United States stands with the entire international community in bearing witness to this brave and determined struggle for the universal rights that we must all uphold, and we will long remember the images of the Tunisian people seeking to make their voices heard. I urge all parties to maintain calm and avoid violence, and call on the Tunisian government to respect human rights, and to hold free and fair elections in the near future that reflect the true will and aspirations of the Tunisian people.

As I have said before, each nation gives life to the principle of democracy in its own way, grounded in the traditions of its own people, and those countries that respect the universal rights of their people are stronger and more successful than those that do not. I have no doubt that Tunisia's future will be brighter if it is guided by the voices of the Tunisian people.

THE PRESIDENT: Good afternoon, everybody. There are very few moments in our lives where we have the privilege to witness history taking place. This is one of those moments. This is one of those times. The people of Egypt have spoken, their voices have been heard, and Egypt will never be the same.

By stepping down, President Mubarak responded to the Egyptian people's hunger for change. But this is not the end of Egypt's transition. It's a beginning. I'm sure there will be difficult days ahead, and many questions remain unanswered. But I am confident

Statement by the President on Events in Tunisia, The White House, Office of the Press Secretary, For Immediate Release, January 14, 2011. http://www.whitehouse.gov/the-press-office/2011/01/14/statement-president-events-tunisia.

Obama's Remarks on Mubarak's Decision to Step Down, White House, February 11, 2011 http://www.aolnews.com/2011/02/11/full-text-of-president-obamas-remarks-Obama's Remarks on Mubarak's decision to Step down on-mubarak-resignation/.

that the people of Egypt can find the answers, and do so peacefully, constructively, and in the spirit of unity that has defined these last few weeks. For Egyptians have made it clear that nothing less than genuine democracy will carry the day.

The military has served patriotically and responsibly as a caretaker to the state, and will now have to ensure a transition that is credible in the eyes of the Egyptian people. That means protecting the rights of Egypt's citizens, lifting the emergency law, revising the constitution and other laws to make this change irreversible, and laying out a clear path to elections that are fair and free. Above all, this transition must bring all of Egypt's voices to the table. For the spirit of peaceful protest and perseverance that the Egyptian people have shown can serve as a powerful wind at the back of this change.

The United States will continue to be a friend and partner to Egypt. We stand ready to provide whatever assistance is necessary—and asked for—to pursue a credible transition to a democracy. I'm also confident that the same ingenuity and entrepreneurial spirit that the young people of Egypt have shown in recent days can be harnessed to create new opportunity—jobs and businesses that allow the extraordinary potential of this generation to take flight. And I know that a democratic Egypt can advance its role of responsible leadership not only in the region but around the world.

Egypt has played a pivotal role in human history for over 6,000 years. But over the last few weeks, the wheel of history turned at a blinding pace as the Egyptian people demanded their universal rights.

We saw mothers and fathers carrying their children on their shoulders to show them what true freedom might look like. We saw a young Egyptian say, "For the first time in my life, I really count. My voice is heard. Even though I'm only one person, this is the way real democracy works."

We saw protesters chant "Selmiyya, selmiyya"—"We are peaceful"—again and again.

We saw a military that would not fire bullets at the people they were sworn to protect. And we saw doctors and nurses rushing into the streets to care for those who were wounded, volunteers checking protesters to ensure that they were unarmed.

We saw people of faith praying together and chanting—Muslims, Christians, We are one." And though we know that the strains between faiths still divide too many in this world and no single event will close that chasm immediately, these scenes remind us that we need not be defined by our differences. We can be defined by the common humanity that we share.

And above all, we saw a new generation emerge—a generation that uses their own creativity and talent and technology to call for a government that represented their hopes and not their fears; a government that is responsive to their boundless aspirations. One Egyptian put it simply: Most people have discovered in the last few days … that they are worth something, and this cannot be taken away from them anymore, ever.

This is the power of human dignity, and it can never be denied. Egyptians have inspired us, and they've done so by putting the lie to the idea that justice is best gained through violence. For in Egypt, it was the moral force of nonviolence—not terrorism, not mindless killing—but nonviolence, moral force that bent the arc of history toward justice once more.

And while the sights and sounds that we heard were entirely Egyptian, we can't help but hear the echoes of history—echoes from Germans tearing down a wall, Indonesian students taking to the streets, Gandhi leading his people down the path of justice.

As Martin Luther King said in celebrating the birth of a new nation in Ghana while trying to perfect his own, "There is something in the soul that cries out for freedom." Those were the cries that came from Tahrir Square, and the entire world has taken note.

Today belongs to the people of Egypt, and the American people are moved by these scenes in Cairo and across Egypt because of who we are as a people and the kind of world that we want our children to grow up in.

The word Tahrir means liberation. It is a word that speaks to that something in our souls that cries out for freedom. And forevermore it will remind us of the Egyptian people—of what they did, of the things that they stood for, and how they changed their country, and in doing so changed the world. Thank you.

President Obama spoke with King Hamad bin Isa Al-Khalifa of Bahrain this evening to discuss the ongoing situation in Bahrain. The President reiterated his condemnation of the violence used against peaceful protesters, and strongly urged the government of Bahrain to show restraint, and to hold those responsible for the violence accountable. As a long-standing partner of Bahrain, the President said that the United States believes that the stability of Bahrain depends upon respect for the universal rights of the people of Bahrain, and a process of meaningful reform that is responsive to the aspirations of all Bahrainis.

THE PRESIDENT: Good afternoon, everybody. Secretary Clinton and I just concluded a meeting that focused on the ongoing situation in Libya. Over the last few days, my national security team has been working around the clock to monitor the situation there and to coordinate with our international partners about a way forward.

Readout of President Obama's Call with the King of Bahrain, The White House, Office of the Press Secretary, For Immediate Release, February 18, 2011. http://www.whitehouse.gov/the-press-office/2011/02/18/readout-president-obamas-call-king-bahrain.

Remarks by the President on Libya, The White House, Office of the Press Secretary, For Immediate Release, February 23, 2011. http://www.whitehouse.gov/the-press-office/2011/02/23/remarks-president-libya.

First, we are doing everything we can to protect American citizens. That is my highest priority. In Libya, we've urged our people to leave the country and the State Department is assisting those in need of support. Meanwhile, I think all Americans should give thanks to the heroic work that's being done by our Foreign Service Officers and the men and women serving in our embassies and consulates around the world. They represent the very best of our country and its values.

Now, throughout this period of unrest and upheaval across the region the United States has maintained a set of core principles which guide our approach. These principles apply to the situation in Libya. As I said last week, we strongly condemn the use of violence in Libya.

The American people extend our deepest condolences to the families and loved ones of all who've been killed and injured. The suffering and bloodshed is outrageous and it is unacceptable. So are threats and orders to shoot peaceful protesters and further punish the people of Libya. These actions violate international norms and every standard of common decency. This violence must stop.

The United States also strongly supports the universal rights of the Libyan people. That includes the rights of peaceful assembly, free speech, and the ability of the Libyan people to determine their own destiny. These are human rights. They are not negotiable. They must be respected in every country. And they cannot be denied through violence or suppression.

In a volatile situation like this one, it is imperative that the nations and peoples of the world speak with one voice, and that has been our focus. Yesterday a unanimous U.N. Security Council sent a clear message that it condemns the violence in Libya, supports accountability for the perpetrators, and stands with the Libyan people.

This same message, by the way, has been delivered by the European Union, the Arab League, the African Union, the Organization of the Islamic Conference, and many individual nations. North and south, east and west, voices are being raised together to oppose suppression and support the rights of the Libyan people.

I've also asked my administration to prepare the full range of options that we have to respond to this crisis. This includes those actions we may take and those we will coordinate with our allies and partners, or those that we'll carry out through multilateral institutions.

Like all governments, the Libyan government has a responsibility to refrain from violence, to allow humanitarian assistance to reach those in need, and to respect the rights of its people. It must be held accountable for its failure to meet those responsibilities, and face the cost of continued violations of human rights.

This is not simply a concern of the United States. The entire world is watching, and we will coordinate our assistance and accountability measures with the international community. To that end, Secretary Clinton and I have asked Bill Burns, our Under

Secretary of State for Political Affairs, to make several stops in Europe and the region to intensify our consultations with allies and partners about the situation in Libya.

I've also asked Secretary Clinton to travel to Geneva on Monday, where a number of foreign ministers will convene for a session of the Human Rights Council. There she'll hold consultations with her counterparts on events throughout the region and continue to ensure that we join with the international community to speak with one voice to the government and the people of Libya.

And even as we are focused on the urgent situation in Libya, let me just say that our efforts continue to address the events taking place elsewhere, including how the international community can most effectively support the peaceful transition to democracy in both Tunisia and in Egypt.

So let me be clear. The change that is taking place across the region is being driven by the people of the region. This change doesn't represent the work of the United States or any foreign power. It represents the aspirations of people who are seeking a better life.

As one Libyan said, "We just want to be able to live like human beings." We just want to be able to live like human beings. It is the most basic of aspirations that is driving this change. And throughout this time of transition, the United States will continue to stand up for freedom, stand up for justice, and stand up for the dignity of all people. Thank you very much.

I strongly condemn the violence that has taken place in Yemen today and call on President Saleh to adhere to his public pledge to allow demonstrations to take place peacefully. Those responsible for today's violence must be held accountable. The United States stands for a set of universal rights, including the freedom of expression and assembly, as well as political change that meets the aspirations of the Yemeni people. It is more important than ever for all sides to participate in an open and transparent process that addresses the legitimate concerns of the Yemeni people, and provides a peaceful, orderly and democratic path to a stronger and more prosperous nation.

I strongly condemn the abhorrent violence committed against peaceful protesters by the Syrian government today and over the past few weeks. I also condemn any use of violence by protesters. The United States extends our condolences to the families

Statement by the President on Violence in Yemen, The White House, Office of the Press Secretary, For Immediate Release, March 18, 2011. http://www.whitehouse.gov/the-press-office/2011/03/18/statement-president-violence-yemen.

Statement from the President on the Violence in Syria, The White House, Office of the Press Secretary, For Immediate Release, April 8, 2011. http://www.whitehouse.gov/the-press-office/2011/04/08/statement-president-violence-syria.

and loved ones of all the victims. I call upon the Syrian authorities to refrain from any further violence against peaceful protestors. Furthermore, the arbitrary arrests, detention, and torture of prisoners that has been reported must end now, and the free flow of information must be permitted so that there can be independent verification of events on the ground.

Throughout this time of upheaval, the American people have heard the voices of the Syrian people, who have demonstrated extraordinary courage and dignity, and who deserve a government that is responsive to their aspirations. Syrians have called for the freedoms that individuals around the world should enjoy: freedom of expression, association, and peaceful assembly; confidence in the rule of law and the equal administration of justice; and a government that is transparent and free of corruption. These rights are universal, and they must be respected in Syria.

Until now, the Syrian government has not addressed the legitimate aspirations of the Syrian people. Violence and detention are not the answer to the grievances of the Syrian people. It is time for the Syrian government to stop repressing its citizens and to listen to the voices of the Syrian people calling for meaningful political and economic reforms.

Chapter 7

Barack Obama and Europe

P **RESIDENT OBAMA:** Earlier today, we finished a very productive summit that will be, I believe, a turning point in our pursuit of global economic recovery. By any measure, the London summit was historic. It was historic because of the size and the scope of the challenges that we face, and because of the timeliness and magnitude of our response.

The challenge is clear. The global economy is contracting. Trade is shrinking. Unemployment is rising. The international finance system is nearly frozen. Even these facts can't fully capture the crisis that we're confronting, because behind them is the pain and uncertainty that so many people are facing. We see it back in the United States. We see it here in London. We see it around the world: families losing their homes, workers losing their jobs and their savings, students who are deferring their dreams. So many have lost so much. Just to underscore this point, back in the United States, jobless claims released today were the highest in 26 years. We owe it to all of our citizens to act, and to act with a sense of urgency.

In an age where our economies are linked more closely than ever before, the whole world has been touched by this devastating downturn. And today, the world's leaders have responded with an unprecedented set of comprehensive and coordinated actions.

Now, just keep in mind some historical context. Faced with similar global challenges in the past, the world was slow to act, and people paid an enormous price. That was true in the Great Depression, when nations prolonged and worsened the crisis by turning inward, waiting for more than a decade to meet the challenge together. Even as recently as the 1980s, the slow global response deepened and widened a debt crisis in Latin America that pushed millions into poverty.

Today, we've learned the lessons of history. I know that in the days leading up to the summit, some of you in the press, some commentators, confused honest and open debate with irreconcilable differences. But after weeks of preparation, and two days

News Conference by President Obama, ExCel Center, London, United Kingdom, The White House, Office of the Press Secretary, For Immediate Release, April 2, 2009. http://www.whitehouse.gov/the_press_office/News-Conference-by-President-Obama-4-02-09/.

of careful negotiation, we have agreed on a series of unprecedented steps to restore growth and prevent a crisis like this from happening again. Let me outline what I think has been most significant.

Number one, we are committed to growth and job creation. All G20 nations have acted to stimulate demand, which will total well over $2 trillion in global fiscal expansion. The United States is also partnering with the private sector to clean out the troubled assets, the legacy assets that are crippling some banks, and using the full force of the government to ensure that our action leads directly to loans to businesses large and small, as well as individuals who depend on credit. And these efforts will be amplified by our G20 partners, who are pursuing similarly comprehensive programs.

And we also agreed on bold action to support developing countries, so that we aren't faced with declining markets that the global economy depends on. Together, the G20 is tripling the IMF's lending capacity and promoting lending by multilateral development banks to increase the purchasing power and expand markets in every country.

We've also rejected the protectionism that could deepen this crisis. History tells us that turning inward can help turn a downturn into a depression. And this cooperation between the world's leading economies signals our support for open markets, as does our multilateral commitment to trade finance that will grow our exports and create new jobs. That's all on the growth front.

And next we made enormous strides in committing ourselves to comprehensive reform of a failed regulatory system. And together, I believe that we must put an end to the bubble-and-bust economy that has stood in the way of sustained growth and enabled abusive risk-taking that endangers our prosperity.

At home, back in the States, our efforts began with the approach that Secretary Geithner proposed last week, the strongest regulatory reforms any nation has contemplated so far to prevent the massive failure of responsibility that we have already seen. Today, these principles have informed and enabled the coordinated action that we will take with our G20 partners.

To prevent future crises, we agreed to increased transparency and capital protections for financial institutions. We're extending supervision to all systemically important institutions, markets and products, including hedge funds. We'll identify jurisdictions that fail to cooperate, including tax havens, and take action to defend our financial system. We will reestablish the Financial Stability Forum with a stronger mandate. And we will reform and expand the IMF and World Bank so they are more efficient, effective and representative.

Finally, we are protecting those who don't always have a voice at the G20, but who have suffered greatly in this crisis. And the United States is ready to lead in this endeavor. In the coming days, I intend to work with Congress to provide $448 million in immediate assistance to vulnerable populations—from Africa to Latin America—and to double support for food safety to over $1 billion so that we are giving people the tools they need to lift themselves out of poverty. We will also support the United Nations and World Bank as they coordinate the rapid assistance necessary to prevent humanitarian catastrophe. I have to say, though, that this is not just charity. These are all future markets for all countries, and future drivers of world economic growth.

Let me also underscore my appreciation to Prime Minister Brown, his entire team, and all my colleagues from around the world who contributed to the summit's success. You know, it's hard for 20 heads of state to bridge their differences. We've all got our own national policies; we all have our own assumptions, our own political cultures. But our citizens are all hurting. They all need us to come together. So I'm pleased that the G20 has agreed to meet again this fall, because I believe that this is just the beginning. Our problems are not going to be solved in one meeting; they're not going to be solved in two meetings. We're going to have to be proactive in shaping events and persistent in monitoring our progress to determine whether further action is needed.

I also want to just make a few remarks about additional meetings I had outside of the G20 context. While here in London I had the opportunity to hold bilateral meetings with leaders of Russia, China, South Korea, Saudi Arabia and India, as well as Great Britain. And these discussions were extraordinarily valuable and productive. Of course, we spoke about additional steps to promote economic recovery and growth. But we also discussed coordinated actions on a range of issues: how we could reduce the nuclear threat; how we could forge a coordinated response to North Korea's planned missile launch; how we can turn back terrorism and stabilize Afghanistan; how we can protect our planet from the scourge of climate change. I'm encouraged that we laid the groundwork for real and lasting progress on a host of these issues.

Ultimately, the challenges of the 21st century can't be met without collective action. Agreement will almost never be easy, and results won't always come quickly. But I am committed to respecting different points of view, and to forging a consensus instead of dictating our terms. That's how we made progress in the last few days. And that's how we will advance and uphold our ideals in the months and years to come.

You know, at home, I've often spoken about a new era of responsibility. And I believe strongly that this era must not end at our borders. In a world that's more and more interconnected, we all have responsibilities to work together to solve common challenges. And although it will take time, I am confident that we will rebuild global prosperity if we act with a common sense of purpose, persistence, and the optimism that the moment demands.

So I appreciate your attention, and I'm going to take a few questions. I've got a list of a few people I'm going to call on and then I will intersperse some folks I'm calling on randomly.

Thank you so much. Thank you for this wonderful welcome. Thank you to the people of Prague. Thank you to the people of the Czech Republic. Today, I'm proud to stand here with you in the middle of this great city, in the center of Europe. And, to paraphrase one of my predecessors, I am also proud to be the man who brought Michelle Obama to Prague.

To Mr. President, Mr. Prime Minister, to all the dignitaries who are here, thank you for your extraordinary hospitality. And to the people of the Czech Republic, thank you for your friendship to the United States.

I've learned over many years to appreciate the good company and the good humor of the Czech people in my hometown of Chicago. Behind me is a statue of a hero of the Czech people—Tomas Masaryk. In 1918, after America had pledged its support for Czech independence, Masaryk spoke to a crowd in Chicago that was estimated to be over 100,000. I don't think I can match his record—but I am honored to follow his footsteps from Chicago to Prague.

For over a thousand years, Prague has set itself apart from any other city in any other place. You've known war and peace. You've seen empires rise and fall. You've led revolutions in the arts and science, in politics and in poetry. Through it all, the people of Prague have insisted on pursuing their own path, and defining their own destiny. And this city—this Golden City which is both ancient and youthful—stands as a living monument to your unconquerable spirit.

When I was born, the world was divided, and our nations were faced with very different circumstances. Few people would have predicted that someone like me would one day become the President of the United States. Few people would have predicted that an American President would one day be permitted to speak to an audience like this in Prague. Few would have imagined that the Czech Republic would become a free nation, a member of NATO, a leader of a united Europe. Those ideas would have been dismissed as dreams.

We are here today because enough people ignored the voices who told them that the world could not change. We're here today because of the courage of those who stood up and took risks to say that freedom is a right for all people, no matter what side of a wall they live on, and no matter what they look like.

Remarks by President Barack Obama, The White House, Office of the Press Secretary, For Immediate Release, April 5, 2009. Hradcany Square Prague, Czech Republic. http://m.whitehouse.gov/the_press_office/Remarks-By-President-Barack-Obama-In-Prague-As-Delivered/

We are here today because of the Prague Spring—because the simple and principled pursuit of liberty and opportunity shamed those who relied on the power of tanks and arms to put down the will of a people.

We are here today because 20 years ago, the people of this city took to the streets to claim the promise of a new day, and the fundamental human rights that had been denied them for far too long. Sametová Revoluce—the Velvet Revolution taught us many things. It showed us that peaceful protest could shake the foundations of an empire, and expose the emptiness of an ideology. It showed us that small countries can play a pivotal role in world events, and that young people can lead the way in overcoming old conflicts. And it proved that moral leadership is more powerful than any weapon. That's why I'm speaking to you in the center of a Europe that is peaceful, united and free—because ordinary people believed that divisions could be bridged, even when their leaders did not. They believed that walls could come down; that peace could prevail.

We are here today because Americans and Czechs believed against all odds that today could be possible. Now, we share this common history. But now this generation—our generation—cannot stand still. We, too, have a choice to make. As the world has become less divided, it has become more interconnected. And we've seen events move faster than our ability to control them—a global economy in crisis, a changing climate, the persistent dangers of old conflicts, new threats and the spread of catastrophic weapons.

None of these challenges can be solved quickly or easily. But all of them demand that we listen to one another and work together; that we focus on our common interests, not on occasional differences; and that we reaffirm our shared values, which are stronger than any force that could drive us apart. That is the work that we must carry on. That is the work that I have come to Europe to begin.

To renew our prosperity, we need action coordinated across borders. That means investments to create new jobs. That means resisting the walls of protectionism that stand in the way of growth. That means a change in our financial system, with new rules to prevent abuse and future crisis.

And we have an obligation to our common prosperity and our common humanity to extend a hand to those emerging markets and impoverished people who are suffering the most, even though they may have had very little to do with financial crises, which is why we set aside over a trillion dollars for the International Monetary Fund earlier this week, to make sure that everybody—everybody—receives some assistance.

Now, to protect our planet, now is the time to change the way that we use energy. Together, we must confront climate change by ending the world's dependence on fossil fuels, by tapping the power of new sources of energy like the wind and sun, and calling upon all nations to do their part. And I pledge to you that in this global effort, the United States is now ready to lead. To provide for our common security, we must strengthen our alliance. NATO was founded 60 years ago, after Communism took over Czechoslovakia. That was when the free world learned too late that it could not afford division. So we came together to forge the strongest alliance that the world has ever known. And we should—stood shoulder to shoulder—year after year, decade after decade—until an Iron Curtain was lifted, and freedom spread like flowing water.

This marks the 10th year of NATO membership for the Czech Republic. And I know that many times in the 20th century, decisions were made without you at the table. Great powers let you down, or determined your destiny without your voice being heard. I am here to say that the United States will never turn its back on the people of this nation. We are bound by shared values, shared history—We are bound by shared values and shared history and the enduring promise of our alliance. NATO's Article V states it clearly: An attack on one is an attack on all. That is a promise for our time, and for all time.

The people of the Czech Republic kept that promise after America was attacked; thousands were killed on our soil, and NATO responded. NATO's mission in Afghanistan is fundamental to the safety of people on both sides of the Atlantic. We are targeting the same al Qaeda terrorists who have struck from New York to London, and helping the Afghan people take responsibility for their future. We are demonstrating that free nations can make common cause on behalf of our common security. And I want you to know that we honor the sacrifices of the Czech people in this endeavor, and mourn the loss of those you've lost.

But no alliance can afford to stand still. We must work together as NATO members so that we have contingency plans in place to deal with new threats, wherever they may come from. We must strengthen our cooperation with one another, and with other nations and institutions around the world, to confront dangers that recognize no borders. And we must pursue constructive relations with Russia on issues of common concern.

Now, one of those issues that I'll focus on today is fundamental to the security of our nations and to the peace of the world—that's the future of nuclear weapons in the 21st century. The existence of thousands of nuclear weapons is the most dangerous legacy of the Cold War. No nuclear war was fought between the United States and the Soviet Union, but generations lived with the knowledge that their world could be erased in a single flash of light. Cities like Prague that existed for centuries, that embodied the beauty and the talent of so much of humanity, would have ceased to exist.

Today, the Cold War has disappeared but thousands of those weapons have not. In a strange turn of history, the threat of global nuclear war has gone down, but the risk of a nuclear attack has gone up. More nations have acquired these weapons. Testing has continued. Black market trade in nuclear secrets and nuclear materials abound. The technology to build a bomb has spread. Terrorists are determined to buy, build or steal one. Our efforts to contain these dangers are centered on a global non-proliferation regime, but as more people and nations break the rules, we could reach the point where the center cannot hold.

Now, understand, this matters to people everywhere. One nuclear weapon exploded in one city—be it New York or Moscow, Islamabad or Mumbai, Tokyo or Tel Aviv, Paris or Prague—could kill hundreds of thousands of people. And no matter where it happens, there is no end to what the consequences might be—for our global safety, our security, our society, our economy, to our ultimate survival.

Some argue that the spread of these weapons cannot be stopped, cannot be checked—that we are destined to live in a world where more nations and more people possess the ultimate tools of destruction. Such fatalism is a deadly adversary, for if we believe that the spread of nuclear weapons is inevitable, then in some way we are admitting to ourselves that the use of nuclear weapons is inevitable.

Just as we stood for freedom in the 20th century, we must stand together for the right of people everywhere to live free from fear in the 21st century. And as nuclear power—as a nuclear power, as the only nuclear power to have used a nuclear weapon, the United States has a moral responsibility to act. We cannot succeed in this endeavor alone, but we can lead it, we can start it.

So today, I state clearly and with conviction America's commitment to seek the peace and security of a world without nuclear weapons. I'm not naive. This goal will not be reached quickly—perhaps not in my lifetime. It will take patience and persistence. But now we, too, must ignore the voices who tell us that the world cannot change. We have to insist, "Yes, we can."

Now, let me describe to you the trajectory we need to be on. First, the United States will take concrete steps towards a world without nuclear weapons. To put an end to Cold War thinking, we will reduce the role of nuclear weapons in our national security strategy, and urge others to do the same. Make no mistake: As long as these weapons exist, the United States will maintain a safe, secure and effective arsenal to deter any adversary, and guarantee that defense to our allies—including the Czech Republic. But we will begin the work of reducing our arsenal.

To reduce our warheads and stockpiles, we will negotiate a new Strategic Arms Reduction Treaty with the Russians this year. President Medvedev and I began this process in London, and will seek a new agreement by the end of this year that is legally binding and sufficiently bold. And this will set the stage for further cuts, and we will seek to include all nuclear weapons states in this endeavor.

To achieve a global ban on nuclear testing, my administration will immediately and aggressively pursue U.S. ratification of the Comprehensive Test Ban Treaty. After more than five decades of talks, it is time for the testing of nuclear weapons to finally be banned.

And to cut off the building blocks needed for a bomb, the United States will seek a new treaty that verifiably ends the production of fissile materials intended for use in state nuclear weapons. If we are serious about stopping the spread of these weapons, then we should put an end to the dedicated production of weapons-grade materials that create them. That's the first step.

Second, together we will strengthen the Nuclear Non-Proliferation Treaty as a basis for cooperation. The basic bargain is sound: Countries with nuclear weapons will move towards disarmament, countries without nuclear weapons will not acquire them, and all countries can access peaceful nuclear energy. To strengthen the treaty, we should embrace several principles. We need more resources and authority to strengthen international inspections. We need real and immediate consequences for countries caught breaking the rules or trying to leave the treaty without cause.

And we should build a new framework for civil nuclear cooperation, including an international fuel bank, so that countries can access peaceful power without increasing the risks of proliferation. That must be the right of every nation that renounces nuclear weapons, especially developing countries embarking on peaceful programs. And no approach will succeed if it's based on the denial of rights to nations that play by the rules. We must harness the power of nuclear energy on behalf of our efforts to combat climate change, and to advance peace opportunity for all people.

But we go forward with no illusions. Some countries will break the rules. That's why we need a structure in place that ensures when any nation does, they will face consequences. Just this morning, we were reminded again of why we need a new and more rigorous approach to address this threat. North Korea broke the rules once again by testing a rocket that could be used for long range missiles. This provocation underscores the need for action—not just this afternoon at the U.N. Security Council, but in our determination to prevent the spread of these weapons.

Rules must be binding. Violations must be punished. Words must mean something. The world must stand together to prevent the spread of these weapons. Now is the time for a strong international response—now is the time for a strong international response, and North Korea must know that the path to security and respect will never come through threats and illegal weapons. All nations must come together to build a stronger, global regime. And that's why we must stand shoulder to shoulder to pressure the North Koreans to change course.

Iran has yet to build a nuclear weapon. My administration will seek engagement with Iran based on mutual interests and mutual respect. We believe in dialogue. But in that dialogue we will present a clear choice. We want Iran to take its rightful place in the community of nations, politically and economically. We will support Iran's right to peaceful nuclear energy with rigorous inspections. That's a path that the Islamic Republic can take. Or the government can choose increased isolation, international pressure, and a potential nuclear arms race in the region that will increase insecurity for all.

So let me be clear: Iran's nuclear and ballistic missile activity poses a real threat, not just to the United States, but to Iran's neighbors and our allies. The Czech Republic and Poland have been courageous in agreeing to host a defense against these missiles. As long as the threat from Iran persists, we will go forward with a missile defense system that is cost-effective and proven. If the Iranian threat is eliminated, we will have a stronger basis for security, and the driving force for missile defense construction in Europe will be removed.

So, finally, we must ensure that terrorists never acquire a nuclear weapon. This is the most immediate and extreme threat to global security. One terrorist with one nuclear weapon could unleash massive destruction. Al Qaeda has said it seeks a bomb and that it would have no problem with using it. And we know that there is unsecured nuclear material across the globe. To protect our people, we must act with a sense of purpose without delay.

So today I am announcing a new international effort to secure all vulnerable nuclear material around the world within four years. We will set new standards, expand our co-operation with Russia, pursue new partnerships to lock down these sensitive materials.

We must also build on our efforts to break up black markets, detect and intercept materials in transit, and use financial tools to disrupt this dangerous trade. Because this threat will be lasting, we should come together to turn efforts such as the Proliferation Security Initiative and the Global Initiative to Combat Nuclear Terrorism into durable international institutions. And we should start by having a Global Summit on Nuclear Security that the United States will host within the next year.

Now, I know that there are some who will question whether we can act on such a broad agenda. There are those who doubt whether true international cooperation is possible, given inevitable differences among nations. And there are those who hear talk of a world without nuclear weapons and doubt whether it's worth setting a goal that seems impossible to achieve.

But make no mistake: We know where that road leads. When nations and peoples allow themselves to be defined by their differences, the gulf between them widens. When we fail to pursue peace, then it stays forever beyond our grasp. We know the path when we choose fear over hope. To denounce or shrug off a call for cooperation is an easy but also a cowardly thing to do. That's how wars begin. That's where human progress ends.

There is violence and injustice in our world that must be confronted. We must confront it not by splitting apart but by standing together as free nations, as free people. I know that a call to arms can stir the souls of men and women more than a call to lay them down. But that is why the voices for peace and progress must be raised together. Those are the voices that still echo through the streets of Prague. Those are the ghosts of 1968. Those were the joyful sounds of the Velvet Revolution. Those were the Czechs who helped bring down a nuclear-armed empire without firing a shot.

Human destiny will be what we make of it. And here in Prague, let us honor our past by reaching for a better future. Let us bridge our divisions, build upon our hopes, accept our responsibility to leave this world more prosperous and more peaceful than we found it. Together we can do it. Thank you very much. Thank you, Prague.

PRESIDENT OBAMA: Good afternoon, everyone. We have just concluded an extremely productive NATO summit, and I want to thank our hosts, the government and the people of Portugal, for their hospitality in this beautiful city of Lisbon. And I thank my fellow leaders for the sense of common purpose that they brought to our work here.

For more than 60 years, NATO has proven itself as the most successful alliance in history. It's defended the independence and freedom of its members. It has nurtured young democracies and welcomed them into Europe that is whole and free. It has acted to end ethnic cleansing beyond our borders. And today we stand united in Afghanistan, so that terrorists who threaten us all have no safe haven and so that the Afghan people can forge a more hopeful future.

At no time during these past six decades was our success guaranteed. Indeed, there have been many times when skeptics have predicted the end of this alliance. But each time NATO has risen to the occasion and adapted to meet the challenges of that time. And now, as we face a new century with very different challenges from the last, we have come together here in Lisbon to take action in four areas that are critical to the future of the alliance.

First, we aligned our approach on the way forward in Afghanistan, particularly on a transition to full Afghan lead that will begin in early 2011 and will conclude in 2014. It is important for the American people to remember that Afghanistan is not just an American battle. We are joined by a NATO-led coalition made up of 48 nations with over 40,000 troops from allied and partner countries. And we honor the service and sacrifice of every single one.

With the additional resources that we've put in place we're now achieving our objective of breaking the Taliban's momentum and doing the hard work of training Afghan security forces and assisting the Afghan people. And I want to thank our allies who committed additional trainers and mentors to support the vital mission of training Afghan forces. With these commitments I am confident that we can meet our objective.

Press Conference of the President after NATO Summit, Feria Internacional de Lisboa, Lisbon, Portugal, The White House, Office of the Press Secretary, For Immediate Release, November 20, 2010. http://www.whitehouse.gov/the-press-office/2010/11/20/press-conference-president-after-nato-summit.

Here in Lisbon we agreed that early 2011 will mark the beginning of a transition to Afghan responsibility, and we adopted the goal of Afghan forces taking the lead for security across the country by the end of 2014. This is a goal that President Karzai has put forward. I've made it clear that even as Americans transition and troop reductions will begin in July, we will also forge a long-term partnership with the Afghan people. And today, NATO has done the same. So this leaves no doubt that as Afghans stand up and take the lead they will not be standing alone.

As we look ahead to a new phase in Afghanistan, we also reached agreement in a second area—a new strategic concept for NATO that recognizes the capabilities and partners that the alliance needs to meet the challenges of the 21st century. I want to give special thanks to Secretary General Rasmussen for his outstanding leadership in forging a vision that preserves the enduring strengths of the alliance while adapting it to meet the missions of the future.

As I said yesterday, we have reaffirmed the central premise of NATO—our Article V commitment that an attack on one is an attack on all. And to ensure this commitment has meaning, we agreed to take action in a third area: to modernize our conventional forces and develop the full range of military capabilities that we need to defend our nations.

We'll invest in technologies so that allied forces can deploy and operate together more effectively. We'll deploy new defenses against threats such as cyber attacks. And we will reform alliance command structures to make them more flexible and more efficient. Most important, we agreed to develop a missile defense capability for NATO territory, which is necessary to defend against the growing threat from ballistic missiles.

The new approach to European missile defense that I announced last year—the phased adaptive approach—will be the United States contribution to this effort and a foundation for greater collaboration. After years of talk about how to meet this objective, we now have a clear plan to protect all of our allies in Europe as well as the United States.

When it comes to nuclear weapons, our strategic concept reflects both today's realities as well as our future aspirations. The alliance will work to create the conditions so that we can reduce nuclear weapons and pursue the vision of a world without them. At the same time, we've made it very clear that so long as these weapons exist, NATO will remain a nuclear alliance, and the United States will maintain a safe, secure and effective nuclear arsenal to defer—deter adversaries and guarantee the defense of all our allies.

Finally, we agreed to keep forging the partnership beyond NATO that helped make our alliance a pillar of global security. We'll continue to enhance NATO's cooperation with the EU—which I will talk about in my summit later this afternoon with EU leaders. After a two-year break, we are also resuming cooperation between NATO and Russia.

I was very pleased that my friend and partner, President Dmitri Medvedev, joined us today at the NATO-Russia Council Summit. Together we've worked hard to reset the relations between the United States and Russia, which has led to concrete benefits for both our nations. Now we're also resetting the NATO-Russia relationship. We see Russia as a partner, not an adversary. And we agreed to deepen our cooperation in several critical areas: on Afghanistan, counternarcotics, and a range of 21st-century security challenges. And perhaps most significantly, we agreed to cooperate on missile defense, which turns a source of past tension into a source of potential cooperation against a shared threat.

So overall, this has been an extremely productive two days. We came to Lisbon with a clear task, and that was to revitalize our alliance to meet the challenges of our time. That's what we've done here. Of course, it's work that cannot end here. And so I'm pleased to announce that the United States will host the next NATO summit in 2012—a summit that will allow us to build on the commitments that we've made here today as we transition to full Afghan lead, build new capabilities, expand our partnerships, and ensure that the most successful alliance in history will continue to advance our security and our prosperity well into the future.

And I said to Prime Minister Socrates that considering he has thrown such a successful summit here in Lisbon, I've been taking notes. You set a very high bar of outstanding hospitality, and so I appreciate everything that the people of Portugal have done, and we will try to reciprocate that hospitality when we host in 2012. So with that, let me take some questions. And I'm going to start with Margaret Warner of PBS. Margaret, why don't you get a microphone.

Q: Thank you, Mr. President. What message do you hope this summit sends to Senator Jon Kyl and other Republicans in the Senate who are resisting voting on and ratifying START in the lame duck session?

PRESIDENT OBAMA: Well, a couple of messages that I just want to send to the American people. Number one, I think that Americans should be proud that an alliance that began 60 years ago, through the extraordinary sacrifices, in part, of American young men and women, sustained throughout a Cold War, has resulted in a Europe that's more unified than it's ever been before, that is an extraordinarily strong ally of the United States, and that continues to be a cornerstone of prosperity not just for the United States and Europe but for the world. This is a direct result of American efforts and American sacrifice. And I think the world appreciates it.

The second message I want to send is that after a period in which relations between the United States and Europe were severely strained, that strain no longer exists. There are occasions where there may be disagreements on certain tactical issues, but in terms of a broad vision of how we achieve transatlantic security that alliance has never been stronger. And that's something that Americans should feel good about.

Number three, I think the Americans should know that American leadership remains absolutely critical to achieving some of these important security objectives. And I think our European partners would be the first to acknowledge that.

What we ratified here today is the direct result of work that we've done over the last two years to get to this point. And just to take the example of Afghanistan. I think that if you said even a year ago or even maybe six months ago that we would have a unified approach on the part of our allies to move forward in Afghanistan with a sustained commitment where we actually increased the resources available and closed the training gap in order to be successful, I think a lot of skeptics would have said that's not going to happen. It has happened, in part because we have rebuilt those strong bonds of trust between the United States and our allies.

The fourth thing—and this finally goes to your specific question—unprompted, I have received overwhelming support from our allies here that START—the New START treaty—is a critical component to U.S. and European security. And they have urged both privately and publicly that this gets done.

And I think you've seen the comments of a wide range of European partners on this issue, including those who live right next to Russia, who used to live behind the Iron Curtain, who have the most cause for concern with respect to Russian intentions and who have uniformly said that they will feel safer and more secure if this treaty gets ratified—in art, because right now we have no verification mechanism on the ground with respect to Russian arsenals. And Ronald Reagan said, trust but verify—we can't verify right now.

In part because, as a consequence of the reset between the United States and Russia, we have received enormous help from the Russians in instituting sanctions on Iran that are tougher than anything we've seen before. We have transit agreements with Russia that allows us to supply our troops. There are a whole range of security interests in which we are cooperating with Russia and it would be a profound mistake for us to slip back into mistrust as a consequence of our failure to ratify.

And the third reason is that with the Cold War over, it is in everybody's interests to work on reducing our nuclear arsenals, which are hugely expensive and contain the possibilities of great damage, if not in terms of direct nuclear war, then in terms of issues of nuclear proliferation.

So we've got our European allies saying this is important. We've got the U.S. military saying this is important. We've got the national security advisors and the secretaries of defense and generals from the Reagan administration, the Bush administration—Bush one and Bush two—as well as from the Clinton administration and my administration saying this is important to our national security. We've got the Republican chairman of the Foreign Relations Committee saying this is in our national interest to get done now. This is an issue that traditionally has received strong bipartisan support. We've gone through 18 hearings; we've answered 1,000 questions. We have met the concerns about modernizing our nuclear stockpile with concrete budget numbers. It's time for us to go ahead and get it done. And my hope is that we will do so.

There's no other reason not to do it than the fact that Washington has become a very partisan place. And this is a classic area where we have to rise above partisanship. Nobody is going to score points in the 2012 election around this issue, but it's something that we should be doing because it helps keep America safe. And my expectation is, is that my Republican friends in the Senate will ultimately conclude that it makes sense for us to do this.

Chapter 8

Barack Obama: Bilateral Relations with China, India, and Russia

On 1 April 2009, President Barack Obama of the United States and President Hu Jintao of China met on the sidelines of the G20 Financial Summit in London, the United Kingdom. The two heads of state had an extensive exchange of views on U.S.-China relations and global issues of common interest, and reached the following points of agreement:

I. Toward Enhanced U.S.-China Relations

The two sides agreed to work together to build a positive, cooperative, and comprehensive U.S.-China relationship for the 21st century and to maintain and strengthen exchanges at all levels. President Hu Jintao invited President Obama to visit China in the second half of this year, and President Obama accepted the invitation with pleasure.

The two sides decided to establish the "U.S.-China Strategic and Economic Dialogue." U.S. Secretary of State Hillary Clinton and Chinese State Councilor Dai Bingguo will chair the "Strategic Track" and U.S. Secretary of the Treasury Timothy Geithner and Chinese Vice Premier Wang Qishan will chair the "Economic Track" of the Dialogue, each as special representatives of their respective presidents. The two sides will hold the first round of the dialogue in Washington DC this summer. The two sides stated that they will continue to advance mutually beneficial cooperation in

Statement on Bilateral Meeting with President Hu of China, The White House, Office of the Press Secretary, For Immediate Release, April 1, 2009. http://www.whitehouse.gov/the_press_office/Statement-On-Bilateral-Meeting-With-President-Hu-Of-China/.

economics and trade through the mechanism of the high-level Joint Commission on Commerce and Trade.

The two sides agreed to further deepen mutually beneficial cooperation in a wide range of areas, including economy and trade, counterterrorism, law enforcement, science and technology, education, culture and health. They also agreed to resume and expand consultations on non-proliferation and other international security topics. They welcomed further exchanges between the national legislatures, local authorities, academics, young people and other sectors. The two sides agreed to resume the human rights dialogue as soon as possible.

Both sides share a commitment to military-to-military relations and will work for their continued improvement and development. The two sides agreed that Admiral Gary Roughead, U.S. Chief of Naval Operations, will visit China upon invitation in April to attend events marking the 60th anniversary of the founding of the Navy of the Chinese People's Liberation Army. The U.S. looks forward to visits by senior Chinese military leaders this year.

The two sides agreed to maintain close communication and coordination and to work together for the settlement of conflicts and reduction of tensions that contribute to global and regional instability, including the denuclearization of the Korean Peninsula, the Iranian nuclear issue, Sudan humanitarian issues, and the situation in South Asia.

The two sides agreed to intensify policy dialogue and practical cooperation in energy, the environment and climate change building on the China-US Ten Year Energy and Environment Cooperation Framework, carry out active cooperation in energy efficiency, renewable energy, and clean energy technologies and work with other parties concerned for positive results at the Copenhagen conference.

II. Strengthening Economic and Financial Cooperation

The two presidents discussed challenges facing the global economy and financial system. They pledged that, as two major economies, the U.S. and China will work together, as well as with other countries, to help the world economy return to strong growth and to strengthen the international financial system so a crisis of this magnitude never happens again.

The two presidents welcomed the fiscal stimulus measures taken by the other, and agreed that these measures were already playing a stabilizing role for the global economy. They also agreed that strong financial systems were essential for restoring growth, and they welcomed the commitment of both countries to address issues in this area. President Obama underlined the commitment of the United States to implement the American Recovery and Reinvestment Act and the Financial Stability Plan. He underscored that once recovery is firmly established, the United States will act to cut the U.S. fiscal deficit in half and bring the deficit down to a level that is sustainable. President Hu emphasized China's commitment to strengthen and improve macroeconomic control and expand domestic demand, particularly consumer demand, to ensure sustainable growth, and ensure steady and relatively fast economic development.

The two presidents agreed the international financial institutions should have more resources to help emerging market and developing nations withstand the shortfall in capital, and the two countries will take actions toward this goal. China and the United States agreed to work together to resolutely support global trade and investment flows that benefit all. To that end, they are committed to resist protectionism and ensure sound and stable U.S.-China trade relations.

President Hu and President Obama discussed regulatory and supervisory changes needed to reform and strengthen the global financial system, including regulatory standards. President Hu welcomed the recent U.S. announcement of a comprehensive financial regulatory reform agenda. President Obama welcomed the commitment of China to continue the development and reform of its financial system.

The Presidents agreed on the need for sweeping changes in the governance structure of international financial institutions. President Obama underscored that such changes were needed so that these organizations better reflect the growing weight of dynamic emerging market economies in the global system.

President Hu and President Obama concluded that continued close cooperation between the United States and China was critical at this time to maintain the health of the world economy and would remain so in the future. They both recognized that as major economies, the United States and China have a need to work together, as well as with other countries, to promote the smooth functioning of the international financial system and the steady growth of the world economy. To this end, the two sides will exchange views and intensify coordination and cooperation on global economic and financial issues, climate change and energy, and other important issues through the Strategic and Economic Dialogue that the two countries have decided to establish.

THE PRESIDENT: Thank you. Good morning. It is a great honor to welcome you to the first meeting of the Strategic Economic Dialogue between the United States and China. This is an essential step in advancing a positive, constructive, and comprehensive relationship between our countries. I'm pleased that President Hu shares my commitment to a sustained dialogue to enhance our shared interests.

Remarks by the President at the U.S./China Strategic and Economic Dialogue, The White House, Office of the Press Secretary, For Immediate Release July 27, 2009, Ronald Reagan Building and International Trade Center, Washington, D.C. http://www.whitehouse.gov/the_press_office/ Remarks-by-the-President-at-the-US/China-Strategic-and-Economic-Dialogue/.

President Hu and I both felt that it was important to get our relationship off to a good start. Of course, as a new President and also as a basketball fan, I have learned from the words of Yao Ming, who said, "No matter whether you are new or an old team member, you need time to adjust to one another." Well, through the constructive meetings that we've already had, and through this dialogue, I'm confident that we will meet Yao's standard.

I want to acknowledge the remarkable American and Chinese leaders who will co-chair this effort. Hillary Clinton and Tim Geithner are two of my closest advisors, and they have both obtained extraordinary experience working with China. And I know that they will have extremely capable and committed Chinese counterparts in State Councilor Dai and Vice Premier Wang. Thank you very much for being here.

I'm also looking forward to the confirmation of an outstanding U.S. Ambassador to China, Governor Jon Huntsman, who is here today. Jon has deep experience living and working in Asia, and—unlike me—he speaks fluent Mandarin Chinese. He also happens to be a Republican who co-chaired Senator McCain's campaign. And I think that demonstrates Jon's commitment to serving his country, and the broad, bipartisan support for positive and productive relations between the United States and China. So thank you, Jon, for your willingness to serve.

Today, we meet in a building that speaks to the history of the last century. It houses a national memorial to President Woodrow Wilson, a man who held office when the 20th century was still young, and America's leadership in the world was emerging. It is named for Ronald Reagan, a man who came of age during two World Wars, and whose presidency helped usher in a new era of history. And it holds a piece of the Berlin Wall, a decades-long symbol of division that was finally torn down, unleashing a rising tide of globalization that continues to shape our world.

One hundred years ago—in the early days of the 20th century—it was clear that there were momentous choices to be made—choices about the borders of nations and the rights of human beings. But in Woodrow Wilson's day, no one could have foreseen the arc of history that led to a wall coming down in Berlin, nor could they have imagined the conflict and upheaval that characterized the years in between. For people everywhere—from Boston to Beijing—the 20th century was a time of great progress, but that progress also came with a great price.

Today, we look out on the horizon of a new century. And as we launch this dialogue, it's important for us to reflect upon the questions that will shape the 21st century. Will growth be stalled by events like our current financial crisis, or will we cooperate to create balanced and sustainable growth, lifting more people out of poverty and creating a broader prosperity around the world? Will the need for energy breed competition and climate change, or will we build partnerships to produce clean power and to protect our planet? Will nuclear weapons spread unchecked, or will we forge a new consensus to use this power for only peaceful purposes? Will extremists be able to stir conflict and division, or will we unite on behalf of our shared security? Will nations and peoples define themselves solely by their differences, or can we find common ground necessary to meet our common challenges, and to respect the dignity of every human being?

We can't predict with certainty what the future will bring, but we can be certain about the issues that will define our times. And we also know this: The relationship between the United States and China will shape the 21st century, which makes it as important as any bilateral relationship in the world. That really must underpin our partnership. That is the responsibility that together we bear.

As we look to the future, we can learn from our past—for history shows us that both our nations benefit from engagement that is grounded in mutual interest and mutual respect. During my time in office, we will mark the 40th anniversary of President Nixon's trip to China. At that time, the world was much different than it is today. America had fought three wars in East Asia in just 30 years, and the Cold War was in a stalemate. China's economy was cut off from the world, and a huge percentage of the Chinese people lived in extreme poverty.

Back then, our dialogue was guided by a narrow focus on our shared rivalry with the Soviet Union. Today, we have a comprehensive relationship that reflects the deepening ties among our people. Our countries have now shared relations for longer than we were estranged. Our people interact in so many ways. And I believe that we are poised to make steady progress on some of the most important issues of our times.

My confidence is rooted in the fact that the United States and China share mutual interests. If we advance those interests through cooperation, our people will benefit and the world will be better off—because our ability to partner with each other is a prerequisite for progress on many of the most pressing global challenges.

Let me name some of those challenges. First, we can cooperate to advance our mutual interests in a lasting economic recovery. The current crisis has made it clear that the choices made within our borders reverberate across the global economy—and this is true not just in New York and Seattle, but in Shanghai and Shenzhen, as well. That is why we must remain committed to strong bilateral and multilateral coordination. And that is the example we have set by acting aggressively to restore growth, to prevent a deeper recession and to save jobs for our people.

Going forward, we can deepen this cooperation. We can promote financial stability through greater transparency and regulatory reform. We can pursue trade that is free and fair, and seek to conclude an ambitious and balanced Doha Round agreement. We can update international institutions so that growing economies like China play a greater role that matches their greater responsibility. And as Americans save more and Chinese are able to spend more, we can put growth on a more sustainable foundation—because just as China has benefited from substantial investment and profitable exports, China can also be an enormous market for American goods.

Second, we can cooperate to advance our mutual interest in a clean, secure, and prosperous energy future. The United States and China are the two largest consumers of energy in the world. We are also the two largest emitters of greenhouse gases in the world. Let's be frank: Neither of us profits from a growing dependence on foreign oil, nor can we spare our people from the ravages of climate change unless we cooperate. Common sense calls upon us to act in concert.

Both of our countries are taking steps to transform our energy economies. Together we can chart a low carbon recovery; we can expand joint efforts at research and development to promote the clean and efficient use of energy; and we can work together to forge a global response at the Climate Change Conference in Copenhagen and beyond. And the best way to foster the innovation that can increase our security and prosperity is to keep our markets open to new ideas, new exchanges, and new sources of energy.

Third, we can cooperate to advance our mutual interests in stopping the spread of nuclear weapons. Make no mistake: The more nations acquire these weapons, the more likely it is that they will be used. Neither America nor China has an interest in a terrorist acquiring a bomb, or a nuclear arms race breaking out in East Asia. That is why we must continue our collaboration to achieve the denuclearization of the Korean Peninsula, and make it clear to North Korea that the path to security and respect can be traveled if they meet their obligations. And that is why we must also be united in preventing Iran from acquiring a nuclear weapon, and urging the Islamic Republic to live up to its international obligations.

This is not about singling out any one nation—it is about the responsibility of all nations. Together, we must cooperate to secure all vulnerable nuclear materials around the world, which will be a focus of our Global Nuclear Summit next year. And together, we must strengthen the Nuclear Non-Proliferation Treaty by renewing its basic bargain: countries with nuclear weapons will move towards disarmament; countries without nuclear weapons will not acquire them; and all countries can access peaceful nuclear energy. A balance of terror cannot hold. In the 21st century, a strong and global regime is the only basis for security from the world's deadliest weapons.

And fourth, we can cooperate to advance our mutual interests in confronting transnational threats. The most pressing dangers we face no longer come from competition among great powers—they come from extremists who would murder innocents; from traffickers and pirates who pursue their own profits at the expense of others; from diseases that know no borders; and from suffering and civil wars that breed instability and terror. These are the threats of the 21st century. And that is why the pursuit of power among nations must no longer be seen as a zero-sum game. Progress—including security—must be shared.

Through increased ties between our militaries, we can diminish causes for dispute while providing a framework for cooperation. Through continued intelligence-sharing, we can disrupt terrorist plots and dismantle terrorist networks. Through early warning and coordination, we can check the spread of disease. And through determined diplomacy, we must meet our responsibility to seek the peaceful resolution of conflict—and that can begin with a renewed push to end the suffering in Darfur, and to promote a comprehensive peace in Sudan.

All of these issues are rooted in the fact that no one nation can meet the challenges of the 21st century on its own, nor effectively advance its interests in isolation. It is this fundamental truth that compels us to cooperate. I have no illusion that the United States and China will agree on every issue, nor choose to see the world in the same way. This was already noted by our previous speaker. But that only makes dialogue more important—so that we can know each other better, and communicate our concerns with candor.

For instance, the United States respects the progress that China has made by lifting hundreds of millions of people out of poverty. Just as we respect China's ancient and remarkable culture, its remarkable achievements, we also strongly believe that the religion and culture of all peoples must be respected and protected, and that all people should be free to speak their minds. And that includes ethnic and religious minorities in China, as surely as it includes minorities within the United States.

Support for human rights and human dignity is ingrained in America. Our nation is made up of immigrants from every part of the world. We have protected our unity and struggled to perfect our union by extending basic rights to all our people. And those rights include the freedom to speak your mind, to worship your God, and to choose your leaders. These are not things that we seek to impose—this is who we are. It guides our openness to one another and to the world.

China has its own distinct story that shapes its own worldview. And Americans know the richness of China's history because it helped to shape the world and it helped to shape America. We know the talent of the Chinese people because they have helped to create this great country. My own Cabinet contains two Chinese Americans. And we know that despite our differences, America is enriched through deeper ties with a country of 1.3 billion people that is at once ancient and dynamic—ties that can be forged through increased exchanges among our people, and constructive bilateral relations between our governments. That is how we will narrow our divisions.

Let us be honest: We know that some are wary of the future. Some in China think that America will try to contain China's ambitions; some in America think that there is something to fear in a rising China. I take a different view. And I believe President Hu takes a different view, as well. I believe in a future where China is a strong, prosperous and successful member of the community of nations; a future when our nations are partners out of necessity, but also out of opportunity. This future is not fixed, but it is a destination that can be reached if we pursue a sustained dialogue like the one that you will commence today, and act on what we hear and what we learn.

Thousands of years ago, the great philosopher Mencius said: "A trail through the mountains, if used, becomes a path in a short time, but, if unused, becomes blocked by grass in an equally short time." Our task is to forge a path to the future that we seek for our children—to prevent mistrust or the inevitable differences of the moment from allowing that trail to be blocked by grass; to always be mindful of the journey that we are undertaking together.

This dialogue will help determine the ultimate destination of that journey. It represents a commitment to shape our young century through sustained cooperation, and not confrontation. I look forward to carrying this effort forward through my first visit to China, where I hope to come to know better your leaders, your people, and your majestic country. Together, I'm confident that we can move steadily in the direction of progress, and meet our responsibility to our people and to the future that we will all share.

Thank you very much.

Barack Obama and India

From the White House, this is a transcript of the remarks President Barack Obama is delivering in India on Monday evening:

Mr. Vice President, Madame Speaker, Mr. Prime Minister, Members of the Lok Sabha and Rajya Sabha, and most of all, the people of India.

I thank you for the great honor of addressing the representatives of more than one billion Indians and the world's largest democracy. I bring the greetings and friendship of the world's oldest democracy—the U.S.A, including nearly three million proud and patriotic Indian Americans.

Over the past three days, my wife Michelle and I have experienced the beauty and dynamism of India and its people. From the majesty of Humayun's Tomb to the advanced technologies that are empowering farmers and women who are the backbone of Indian society. From a Diwali celebration with schoolchildren to the innovators who are fueling India's economic rise. From the university students who will chart India's future, to you—leaders who helped to bring India to this moment of promise.

At every stop, we have been welcomed with the hospitality for which Indians have always been known. So to you and the people of India, on behalf of me, Michelle and the American people, please accept our deepest thanks. Bahoot dhanyavad.

I am not the first American president to visit India. Nor will I be the last. But I am proud to visit India so early in my presidency. It is no coincidence that India is my first

Remarks of President Barack Obama—As Prepared for Delivery, Address to a Joint Session of the Indian Parliament, New Delhi, India, Monday, November 8, 2010. http://blogs.wsj.com/indiarealtime/2010/11/08/president-barack-obamas-remarks-to-indias-parliament/.

stop on a visit to Asia, or that this has been my longest visit to another country since becoming President.

For in Asia and around the world, India is not simply emerging; India has already emerged. And it is my firm belief that the relationship between the United States and India—bound by our shared interests and values—will be one of the defining partnerships of the 21st century. This is the partnership I have come here to build. This is the vision that our nations can realize together.

My confidence in our shared future is grounded in my respect for India's treasured past—a civilization that has been shaping the world for thousands of years. Indians unlocked the intricacies of the human body and the vastness of our universe. And it is no exaggeration to say that our information age is rooted in Indian innovations—including the number zero.

India not only opened our minds, she expanded our moral imagination. With religious texts that still summon the faithful to lives of dignity and discipline. With poets who imagined a future "where the mind is without fear and the head is held high." And with a man whose message of love and justice endures—the Father of your Nation, Mahatma Gandhi.

For me and Michelle, this visit has therefore held special meaning. Throughout my life, including my work as a young man on behalf of the urban poor, I have always found inspiration in the life of Gandhi and in his simple and profound lesson to be the change we seek in the world. And just as he summoned Indians to seek their destiny, he influenced champions of equality in my own country, including a young Martin Luther King. After making his pilgrimage to India a half century ago, Dr. King called Gandhi's philosophy of non-violent resistance "the only logical and moral approach" in the struggle for justice and progress.

So we were honored to visit the residence where Gandhi and King both stayed—Mani Bhavan. We were humbled to pay our respects at Raj Ghat. And I am mindful that I might not be standing before you today, as President of the United States, had it not been for Gandhi and the message he shared with America and the world.

An ancient civilization of science and innovation. A fundamental faith in human progress. This is the sturdy foundation upon which you have built ever since that stroke of midnight when the tricolor was raised over a free and independent India. And despite the skeptics who said that this country was simply too poor, too vast, too diverse to succeed, you surmounted overwhelming odds and became a model to the world.

Instead of slipping into starvation, you launched a Green Revolution that fed millions. Instead of becoming dependent on commodities and exports, you invested in science and technology and in your greatest resource—the Indian people. And the world sees the results, from the supercomputers you build to the Indian flag that you put on the moon.

Instead of resisting the global economy, you became one of its engines—reforming the licensing *raj* and unleashing an economic marvel that has lifted tens of millions from poverty and created one of the world's largest middle classes.

Instead of succumbing to division, you have shown that the strength of India—the very idea of India—is its embrace of all colors, castes and creeds. It's the diversity represented in this chamber today. It's the richness of faiths celebrated by a visitor to my hometown of Chicago more than a century ago—the renowned Swami Vivekananda. He said that, "holiness, purity and charity are not the exclusive possessions of any church in the world, and that every system has produced men and women of the most exalted character."

And instead of being lured by the false notion that progress must come at the expense of freedom, you built the institutions upon which true democracy depends—free and fair elections, which enable citizens to choose their own leaders without recourse to arms; an independent judiciary and the rule of law, which allows people to address their grievances; and a thriving free press and vibrant civil society which allows every voice to be heard. And this year, as India marks 60 years with a strong and democratic constitution, the lesson is clear: India has succeeded, not in spite of democracy; India has succeeded because of democracy.

Just as India has changed, so too has the relationship between our two nations. In the decades after independence, India advanced its interests as a proud leader of the nonaligned movement. Yet too often, the United States and India found ourselves on opposite sides of a North-South divide and estranged by a long Cold War. Those days are over.

Here in India, two successive governments led by different parties have recognized that deeper partnership with America is both natural and necessary. In the United States, both of my predecessors—one Democrat, one Republican—worked to bring us closer, leading to increased trade and a landmark civil nuclear agreement.

Since then, people in both our countries have asked: what next? How can we build on this progress and realize the full potential of our partnership? That is what I want to address today—the future that the United States seeks in an interconnected world; why I believe that India is indispensable to this vision; and how we can forge a truly global partnership—not in just one or two areas, but across many; not just for our mutual benefit, but for the world's.

Of course, only Indians can determine India's national interests and how to advance them on the world stage. But I stand before you today because I am convinced that the interests of the United States—and the interests we share with India—are best advanced in partnership.

The United States seeks security—the security of our country, allies and partners. We seek prosperity—a strong and growing economy in an open international economic system. We seek respect for universal values. And we seek a just and sustainable international order that promotes peace and security by meeting global challenges through stronger global cooperation.

To advance these interests, I have committed the United States to comprehensive engagement with the world, based on mutual interest and mutual respect. And a central pillar of this engagement is forging deeper cooperation with 21st century centers of influence—and that includes India. This is why I believe that India and America are indispensable partners in meeting the challenges of our time.

Since taking office, I've therefore made our relationship a priority. I was proud to welcome Prime Minister Singh for the first official state visit of my presidency. For the first time ever, our governments are working together across the whole range of common challenges we face. And let me say it as clearly as I can: the United States not only welcomes India as a rising global power, we fervently support it, and we have worked to help make it a reality.

Together with our partners, we have made the G20 the premier forum for international economic cooperation, bringing more voices to the table of global economic decision-making, including India. We have increased the role of emerging economies like India at international financial institutions. We valued India's important role at Copenhagen, where, for the first time, all major economies committed to take action to confront climate change—and to stand by those actions. We salute India's long history as a leading contributor to United Nations peacekeeping missions. And we welcome India as it prepares to take its seat on the United Nations Security Council.

In short, with India assuming its rightful place in the world, we have an historic opportunity to make the relationship between our two countries a defining partnership of the century ahead. And I believe we can do so by working together in three important areas.

First, as global partners we can promote prosperity in both our countries. Together, we can create the high-tech, high-wage jobs of the future. With my visit, we are now ready to begin implementing our civil nuclear agreement. This will help meet India's growing energy needs and create thousands of jobs in both our countries.

We need to forge partnerships in high-tech sectors like defense and civil space. So we have removed Indian organizations from our so-called "entity list." And we'll work to reform our controls on exports. Both of these steps will ensure that Indian companies seeking high-tech trade and technologies from America are treated the same as our closest allies and partners.

We can pursue joint research and development to create green jobs; give Indians more access to cleaner, affordable energy; meet the commitments we made at Copenhagen; and show the possibilities of low-carbon growth.

Together, we can resist the protectionism that stifles growth and innovation. The United States remains—and will continue to remain—one of the most open economies in the world. And by opening markets and reducing barriers to foreign investment,

India can realize its full economic potential as well. As G20 partners, we can make sure the global economic recovery is strong and durable. And we can keep striving for a Doha Round that is ambitious and balanced—with the courage to make the compromises that are necessary so global trade works for all economies.

Together, we can strengthen agriculture. Cooperation between Indian and American researchers and scientists sparked the Green Revolution. Today, India is a leader in using technology to empower farmers, like those I met yesterday who get free updates on market and weather conditions on their cell phones. And the United States is a leader in agricultural productivity and research. Now, as farmers and rural areas face the effects of climate change and drought, we'll work together to spark a second, more sustainable Evergreen Revolution.

Together, we're going to improve Indian weather forecasting systems before the next monsoon season. We aim to help millions of Indian farming households save water and increase productivity; improve food processing so crops don't spoil on the way to market; and enhance climate and crop forecasting to avoid losses that cripple communities and drive up food prices.

Because the wealth of a nation also depends on the health of its people, we'll continue to support India's efforts against diseases like tuberculosis and HIV/AIDS, and as global partners, we'll work to improve global health by preventing the spread of pandemic flu. And because knowledge is the currency of the 21st century, we'll increase exchanges between our students, colleges and universities, which are among the best in the world.

As we work to advance our shared prosperity, we can partner to address a second priority—our shared security. In Mumbai, I met with the courageous families and survivors of that barbaric attack. And here in this Parliament, which was itself targeted because of the democracy it represents, we honor the memory of all those who have been taken from us, including American citizens on 26/11 and Indian citizens on 9/11.

This is the bond we share. It's why we insist that nothing ever justifies the slaughter of innocent men, women and children. It's why we're working together, more closely than ever, to prevent terrorist attacks and to deepen our cooperation even further. And it's why, as strong and resilient societies, we refuse to live in fear, we will not sacrifice the values and rule of law that defines us, and we will never waver in the defense of our people.

America's fight against al Qaeda and its terrorist affiliates is why we persevere in Afghanistan, where major development assistance from India has improved the lives of the Afghan people. We're making progress in our mission to break the Taliban's momentum and to train Afghan forces so they can take the lead for their security. And while I have made it clear that American forces will begin the transition to Afghan responsibility next summer, I have also made it clear that America's commitment to the Afghan people will endure. The United States will not abandon the people of Afghanistan—or the region—to the violent extremists who threaten us all.

Our strategy to disrupt, dismantle and defeat al Qaeda and its affiliates has to succeed on both sides of the border. That is why we have worked with the Pakistani government to address the threat of terrorist networks in the border region. The Pakistani government increasingly recognizes that these networks are not just a threat outside of Pakistan—they are a threat to the Pakistani people, who have suffered greatly at the hands of violent extremists.

And we will continue to insist to Pakistan's leaders that terrorist safe-havens within their borders are unacceptable, and that the terrorists behind the Mumbai attacks be brought to justice. We must also recognize that all of us have and interest in both an Afghanistan and a Pakistan that is stable, prosperous and democratic—and none more so than India.

More broadly, India and the United States can partner in Asia. Today, the United States is once again playing a leadership role in Asia—strengthening old alliances; deepening relationships, as we are doing with China; and we're reengaging with regional organizations like ASEAN and joining the East Asia summit—organizations in which India is also a partner. Like your neighbors in Southeast Asia, we want India to not only "look East," we want India to "engage East"—because it will increase the security and prosperity of all our nations.

And as two global leaders, the United States and India can partner for global security—especially as India serves on the Security Council over the next two years. Indeed, the just and sustainable international order that America seeks includes a United Nations that is efficient, effective, credible and legitimate. That is why I can say today—in the years ahead, I look forward to a reformed U.N. Security Council that includes India as a permanent member.

Now, let me suggest that with increased power comes increased responsibility. The United Nations exists to fulfill its founding ideals of preserving peace and security, promoting global cooperation, and advancing human rights. These are the responsibilities of all nations, but especially those that seek to lead in the 21st century. And so we look forward to working with India—and other nations that aspire to Security Council membership—to ensure that the Security Council is effective; that resolutions are implemented and sanctions enforced; and that we strengthen the international norms which recognize the rights and responsibilities of all nations and individuals.

This includes our responsibility to prevent the spread of nuclear weapons. Since I took office, the United States has reduced the role of nuclear weapons in our national security strategy, and agreed with Russia to reduce our arsenals. We have put preventing nuclear proliferation and nuclear terrorism at the top of our nuclear agenda, and strengthened the cornerstone of the global non-proliferation regime—the Nuclear Non-Proliferation Treaty.

Together, the United States and India can pursue our goal of securing the world's vulnerable nuclear materials. We can make it clear that even as every nation has the right to peaceful nuclear energy, every nation must also meet its international obligations—and that includes the Islamic Republic of Iran. And together, we can pursue a vision that Indian leaders have espoused since independence—a world without nuclear weapons. This leads me to the final area where our countries can partner—strengthening the foundations of democratic governance, not only at home but abroad.

Now, in a new collaboration on open government, our two countries are going to share our experience, identify what works, and develop the next-generation of tools to empower citizens. And in another example of how American and Indian partnership can address global challenges, we're going to share these innovations with civil society groups and countries around the world. We're going to show that democracy, more than any other form of government, delivers for the common man—and woman.

As the world's two largest democracies, we must also never forget that the price of our own freedom is standing up for the freedom of others. Indians know this, for it is the story of your nation. Before he ever began his struggle for Indian independence, Gandhi stood up for the rights of Indians in South Africa. Just as others, including the United States, supported Indian independence, India championed the self-determination of peoples from Africa to Asia as they too broke free from colonialism. And along with the United States, you've been a leader in supporting democratic development and civil society groups around the world. This, too, is part of India's greatness.

Every country will follow its own path. No one nation has a monopoly on wisdom, and no nation should ever try to impose its values on another. But when peaceful democratic movements are suppressed—as in Burma—then the democracies of the world cannot remain silent. For it is unacceptable to gun down peaceful protestors and incarcerate political prisoners decade after decade. It is unacceptable to hold the aspirations of an entire people hostage to the greed and paranoia of a bankrupt regime. It is unacceptable to steal an election, as the regime in Burma has done again for all the world to see.

Faced with such gross violations of human rights, it is the responsibility of the international community—especially leaders like the United States and India—to condemn it. If I can be frank, in international fora, India has often avoided these issues. But speaking up for those who cannot do so for themselves is not interfering in the affairs of other countries. It's not violating the rights of sovereign nations. It's staying true to our democratic principles. It's giving meaning to the human rights that we say are universal. And it sustains the progress that in Asia and around the world has helped turn dictatorships into democracies and ultimately increased our security in the world.

Promoting shared prosperity. Preserving peace and security. Strengthening democratic governance and human rights. These are the responsibilities of leadership. And, as global partners, this is the leadership that the United States and India can offer in the 21ˢᵗ century. Ultimately, however, this cannot be a relationship only between presidents and prime ministers, or in the halls of this parliament. Ultimately, this must be a partnership between our peoples. So I want to conclude by speaking directly to the people of India watching today.

In your lives, you have overcome odds that might have overwhelmed a lesser country. In just decades, you have achieved progress and development that took other nation's centuries. And now you are assuming your rightful place as a leader among nations. Your parents and grandparents imagined this. Your children and grandchildren will look back on this. But only you—this generation of Indians—can seize the possibility of this moment.

As you carry on with the hard work ahead, I want every Indian citizen to know: the United States of America will not simply be cheering you on from the sidelines. We will be right there with you, shoulder to shoulder. Because we believe in the promise of India. And we believe that the future is what we make it.

We believe that no matter who you are or where you come from, every person can fulfill their God-given potential, just as a Dalit like Dr. Ambedkar could lift himself up and pen the words of the Constitution that protects the rights of all Indians.

We believe that no matter where you live—whether a village in Punjab or the bylanes of Chandni Chowk ... an old section of Kolkata or a new high-rise in Bangalore—every person deserves the same chance to live in security and dignity, to get an education, to find work, and to give their children a better future.

And we believe that when countries and cultures put aside old habits and attitudes that keep people apart, when we recognize our common humanity, then we can begin to fulfill the aspirations we share. It's a simple lesson contained in that collection of stories which has guided Indians for centuries—the Panchtantra. And it's the spirit of the inscription seen by all who enter this great hall: "That one is mine and the other a stranger is the concept of little minds. But to the large-hearted, the world itself is their family."

This is the story of India; it's the story of America—that despite their differences, people can see themselves in one another, and work together and succeed together as one proud nation. And it can be the spirit of the partnership between our nations—that even as we honor the histories which in different times kept us apart, even as we preserve what makes us unique in a globalized world, we can recognize how much we can achieve together. Thank you, Jai Hind!, and long live the partnership between India and the United States.

Barack Obama and U.S.-Russian Relations

Thank you so much. Well, congratulations, Oxana. And to the entire Class of 2009, congratulations to you. I don't know if anybody else will meet their future wife or husband in class like I did, but I'm sure that you're all going to have wonderful careers.

I want to acknowledge a few people who are here. We have President Mikhail Gorbachev is here today, and I want everybody to give him a big round of applause. I want to thank Sergei Gurief, Director of the New Economic School. Max Boiko, their Chairman of the Board. And Arkady Dvorkovich, who is the NES board member, President of the Alumni Association and is doing an excellent job for President Medvedev, because he was in our meeting yesterday.

Good morning. It is a great honor for me to join you at the New Economic School. Michelle and I are so pleased to be in Moscow. And as somebody who was born in Hawaii, I'm glad to be here in July instead of January.

I know that NES is a young school, but I speak to you today with deep respect for Russia's timeless heritage. Russian writers have helped us understand the complexity of the human experience and recognize eternal truths. Russian painters, composers and dancers have introduced us to new forms of beauty. Russian scientists have cured disease, sought new frontiers of progress and helped us go to space.

These are contributions that are not contained by Russia's borders, as vast as those borders are. Indeed, Russia's heritage has touched every corner of the world, and speaks to the humanity that we share. That includes my own country, which has been blessed with Russian immigrants for decades; we've been enriched by Russian culture, and enhanced by Russian cooperation. And as a resident of Washington, D.C., I continue to benefit from the contributions of Russians—specifically, from Alexander Ovechkin. We're very pleased to have him in Washington, D.C.

Here at NES, you have inherited this great cultural legacy, but your focus on economics is no less fundamental to the future of humanity. As Pushkin said, "Inspiration is needed in geometry just as much as poetry." And today, I want particularly to speak to those of you preparing to graduate. You're poised to be leaders in academia and industry; in finance and government. But before you move forward, it's worth reflecting on what has already taken place during your young lives.

Obama's Speech on U.S.-Russia Relations, Remarks by the President at the New Economic School Graduation, Gostinny Dvor, Moscow, Russia, The White House, Office of the Press Secretary, For Immediate Release, July 7, 2009. http://www.whitehouse.gov/the_press_office/ Remarks-By-The-President-At-The-New-Economic-School-Graduation/.

Like President Medvedev and myself, you're not old enough to have witnessed the darkest hours of the Cold War, when hydrogen bombs were tested in the atmosphere, and children drilled in fallout shelters, and we reached the brink of nuclear catastrophe. But you are the last generation born when the world was divided. At that time, the American and Soviet armies were still massed in Europe, trained and ready to fight. The ideological trenches of the last century were roughly in place. Competition in everything from astrophysics to athletics was treated as a zero-sum game. If one person won, then the other person had to lose.

And then, within a few short years, the world as it was ceased to be. Now, make no mistake: This change did not come from any one nation. The Cold War reached a conclusion because of the actions of many nations over many years, and because the people of Russia and Eastern Europe stood up and decided that its end would be peaceful.

With the end of the Cold War, there were extraordinary expectations—for peace and for prosperity; for new arrangements among nations, and new opportunities for individuals. Like all periods of great change, it was a time of ambitious plans and endless possibilities. But, of course, things don't always work out exactly as planned. Back in 1993, shortly after this school opened, one NES student summed up the difficulty of change when he told a reporter, and I quote him: "The real world is not so rational as on paper." The real world is not so rational as on paper.

Over two tumultuous decades, that truth has been borne out around the world. Great wealth has been created, but it has not eliminated vast pockets of crushing poverty. Poverty exists here, it exists in the United States, and it exists all around the world. More people have gone to the ballot box, but too many governments still fail to protect the rights of their people. Ideological struggles have diminished, but they've been replaced by conflicts over tribe and ethnicity and religion. A human being with a computer can hold the same amount of information stored in the Russian State Library, but that technology can also be used to do great harm.

In a new Russia, the disappearance of old political and economic restrictions after the end of the Soviet Union brought both opportunity and hardship. A few prospered, but many more did not. There were tough times. But the Russian people showed strength and made sacrifices, and you achieved hard-earned progress through a growing economy and greater confidence. And despite painful times, many in Eastern Europe and Russia are much better off today than 20 years ago.

We see that progress here at NES—a school founded with Western support that is now distinctly Russian; a place of learning and inquiry where the test of an idea is not whether it is Russian or American or European, but whether it works. Above all, we see that progress in all of you—young people with a young century to shape as you see fit.

Your lifetime coincides with this era of transition. But think about the fundamental questions asked when this school was founded. What kind of future is Russia going to have? What kind of future are Russia and America going to have together? What world order will replace the Cold War? Those questions still don't have clear answers, and so now they must be answered by you—by your generation in Russia, in America, and around the world. You get to decide. And while I cannot answer those questions for you, I can speak plainly about the future that America is seeking.

To begin with, let me be clear: America wants a strong, peaceful and prosperous Russia. This belief is rooted in our respect for the Russian people, and a shared history between our nations that goes beyond competition. Despite our past rivalry, our people were allies in the greatest struggle of the last century. Recently, I noted this when I was in Normandy—for just as men from Boston and Birmingham risked all that they had to storm those beaches and scale those cliffs, Soviet soldiers from places like Kazan and Kiev endured unimaginable hardships to repeal—to repel an invasion, and turn the tide in the east. As President John Kennedy said, "No nation in history of battle ever suffered more than the Soviet Union in the Second World War."

So as we honor this past, we also recognize the future benefit that will come from a strong and vibrant Russia. Think of the issues that will define your lives: security from nuclear weapons and extremism; access to markets and opportunity; health and the environment; an international system that protects sovereignty and human rights, while promoting stability and prosperity. These challenges demand global partnership, and that partnership will be stronger if Russia occupies its rightful place as a great power.

Yet unfortunately, there is sometimes a sense that old assumptions must prevail, old ways of thinking; a conception of power that is rooted in the past rather than in the future. There is the 20th century view that the United States and Russia are destined to be antagonists, and that a strong Russia or a strong America can only assert themselves in opposition to one another. And there is a 19th century view that we are destined to vie for spheres of influence, and that great powers must forge competing blocs to balance one another.

These assumptions are wrong. In 2009, a great power does not show strength by dominating or demonizing other countries. The days when empires could treat sovereign states as pieces on a chess board are over. As I said in Cairo, given our independence, any world order that—given our interdependence, any world order that tries to elevate one nation or one group of people over another will inevitably fail. The pursuit of power is no longer a zero-sum game—progress must be shared.

That's why I have called for a "reset" in relations between the United States and Russia. This must be more than a fresh start between the Kremlin and the White House—though that is important and I've had excellent discussions with both your President and your Prime Minister. It must be a sustained effort among the American and Russian people to identify mutual interests, and expand dialogue and cooperation that can pave the way to progress.

This will not be easy. It's difficult to forge a lasting partnership between former adversaries, it's hard to change habits that have been ingrained in our governments and our bureaucracies for decades. But I believe that on the fundamental issues that will shape this century, Americans and Russians share common interests that form a basis for cooperation. It is not for me to define Russia's national interests, but I can tell you about America's national interests, and I believe that you will see that we share common ground.

First, America has an interest in reversing the spread of nuclear weapons and preventing their use. In the last century, generations of Americans and Russians inherited the power to destroy nations, and the understanding that using that power would bring about our own destruction. In 2009, our inheritance is different. You and I don't have to ask whether American and Russian leaders will respect a balance of terror—we understand the horrific consequences of any war between our two countries. But we do have to ask this question: We have to ask whether extremists who have killed innocent civilians in New York and in Moscow will show that same restraint. We have to ask whether 10 or 20 or 50 nuclear-armed nations will protect their arsenals and refrain from using them.

This is the core of the nuclear challenge in the 21st century. The notion that prestige comes from holding these weapons, or that we can protect ourselves by picking and choosing which nations can have these weapons, is an illusion. In the short period since the end of the Cold War, we've already seen India, Pakistan and North Korea conduct nuclear tests. Without a fundamental change, do any of us truly believe that the next two decades will not bring about the further spread of these nuclear weapons?

That's why America is committed to stopping nuclear proliferation, and ultimately seeking a world without nuclear weapons. That is consistent with our commitment under the Nuclear Non-Proliferation Treaty. That is our responsibility as the world's two leading nuclear powers. And while I know this goal won't be met soon, pursuing it provides the legal and moral foundation to prevent the proliferation and eventual use of nuclear weapons.

We're already taking important steps to build this foundation. Yesterday, President Medvedev and I made progress on negotiating a new treaty that will substantially reduce our warheads and delivery systems. We renewed our commitment to clean, safe and peaceful nuclear energy, which must be a right for all nations that live up to their responsibilities under the NPT. And we agreed to increase cooperation on nuclear security, which is essential to achieving the goal of securing all vulnerable nuclear material within four years.

As we keep our own commitments, we must hold other nations accountable for theirs. Whether America or Russia, neither of us would benefit from a nuclear arms race in East Asia or the Middle East. That's why we should be united in opposing

North Korea's efforts to become a nuclear power, and opposing Iran's efforts to acquire a nuclear weapon. And I'm pleased that President Medvedev and I agreed upon a joint threat assessment of the ballistic challenges—ballistic missile challenges of the 21st century, including from Iran and North Korea. This is not about singling out individual nations—it's about the responsibilities of all nations. If we fail to stand together, then the NPT and the Security Council will lose credibility, and international law will give way to the law of the jungle. And that benefits no one. As I said in Prague, rules must be binding, violations must be punished and words must mean something.

The successful enforcement of these rules will remove causes of disagreement. I know Russia opposes the planned configuration for missile defense in Europe. And my administration is reviewing these plans to enhance the security of America, Europe and the world. And I've made it clear that this system is directed at preventing a potential attack from Iran. It has nothing to do with Russia. In fact, I want to work together with Russia on a missile defense architecture that makes us all safer. But if the threat from Iran's nuclear and ballistic missile program is eliminated, the driving force for missile defense in Europe will be eliminated, and that is in our mutual interests.

Now, in addition to securing the world's most dangerous weapons, a second area where America has a critical national interest is in isolating and defeating violent extremists. For years, al-Qaeda and its affiliates have defiled a great religion of peace and justice, and ruthlessly murdered men, women and children of all nationalities and faiths. Indeed, above all, they have murdered Muslims. And these extremists have killed in Amman and Bali; Islamabad and Kabul; and they have the blood of Americans and Russians on their hands. They're plotting to kill more of our people, and they benefit from safe havens that allow them to train and operate—particularly along the border of Pakistan and Afghanistan.

And that's why America has a clear goal: to disrupt, dismantle and defeat al-Qaeda and its allies in Afghanistan and Pakistan. We seek no bases, nor do we want to control these nations. Instead, we want to work with international partners, including Russia, to help Afghans and Pakistanis advance their own security and prosperity. And that's why I'm pleased that Russia has agreed to allow the United States to supply our coalition forces through your territory. Neither America nor Russia has an interest in an Afghanistan or Pakistan governed by the Taliban. It's time to work together on behalf of a different future—a future in which we leave behind the great game of the past and the conflict of the present; a future in which all of us contribute to the security of Central Asia.

Now, beyond Afghanistan, America is committed to promoting the opportunity that will isolate extremists. We are helping the Iraqi people build a better future, and leaving Iraq to the Iraqis. We're pursuing the goal of two states, Israel and Palestine, living in peace and security. We're partnering with Muslim communities around the world to advance education, health, and economic development. In each of these endeavors, I believe that the Russian people share our goals, and will benefit from success—and we need to partner together.

Now, in addition to these security concerns, the third area that I will discuss is America's interest in global prosperity. And since we have so many economists and future businessmen and women in the room, I know this is of great interest to you.

We meet in the midst of the worst global recession in a generation. I believe that the free market is the greatest force for creating and distributing wealth that the world has known. But wherever the market is allowed to run rampant—through excessive risk-taking, a lack of regulation, or corruption—then all are endangered, whether we live on the Mississippi or on the Volga.

In America, we're now taking unprecedented steps to jump-start our economy and reform our system of regulation. But just as no nation can wall itself off from the consequences of a global crisis, no one can serve as the sole engine of global growth. You see, during your lives, something fundamental has changed. And while this crisis has shown us the risks that come with change, that risk is overwhelmed by opportunity.

Think of what's possible today that was unthinkable two decades ago. A young woman with an Internet connection in Bangalore, India, can compete with anybody anywhere in the world. An entrepreneur with a startup company in Beijing can take his business global. An NES professor in Moscow can collaborate with colleagues at Harvard or Stanford. That's good for all of us, because when prosperity is created in India, that's a new market for our goods; when new ideas take hold in China, that pushes our businesses to innovate; when new connections are forged among people, all of us are enriched.

There is extraordinary potential for increased cooperation between Americans and Russians. We can pursue trade that is free and fair and integrated with the wider world. We can boost investment that creates jobs in both our countries, we can forge partnerships on energy that tap not only traditional resources, like oil and gas, but new sources of energy that will drive growth and combat climate change. All of that, Americans and Russians can do together.

Now, government can promote this cooperation, but ultimately individuals must advance this cooperation, because the greatest resource of any nation in the 21st century is you. It's people; it's young people especially. And the country which taps that resource will be the country that will succeed. That success depends upon economies that function within the rule of law. As President Medvedev has rightly said, a mature and effective legal system is a condition for sustained economic development. People everywhere should have the right to do business or get an education without paying a bribe. Whether they are in America or Russia or Africa or Latin America, that's not an American idea or a Russian idea—that's how people and countries will succeed in the 21st century.

And this brings me to the fourth issue that I will discuss—America's interest in democratic governments that protect the rights of their people. By no means is America perfect. But it is our commitment to certain universal values which allows us to correct our imperfections, to improve constantly, and to grow stronger over time. Freedom of speech and assembly has allowed women, and minorities, and workers to protest for full and equal rights at a time when they were denied. The rule of law and equal administration of justice has busted monopolies, shut down political machines that were corrupt, ended abuses of power. Independent media have exposed corruption at all levels of business and government. Competitive elections allow us to change course and hold our leaders accountable. If our democracy did not advance those rights, then I, as a person of African ancestry, wouldn't be able to address you as an American citizen, much less a President. Because at the time of our founding, I had no rights—people who looked like me. But it is because of that process that I can now stand before you as President of the United States.

So around the world, America supports these values because they are moral, but also because they work. The arc of history shows that governments which serve their own people survive and thrive; governments which serve only their own power do not. Governments that represent the will of their people are far less likely to descend into failed states, to terrorize their citizens, or to wage war on others. Governments that promote the rule of law, subject their actions to oversight, and allow for independent institutions are more dependable trading partners. And in our own history, democracies have been America's most enduring allies, including those we once waged war with in Europe and Asia—nations that today live with great security and prosperity.

Now let me be clear: America cannot and should not seek to impose any system of government on any other country, nor would we presume to choose which party or individual should run a country. And we haven't always done what we should have on that front. Even as we meet here today, America supports now the restoration of the democratically elected President of Honduras, even though he has strongly opposed American policies. We do so not because we agree with him. We do so because we respect the universal principle that people should choose their own leaders, whether they are leaders we agree with or not.

And that leads me to the final area that I will discuss, which is America's interest in an international system that advances cooperation while respecting the sovereignty of all nations.

State sovereignty must be a cornerstone of international order. Just as all states should have the right to choose their leaders, states must have the right to borders that are secure, and to their own foreign policies. That is true for Russia, just as it is true for the United States. Any system that cedes those rights will lead to anarchy. That's why we must apply this principle to all nations—and that includes nations like Georgia and Ukraine. America will never impose a security arrangement on another country. For any country to become a member of an organization like NATO, for example, a majority of its people must choose to; they must undertake reforms; they must be able to contribute to the Alliance's mission. And let me be clear: NATO should be seeking collaboration with Russia, not confrontation.

And more broadly, we need to foster cooperation and respect among all nations and peoples. As President of the United States, I will work tirelessly to protect America's security and to advance our interests. But no one nation can meet the challenges of the 21st century on its own, nor dictate its terms to the world. That is something that America now understands, just as Russia understands. That's why America seeks an international system that lets nations pursue their interests peacefully, especially when those interests diverge; a system where the universal rights of human beings are respected, and violations of those rights are opposed; a system where we hold ourselves to the same standards that we apply to other nations, with clear rights and responsibilities for all.

There was a time when Roosevelt, Churchill and Stalin could shape the world in one meeting. Those days are over. The world is more complex today. Billions of people have found their voice, and seek their own measure of prosperity and self-determination in every corner of the planet. Over the past two decades, we've witnessed markets grow, wealth spread and technology used to build—not destroy. We've seen old hatreds pass, illusions of differences between people lift and fade away; we've seen the human destiny in the hands of more and more human beings who can shape their own destinies. Now, we must see that the period of transition which you have lived through ushers in a new era in which nations live in peace, and people realize their aspirations for dignity, security, and a better life for their children. That is America's interest, and I believe that it is Russia's interest as well.

I know that this future can seem distant. Change is hard. In the words of that NES student back in 1993, the real world is not so rational as on paper. But think of the change that has unfolded with the passing of time. One hundred years ago, a czar ruled Russia, and Europe was a place of empire. When I was born, segregation was still the law of the land in parts of America, and my father's Kenya was still a colony. When you were born, a school like this would have been impossible, and the Internet was only known to a privileged few.

You get to decide what comes next. You get to choose where change will take us, because the future does not belong to those who gather armies on a field of battle or bury missiles in the ground; the future belongs to young people with an education and the imagination to create. That is the source of power in this century. And given all that has happened in your two decades on Earth, just imagine what you can create in the years to come. Every country charts its own course. Russia has cut its way through time like a mighty river through a canyon, leaving an indelible mark on human history as it goes. As you move this story forward, look to the future that can be built if we refuse to be burdened by the old obstacles and old suspicions; look to the future that can be built if we partner on behalf of the aspirations we hold in common. Together, we can build a world where people are protected, prosperity is enlarged, and our power truly serves progress. And it is all in your hands. Good luck to all of you. Thank you very much.

Chapter 9

Barack Obama and Nobel Peace Prize—Toward
an Obama Doctrine?

THE PRESIDENT: **Your Majesties**, Your Royal Highnesses, distinguished members of the Norwegian Nobel Committee, citizens of America, and citizens of the world: I receive this honor with deep gratitude and great humility. It is an award that speaks to our highest aspirations—that for all the cruelty and hardship of our world, we are not mere prisoners of fate. Our actions matter, and can bend history in the direction of justice.

And yet I would be remiss if I did not acknowledge the considerable controversy that your generous decision has generated. In part, this is because I am at the beginning, and not the end, of my labors on the world stage. Compared to some of the giants of history who've received this prize—Schweitzer and King; Marshall and Mandela—my accomplishments are slight. And then there are the men and women around the world who have been jailed and beaten in the pursuit of justice; those who toil in humanitarian organizations to relieve suffering; the unrecognized millions whose quiet acts of courage and compassion inspire even the most hardened cynics. I cannot argue with those who find these men and women—some known, some obscure to all but those they help—to be far more deserving of this honor than I.

But perhaps the most profound issue surrounding my receipt of this prize is the fact that I am the Commander-in-Chief of the military of a nation in the midst of two wars. One of these wars is winding down. The other is a conflict that America did not seek; one in which we are joined by 42 other countries—including Norway—in an effort to defend ourselves and all nations from further attacks.

Still, we are at war, and I'm responsible for the deployment of thousands of young Americans to battle in a distant land. Some will kill, and some will be killed. And so

Remarks by the President at the Acceptance of the Nobel Peace Prize, Oslo City Hall, Oslo, Norway. The White House, Office of the Press Secretary, For Immediate Release, December 10, 2009. http://www.whitehouse.gov/the-press-office/remarks-president-acceptance-nobel-peace-prize.

I come here with an acute sense of the costs of armed conflict—filled with difficult questions about the relationship between war and peace, and our effort to replace one with the other.

Now these questions are not new. War, in one form or another, appeared with the first man. At the dawn of history, its morality was not questioned; it was simply a fact, like drought or disease—the manner in which tribes and then civilizations sought power and settled their differences.

And over time, as codes of law sought to control violence within groups, so did philosophers and clerics and statesmen seek to regulate the destructive power of war. The concept of a "just war" emerged, suggesting that war is justified only when certain conditions were met: if it is waged as a last resort or in self-defense; if the force used is proportional; and if, whenever possible, civilians are spared from violence.

Of course, we know that for most of history, this concept of "just war" was rarely observed. The capacity of human beings to think up new ways to kill one another proved inexhaustible, as did our capacity to exempt from mercy those who look different or pray to a different God. Wars between armies gave way to wars between nations—total wars in which the distinction between combatant and civilian became blurred. In the span of 30 years, such carnage would twice engulf this continent. And while it's hard to conceive of a cause more just than the defeat of the Third Reich and the Axis powers, World War II was a conflict in which the total number of civilians who died exceeded the number of soldiers who perished.

In the wake of such destruction, and with the advent of the nuclear age, it became clear to victor and vanquished alike that the world needed institutions to prevent another world war. And so, a quarter century after the United States Senate rejected the League of Nations—an idea for which Woodrow Wilson received this prize—America led the world in constructing an architecture to keep the peace: a Marshall Plan and a United Nations, mechanisms to govern the waging of war, treaties to protect human rights, prevent genocide, restrict the most dangerous weapons.

In many ways, these efforts succeeded. Yes, terrible wars have been fought, and atrocities committed. But there has been no Third World War. The Cold War ended with jubilant crowds dismantling a wall. Commerce has stitched much of the world together. Billions have been lifted from poverty. The ideals of liberty and self-determination, equality and the rule of law have haltingly advanced. We are the heirs of the fortitude and foresight of generations past, and it is a legacy for which my own country is rightfully proud.

And yet, a decade into a new century, this old architecture is buckling under the weight of new threats. The world may no longer shudder at the prospect of war between two nuclear superpowers, but proliferation may increase the risk of catastrophe. Terrorism has long been a tactic, but modern technology allows a few small men with outsized rage to murder innocents on a horrific scale.

Moreover, wars between nations have increasingly given way to wars within nations. The resurgence of ethnic or sectarian conflicts; the growth of secessionist movements, insurgencies, and failed states—all these things have increasingly trapped civilians in unending chaos. In today's wars, many more civilians are killed than soldiers; the seeds of future conflict are sown, economies are wrecked, civil societies torn asunder, refugees amassed, children scarred.

I do not bring with me today a definitive solution to the problems of war. What I do know is that meeting these challenges will require the same vision, hard work, and persistence of those men and women who acted so boldly decades ago. And it will require us to think in new ways about the notions of just war and the imperatives of a just peace.

We must begin by acknowledging the hard truth: We will not eradicate violent conflict in our lifetimes. There will be times when nations—acting individually or in concert—will find the use of force not only necessary but morally justified.

I make this statement mindful of what Martin Luther King Jr. said in this same ceremony years ago: "Violence never brings permanent peace. It solves no social problem: it merely creates new and more complicated ones." As someone who stands here as a direct consequence of Dr. King's life work, I am living testimony to the moral force of non-violence. I know there's nothing weak—nothing passive—nothing naïve—in the creed and lives of Gandhi and King.

But as a head of state sworn to protect and defend my nation, I cannot be guided by their examples alone. I face the world as it is, and cannot stand idle in the face of threats to the American people. For make no mistake: Evil does exist in the world. A non-violent movement could not have halted Hitler's armies. Negotiations cannot convince al Qaeda's leaders to lay down their arms. To say that force may sometimes be necessary is not a call to cynicism—it is a recognition of history; the imperfections of man and the limits of reason.

I raise this point, I begin with this point because in many countries there is a deep ambivalence about military action today, no matter what the cause. And at times, this is joined by a reflexive suspicion of America, the world's sole military superpower.

But the world must remember that it was not simply international institutions—not just treaties and declarations—that brought stability to a post-World War II world. Whatever mistakes we have made, the plain fact is this: The United States of America has helped underwrite global security for more than six decades with the blood of our citizens and the strength of our arms. The service and sacrifice of our men and women in uniform has promoted peace and prosperity from Germany to Korea, and enabled democracy to take hold in places like the Balkans. We have borne this burden not because we seek to impose our will. We have done so out of enlightened self-interest—because we seek a better future for our children and grandchildren, and we believe that their lives will be better if others' children and grandchildren can live in freedom and prosperity.

So yes, the instruments of war do have a role to play in preserving the peace. And yet this truth must coexist with another—that no matter how justified, war promises human tragedy. The soldier's courage and sacrifice is full of glory, expressing devotion to country, to cause, to comrades in arms. But war itself is never glorious, and we must never trumpet it as such.

So part of our challenge is reconciling these two seemingly irreconcilable truths—that war is sometimes necessary, and war at some level is an expression of human folly. Concretely, we must direct our effort to the task that President Kennedy called for long ago. "Let us focus," he said, "on a more practical, more attainable peace, based not on a sudden revolution in human nature but on a gradual evolution in human institutions." A gradual evolution of human institutions.

What might this evolution look like? What might these practical steps be? To begin with, I believe that all nations—strong and weak alike—must adhere to standards that govern the use of force. I—like any head of state—reserve the right to act unilaterally if necessary to defend my nation. Nevertheless, I am convinced that adhering to standards, international standards, strengthens those who do, and isolates and weakens those who don't.

The world rallied around America after the 9/11 attacks, and continues to support our efforts in Afghanistan, because of the horror of those senseless attacks and the recognized principle of self-defense. Likewise, the world recognized the need to confront Saddam Hussein when he invaded Kuwait—a consensus that sent a clear message to all about the cost of aggression.

Furthermore, America—in fact, no nation—can insist that others follow the rules of the road if we refuse to follow them ourselves. For when we don't, our actions appear arbitrary and undercut the legitimacy of future interventions, no matter how justified.

And this becomes particularly important when the purpose of military action extends beyond self-defense or the defense of one nation against an aggressor. More and more, we all confront difficult questions about how to prevent the slaughter of civilians by their own government, or to stop a civil war whose violence and suffering can engulf an entire region.

I believe that force can be justified on humanitarian grounds, as it was in the Balkans, or in other places that have been scarred by war. Inaction tears at our conscience and can lead to more costly intervention later. That's why all responsible nations must embrace the role that militaries with a clear mandate can play to keep the peace.

America's commitment to global security will never waver. But in a world in which threats are more diffuse, and missions more complex, America cannot act alone. America alone cannot secure the peace. This is true in Afghanistan. This is true in failed states like Somalia, where terrorism and piracy is joined by famine and human suffering. And sadly, it will continue to be true in unstable regions for years to come.

The leaders and soldiers of NATO countries, and other friends and allies, demonstrate this truth through the capacity and courage they've shown in Afghanistan. But in many countries, there is a disconnect between the efforts of those who serve and the ambivalence of the broader public. I understand why war is not popular, but I also know this: The belief that peace is desirable is rarely enough to achieve it. Peace requires responsibility. Peace entails sacrifice. That's why NATO continues to be indispensable. That's why we must strengthen U.N. and regional peacekeeping, and not leave the task to a few countries. That's why we honor those who return home from peacekeeping and training abroad to Oslo and Rome; to Ottawa and Sydney; to Dhaka and Kigali—we honor them not as makers of war, but of wagers—but as wagers of peace.

Let me make one final point about the use of force. Even as we make difficult decisions about going to war, we must also think clearly about how we fight it. The Nobel Committee recognized this truth in awarding its first prize for peace to Henry Dunant—the founder of the Red Cross, and a driving force behind the Geneva Conventions.

Where force is necessary, we have a moral and strategic interest in binding ourselves to certain rules of conduct. And even as we confront a vicious adversary that abides by no rules, I believe the United States of America must remain a standard bearer in the conduct of war. That is what makes us different from those whom we fight. That is a source of our strength. That is why I prohibited torture. That is why I ordered the prison at Guantanamo Bay closed. And that is why I have reaffirmed America's commitment to abide by the Geneva Conventions. We lose ourselves when we compromise the very ideals that we fight to defend. And we honor—we honor those ideals by upholding them not when it's easy, but when it is hard.

I have spoken at some length to the question that must weigh on our minds and our hearts as we choose to wage war. But let me now turn to our effort to avoid such tragic choices, and speak of three ways that we can build a just and lasting peace.

First, in dealing with those nations that break rules and laws, I believe that we must develop alternatives to violence that are tough enough to actually change behavior—for if we want a lasting peace, then the words of the international community must mean something. Those regimes that break the rules must be held accountable. Sanctions must exact a real price. Intransigence must be met with increased pressure—and such pressure exists only when the world stands together as one.

One urgent example is the effort to prevent the spread of nuclear weapons, and to seek a world without them. In the middle of the last century, nations agreed to be bound by a treaty whose bargain is clear: All will have access to peaceful nuclear power; those without nuclear weapons will forsake them; and those with nuclear weapons will work towards disarmament. I am committed to upholding this treaty. It is a centerpiece of my foreign policy. And I'm working with President Medvedev to reduce America and Russia's nuclear stockpiles.

But it is also incumbent upon all of us to insist that nations like Iran and North Korea do not game the system. Those who claim to respect international law cannot avert their eyes when those laws are flouted. Those who care for their own security cannot ignore the danger of an arms race in the Middle East or East Asia. Those who seek peace cannot stand idly by as nations arm themselves for nuclear war.

The same principle applies to those who violate international laws by brutalizing their own people. When there is genocide in Darfur, systematic rape in Congo, repression in Burma—there must be consequences. Yes, there will be engagement; yes, there will be diplomacy—but there must be consequences when those things fail. And the closer we stand together, the less likely we will be faced with the choice between armed intervention and complicity in oppression.

This brings me to a second point—the nature of the peace that we seek. For peace is not merely the absence of visible conflict. Only a just peace based on the inherent rights and dignity of every individual can truly be lasting.

It was this insight that drove drafters of the Universal Declaration of Human Rights after the Second World War. In the wake of devastation, they recognized that if human rights are not protected, peace is a hollow promise.

And yet too often, these words are ignored. For some countries, the failure to uphold human rights is excused by the false suggestion that these are somehow Western principles, foreign to local cultures or stages of a nation's development. And within America, there has long been a tension between those who describe themselves as realists or idealists—a tension that suggests a stark choice between the narrow pursuit of interests or an endless campaign to impose our values around the world.

I reject these choices. I believe that peace is unstable where citizens are denied the right to speak freely or worship as they please; choose their own leaders or assemble without fear. Pent-up grievances fester, and the suppression of tribal and religious identity can lead to violence. We also know that the opposite is true. Only when Europe became free did it finally find peace. America has never fought a war against a democracy, and our closest friends are governments that protect the rights of their citizens. No matter how callously defined, neither America's interests—nor the world's—are served by the denial of human aspirations.

So even as we respect the unique culture and traditions of different countries, America will always be a voice for those aspirations that are universal. We will bear witness to the quiet dignity of reformers like Aung Sang Suu Kyi; to the bravery of Zimbabweans who cast their ballots in the face of beatings; to the hundreds of thousands who have marched silently through the streets of Iran. It is telling that the leaders of these governments fear the aspirations of their own people more than the power of any other nation. And it is the responsibility of all free people and free nations to make clear that these movements—these movements of hope and history—they have us on their side.

Let me also say this: The promotion of human rights cannot be about exhortation alone. At times, it must be coupled with painstaking diplomacy. I know that engagement with repressive regimes lacks the satisfying purity of indignation. But I also know that sanctions without outreach—condemnation without discussion—can carry forward only a crippling status quo. No repressive regime can move down a new path unless it has the choice of an open door.

In light of the Cultural Revolution's horrors, Nixon's meeting with Mao appeared inexcusable—and yet it surely helped set China on a path where millions of its citizens have been lifted from poverty and connected to open societies. Pope John Paul's engagement with Poland created space not just for the Catholic Church, but for labor leaders like Lech Walesa. Ronald Reagan's efforts on arms control and embrace of perestroika not only improved relations with the Soviet Union, but empowered dissidents throughout Eastern Europe. There's no simple formula here. But we must try as best we can to balance isolation and engagement, pressure and incentives, so that human rights and dignity are advanced over time.

Third, a just peace includes not only civil and political rights—it must encompass economic security and opportunity. For true peace is not just freedom from fear, but freedom from want.

It is undoubtedly true that development rarely takes root without security; it is also true that security does not exist where human beings do not have access to enough food, or clean water, or the medicine and shelter they need to survive. It does not exist where children can't aspire to a decent education or a job that supports a family. The absence of hope can rot a society from within.

And that's why helping farmers feed their own people—or nations educate their children and care for the sick—is not mere charity. It's also why the world must come together to confront climate change. There is little scientific dispute that if we do nothing, we will face more drought, more famine, more mass displacement—all of which will fuel more conflict for decades. For this reason, it is not merely scientists and environmental activists who call for swift and forceful action—it's military leaders in my own country and others who understand our common security hangs in the balance.

Agreements among nations. Strong institutions. Support for human rights. Investments in development. All these are vital ingredients in bringing about the evolution that President Kennedy spoke about. And yet, I do not believe that we will have the will, the determination, the staying power, to complete this work without something more—and that's the continued expansion of our moral imagination; an insistence that there's something irreducible that we all share.

As the world grows smaller, you might think it would be easier for human beings to recognize how similar we are; to understand that we're all basically seeking the same things; that we all hope for the chance to live out our lives with some measure of happiness and fulfillment for ourselves and our families.

And yet somehow, given the dizzying pace of globalization, the cultural leveling of modernity, it perhaps comes as no surprise that people fear the loss of what they cherish in their particular identities—their race, their tribe, and perhaps most powerfully their religion. In some places, this fear has led to conflict. At times, it even feels like we're moving backwards. We see it in the Middle East, as the conflict between Arabs and Jews seems to harden. We see it in nations that are torn asunder by tribal lines.

And most dangerously, we see it in the way that religion is used to justify the murder of innocents by those who have distorted and defiled the great religion of Islam, and who attacked my country from Afghanistan. These extremists are not the first to kill in the name of God; the cruelties of the Crusades are amply recorded. But they remind us that no Holy War can ever be a just war. For if you truly believe that you are carrying out divine will, then there is no need for restraint—no need to spare the pregnant mother, or the medic, or the Red Cross worker, or even a person of one's own faith. Such a warped view of religion is not just incompatible with the concept of peace, but I believe it's incompatible with the very purpose of faith—for the one rule that lies at the heart of every major religion is that we do unto others as we would have them do unto us.

Adhering to this law of love has always been the core struggle of human nature. For we are fallible. We make mistakes, and fall victim to the temptations of pride, and power, and sometimes evil. Even those of us with the best of intentions will at times fail to right the wrongs before us.

But we do not have to think that human nature is perfect for us to still believe that the human condition can be perfected. We do not have to live in an idealized world to still reach for those ideals that will make it a better place. The non-violence practiced by men like Gandhi and King may not have been practical or possible in every circumstance, but the love that they preached—their fundamental faith in human progress—that must always be the North Star that guides us on our journey.

For if we lose that faith—if we dismiss it as silly or naïve; if we divorce it from the decisions that we make on issues of war and peace—then we lose what's best about humanity. We lose our sense of possibility. We lose our moral compass.

Like generations have before us, we must reject that future. As Dr. King said at this occasion so many years ago, "I refuse to accept despair as the final response to the ambiguities of history. I refuse to accept the idea that the 'isness' of man's present condition makes him morally incapable of reaching up for the eternal 'oughtness' that forever confronts him."

Let us reach for the world that ought to be—that spark of the divine that still stirs within each of our souls. Somewhere today, in the here and now, in the world as it is, a soldier sees he's outgunned, but stands firm to keep the peace. Somewhere today, in this world, a young protestor awaits the brutality of her government, but has the courage to march on. Somewhere today, a mother facing punishing poverty still takes the time to teach her child, scrapes together what few coins she has to send that child to school—because she believes that a cruel world still has a place for that child's dreams.

Let us live by their example. We can acknowledge that oppression will always be with us, and still strive for justice. We can admit the intractability of depravation, and still strive for dignity. Clear-eyed, we can understand that there will be war, and still strive for peace. We can do that—for that is the story of human progress; that's the hope of all the world; and at this moment of challenge, that must be our work here on Earth. Thank you very much.

Chapter 10

Barack Obama and Nuclear Proliferation: Iran and North Korea

THE PRESIDENT: **Good morning, everybody.** We are on our way to Arlington to remember the fallen and those who have served America with extraordinary valor. But before I go there I wanted to say a few words about North Korea's announcement that it has conducted a nuclear test, as well as its decision to attempt a short-range missile launch.

North Korea's nuclear ballistic missile programs pose a great threat to the peace and security of the world and I strongly condemn their reckless action. North Korea's actions endanger the people of Northeast Asia, they are a blatant violation of international law, and they contradict North Korea's own prior commitments.

Now, the United States and the international community must take action in response. The record is clear: North Korea has previously committed to abandoning its nuclear program. Instead of following through on that commitment it has chosen to ignore that commitment. These actions have also flown in the face of United Nations resolutions. As a result North Korea is not only deepening its own isolation, it's also inviting stronger international pressure—that's evident overnight, as Russia and China, as well as our traditional allies of South Korea and Japan, have all come to the same conclusion: North Korea will not find security and respect through threats and illegal weapons.

We will work with our friends and our allies to stand up to this behavior and we will redouble our efforts toward a more robust international nonproliferation regime that all countries have responsibilities to meet. In this effort the United States will never waiver from our determination to protect our people and the peace and security of the world. Thank you.

Remarks by the President by the President on North Korea, Rose Garden, The White House, The Office of the Press Secretary, For Immediate Release, May 25, 2009. http://www.whitehouse.gov/the_press_office/Remarks-by-the-President-on-North-Korea/.

PRESIDENT OBAMA: Well, it's a great honor to be making my first trip to the Republic of Korea as President of the United States. I want to thank my good friend, President Lee, and the Korean people, for their extraordinary hospitality. And I have to say that the arrival ceremony for our state visit was as spectacular as any that we've seen.

I was privileged to host President Lee in Washington in June. As he mentioned, we've seen each other in many multilateral forums, as well, and we've developed a strong working relationship and friendship. And it's a great pleasure to visit this beautiful city.

The Republic of Korea is a close and valued friend and ally of the United States. The strong bonds between our people were forged in the battles of the Korean War nearly 60 years ago. Our alliance, which is grounded in shared interests and values, has provided peace and security on this peninsula and in the region for many decades. And I'm pleased to say that our alliance has never been stronger than it is today.

The 60th anniversary of the outbreak of the Korean War presents an important opportunity to honor the service of our veterans, to reflect on the principles for which they fought, and to move forward in adapting our alliance to meet the challenges of the 21st century. As part of this process, we agreed that Secretaries Clinton and Gates will meet with their Korean counterparts next year to work on realizing our shared vision for the alliance going forward.

The Republic of Korea has made extraordinary progress in the six decades since the Korean War. Evidence of that progress can be seen in Korea's strong democracy, its vibrant economy, but it can also be seen in Korea's increasingly prominent role in global affairs. Indeed, in just one generation, the Republic of Korea has gone from a recipient of aid to a donor nation and—under the leadership of President Lee, a leader within the G20.

The United States has been proud to stand as a friend and ally of the Korean people throughout this period. And later today, I'll also visit some of our servicemen and women, who represent America's unwavering commitment to the security of this country. In going forward, I know that our two nations can strengthen our cooperation on a range of critical issues, including several that we discussed today.

On North Korea, our governments have maintained extraordinarily close cooperation, and President Lee and I are in full agreement on our common approach going forward. I reaffirmed my commitment to continue working together in the six-party process to achieve a definitive and comprehensive resolution of the nuclear issue. As

Remarks by President Barack Obama and President Lee Myung-Bak of Republic of Korea in Joint Press Conference, Blue House, Seoul, South Korea, The White House, Office of the Press Secretary, For Immediate Release, November 19, 2009. http://www.whitehouse.gov/the-press-office/remarks-president-barack-obama-and-president-lee-myung-bak-republic-korea-joint-pre.

a part of that effort, we will be sending Ambassador Bosworth to North Korea on December 8th to engage in direct talks with the North Koreans.

Our message is clear: If North Korea is prepared to take concrete and irreversible steps to fulfill its obligations and eliminate its nuclear weapons program, the United States will support economic assistance and help promote its full integration into the community of nations. That opportunity and respect will not come with threats— North Korea must live up to its obligations.

The Republic of Korea is also, obviously, a close trading partner of the United States, and the relationship between our nations advance our common prosperity. To strengthen those ties, President Lee and I discussed the U.S.-Korea free trade agreement, which holds out the promise of serving our mutual interests. And together, we're committed to working together to move the agreement forward.

PRESIDENT OBAMA: Good morning. We are here to announce that yesterday in Vienna, the United States, the United Kingdom, and France presented detailed evidence to the IAEA demonstrating that the Islamic Republic of Iran has been building a covert uranium enrichment facility near Qom for several years.

Earlier this week, the Iranian government presented a letter to the IAEA that made reference to a new enrichment facility, years after they had started its construction. The existence of this facility underscores Iran's continuing unwillingness to meet its obligations under U.N. Security Council resolutions and IAEA requirements. We expect the IAEA to immediately investigate this disturbing information, and to report to the IAEA Board of Governors.

Now, Iran's decision to build yet another nuclear facility without notifying the IAEA represents a direct challenge to the basic compact at the center of the non-proliferation regime. These rules are clear: All nations have the right to peaceful nuclear energy; those nations with nuclear weapons must move towards disarmament; those nations without nuclear weapons must forsake them. That compact has largely held for decades, keeping the world far safer and more secure. And that compact depends on all nations living up to their responsibilities.

This site deepens a growing concern that Iran is refusing to live up to those international responsibilities, including specifically revealing all nuclear-related activities. As the international community knows, this is not the first time that Iran has concealed information about its nuclear program. Iran has a right to peaceful nuclear power that meets the energy needs of its people. But the size and configuration of this facility

Statements by President Obama, French President Sarkozy, and British Prime Minister Brown, on Iranian Nuclear Facility, Pittsburgh Convention Center, Pittsburgh, Pennsylvania The White House, Office of the Press Secretary, For Immediate Release, September 25, 2009. http://www.whitehouse. gov/the_press_office/Statements-By-President-Obama-French-President-Sarkozy-And-British-Prime-Minister-Brown-On-Iranian-Nuclear-Facility/.

is inconsistent with a peaceful program. Iran is breaking rules that all nations must follow—endangering the global non-proliferation regime, denying its own people access to the opportunity they deserve, and threatening the stability and security of the region and the world.

It is time for Iran to act immediately to restore the confidence of the international community by fulfilling its international obligations. We remain committed to serious, meaningful engagement with Iran to address the nuclear issue through the P5-plus-1 negotiations. Through this dialogue, we are committed to demonstrating that international law is not an empty promise; that obligations must be kept; and that treaties will be enforced.

And that's why there's a sense of urgency about the upcoming meeting on October 1st between Iran, the permanent members of the U.N. Security Council, and Germany. At that meeting, Iran must be prepared to cooperate fully and comprehensively with the IAEA to take concrete steps to create confidence and transparency in its nuclear program and to demonstrate that it is committed to establishing its peaceful intentions through meaningful dialogue and concrete actions.

To put it simply: Iran must comply with U.N. Security Council resolutions and make clear it is willing to meet its responsibilities as a member of the community of nations. We have offered Iran a clear path toward greater international integration if it lives up to its obligations, and that offer stands. But the Iranian government must now demonstrate through deeds its peaceful intentions or be held accountable to international standards and international law.

I should point out that although the United Kingdom, France, and the United States made the presentation to Vienna, that Germany, a member of the P5-plus-1, and Chancellor Merkel in particular, who could not be here this morning, wished to associate herself with these remarks.

THE PRESIDENT: Good afternoon, everybody. Today, the United Nations Security Council voted overwhelmingly to sanction Iran for its continued failure to live up to its obligations. This resolution will put in place the toughest sanctions ever faced by the Iranian government, and it sends an unmistakable message about the international community's commitment to stopping the spread of nuclear weapons.

For years, the Iranian government has failed to live up to its obligations under the Nuclear Non-Proliferation Treaty. It has violated its commitments to the International Atomic Energy Agency. It has ignored U.N. Security Council resolutions. And while Iran's leaders hide behind outlandish rhetoric, their actions have been deeply troubling.

Remarks by the President on United Nations Security Council Resolution on Iran Sanctions, Diplomatic Reception Room, The White House, Office of the Press Secretary, For Immediate Release, June 9, 2010. http://www.whitehouse.gov/the-press-office/remarks-president-united-nations-security-council-resolution-iran-sanctions.

Indeed, when I took office just over 16 months ago, Iranian intransigence was well-established. Iran had gone from zero centrifuges spinning to several thousand, and the international community was divided about how to move forward.

Yet this day was not inevitable. We made clear from the beginning of my administration that the United States was prepared to pursue diplomatic solutions to address the concerns over Iranian nuclear programs. I extended the offer of engagement on the basis of mutual interest and mutual respect. And together with the United Kingdom, with Russia, China, and Germany, we sat down with our Iranian counterparts. We offered the opportunity of a better relationship between Iran and the international community—one that reduced Iran's political isolation, and increased its economic integration with the rest of the world. In short, we offered the Iranian government the prospect of a better future for its people, if—and only if—it lives up to its international obligations.

So there is no double standard at play here. We've made it clear, time and again, that we respect Iran's right, like all countries, to access peaceful nuclear energy. That is a right embedded in the NPT—a treaty that has to serve as the safeguard against a world in which more nations acquire the world's most deadly weapons, and international law is treated as an empty promise. That NPT treaty was signed by all the parties involved, and it is a treaty that the United States has sought to strengthen from the day I took office, including through our own commitments to reduce America's nuclear arsenal.

So let me repeat: We recognize Iran's rights. But with those rights come responsibilities. And time and again, the Iranian government has failed to meet those responsibilities. Iran concealed a nuclear enrichment facility in Qom that raised serious questions about the nature of its program. Iran further violated its own obligations under U.N. Security Council resolutions to suspend uranium enrichment. Instead, they're enriching up to 20 percent. It has failed to comply fully with IAEA's requirements. Indeed, Iran is the only NPT signatory in the world—the only one—that cannot convince the IAEA that its nuclear program is intended for peaceful purposes.

That's why the international community was compelled to impose these serious consequences. These are the most comprehensive sanctions that the Iranian government has faced. They will impose restrictions on Iran's nuclear activities, its ballistic missile program, and, for the first time, its conventional military. They will put a new framework in place to stop Iranian smuggling, and crack down on Iranian banks and financial transactions. They target individuals, entities, and institutions—including those associated with the Revolutionary Guard—that have supported Iran's nuclear program and prospered from illicit activities at the expense of the Iranian people. And we will ensure that these sanctions are vigorously enforced, just as we continue to refine and enforce our own sanctions on Iran alongside our friends and our allies.

The strong resolution that was passed today benefited from strong international support. In voting for it, we were joined by nations from Asia, Africa, Europe, and

Latin America—including Russia and China. And these sanctions show the united view of the international community that a nuclear arms race in the Middle East is in nobody's interest, and that nations must be held accountable for challenging the global non-proliferation regime. The Iranian government must understand that true security will not come through the pursuit of nuclear weapons. True security will come through adherence to international law and the demonstration of its peaceful intent.

We know that the Iranian government will not change its behavior overnight, but today's vote demonstrates the growing costs that will come with Iranian intransigence. And I want to be clear: These sanctions do not close the door on diplomacy. Iran continues to have the opportunity to take a different and better path. I would like nothing more than to reach the day when the Iranian government fulfills its international obligations—a day when these sanctions are lifted, previous sanctions are lifted, and the Iranian people can finally fulfill the greatness of the Iranian nation.

Indeed, these sanctions are not directed at the Iranian people. As I said in Cairo, for decades the Iranian government has defined itself in opposition to my country. But faced with the opportunity to find a new way forward—one that would benefit its own people—the Iranian government has chosen instead to remain a prisoner of the past.

Saturday will mark one year from the day that an election captivated the attention of the world—an event that should have been remembered for how the Iranian people participated with remarkable enthusiasm, but will instead be remembered for how the Iranian government brutally suppressed dissent and murdered the innocent, including a young woman left to die in the street.

Actions do have consequences, and today the Iranian government will face some of those consequences. Because whether it is threatening the nuclear non-proliferation regime, or the human rights of its own citizens, or the stability of its own neighbors by supporting terrorism, the Iranian government continues to demonstrate that its own unjust actions are a threat to justice everywhere.

I want and hope for the people of Iran that the government of Iran will make a different choice. It can make a different choice and pursue a course that will reaffirm the NPT as the basis of global non-proliferation and disarmament—a course that will advance Iran's own security and prosperity, and the peace of the wider world. Today's sanctions are yet another signal that if the Iranian government continues to undermine the NPT and the peace that it protects, then Iran will find itself more isolated, less prosperous and less secure. Thank you.

Chapter 11

Barack Obama and Terrorism

THE PRESIDENT: **Thank you, everybody.** Thank you. Please be seated. Thank you so much. It is great to be here today and I am honored to spend some time with the men and women who are working so hard, around the clock, to keep not only this city but also this country safe from terrorism.

I want to thank our outstanding FBI Director, Robert Mueller, for that kind and brief introduction. As I've said before, these are incredibly challenging times for the FBI. And for the last eight years, Bob has worked tirelessly to prevent additional attacks and keep this nation safe. He's been doing a unbelievable job under very difficult and trying circumstances and we are grateful to him.

I also want to commend Police Commissioner Kelly, Assistant Director in Charge Joe Demarest, and all the leaders who've helped put together a team that is more integrated, more collaborative, and more effective than ever before.

Here at the Joint Terrorism Task Force, we have folks from the FBI working side by side with some of New York's finest, as well as countless federal, state, and local partners—I was taking a look at the list and it looks like 45, 46 different agencies represented here. Together, your success at thwarting terrorist attacks—the strong intelligence you've gathered and the hard-nosed investigations you've pursued—has proved to be a model for law enforcement officials across the country, and for that you should all be extremely proud.

No one knows better than you how important this work is, because you've always been on the front lines in fighting extremism. Last month, we marked the eighth anniversary of the attacks on 9/11. And on that terrible day, when terrorists brought so much death and destruction on our shores and so many lives were lost, many of you were the first on the scenes—saving lives, working tirelessly to bring those responsible to justice, and guarding against future attacks in subsequent weeks and months and years.

Remarks by the President to Joint Terrorism Task Force Staff Members, The White House, Office of the Press Secretary, For Immediate Release, Joint Terrorism Task Force Headquarters New York, New York, October 20, 2009. http://www.whitehouse.gov/the-press-office/remarks-president-joint-terrorism-task-force-staff-members.

That effort continues to this day—quietly doggedly, courageously. Most New Yorkers, much less most Americans, probably don't know this office is here and they don't know what you do. Obviously you're not doing it for the glamour or the glory or the pay. You do it to serve and protect your country. And because of the effort and the sacrifices that you're making on a daily basis, we are making real progress on our core missions: disrupting and dismantling and ultimately defeating al Qaeda and its extremist allies.

I said this when I had a chance to speak to some of the NYPD leadership team last month over the phone, but I particularly want to express my appreciation and admiration for your terrific work—especially in recent weeks. Working together, you save countless lives, and your collaboration earned the respect and gratitude not just of New Yorkers but Americans everywhere.

This level of cooperation and integration is going to be critical in defeating the type of determined and resourceful—and oftentimes in the shadows—opponents that you're up against every day. Nerve centers like this one help you share intelligence, answer questions, and give support instantly. And because each organization is on its own, this task force has shown how much stronger all of you can be when you're actually working together.

You're setting the standard for everybody else, as I said, and you're showing us what focused and integrated counterterrorism work really looks like. And the record of your service is written in the attacks that never occur--because you thwarted them; and because of the countless Americans who are alive today as a consequence of that work. And so America is in your debt for that.

Of course, we all know that we're facing a determined adversary. They are resourceful, they are resilient, they are still plotting, as we have become all too aware. No one can ever promise that there won't be another attack on America's soil. But I can promise you this: I pledge to do everything in my power as President of the United States to keep the American people safe. And that means I pledge to give all of you the tools and the support that you need to get the job done, both here at home and around the world. And I pledge that I will stay as focused on this mission as you are.

So we all have to redouble our efforts in the face of threats that persist. We're going to have to draw strength from the values that we hold dear. We're going to have to keep our eye fixed on the world we seek to build—one that not just—not only defeats our adversaries, but that also promotes dignity and opportunity and justice for all who stand with us.

To do that, I'm going to need all of you to continue the extraordinary work you do and the collaborations you do. That's how we're going to prevail in this fight. That's how we're going to protect this country that we love.

So I know that all of you are extraordinarily busy and I do not want to draw you away from the work that you do. I just want to let you know that we appreciate it, we acknowledge it, we thank you for it, and I am going to continue to be standing behind you each and every step of the way. So thank you very much, everybody. Thank you.

WASHINGTON—In his weekly address, President Barack Obama discussed his solemn responsibility to protect the nation and the steps the administration has taken to that end. From ordering reviews into the attempted act of terrorism in Detroit to a comprehensive strategy that has refocused our efforts on the fight against al Qaeda in Afghanistan and Pakistan and strengthened international partnerships to keep unrelenting pressure on extremists across the globe, the President will continue to do everything in his power to uphold the nation's security.

It has now been more than a week since the attempted act of terrorism aboard that flight to Detroit on Christmas Day. On Thursday, I received the preliminary findings of the reviews that I ordered into our terrorist watchlist system and air travel screening. I've directed my counterterrorism and homeland security advisor at the White House, John Brennan, to lead these reviews going forward and to present the final results and recommendations to me in the days to come.

As I said this week, I will do everything in my power to make sure our hard-working men and women in our intelligence, law enforcement and homeland security communities have the tools and resources they need to keep America safe. This includes making sure these communities—and the people in them—are coordinating effectively and are held accountable at every level. And as President, that is what I will do.

Meanwhile, the investigation into the Christmas Day incident continues, and we're learning more about the suspect. We know that he traveled to Yemen, a country grappling with crushing poverty and deadly insurgencies. It appears that he joined an affiliate of al Qaeda, and that this group—al Qaeda in the Arabian Peninsula—trained him, equipped him with those explosives and directed him to attack that plane headed for America.

This is not the first time this group has targeted us. In recent years, they have bombed Yemeni government facilities and Western hotels, restaurants and embassies—including our embassy in 2008, killing one American. So, as President, I've made it a priority to strengthen our partnership with the Yemeni government—training and equipping their security forces, sharing intelligence and working with them to strike al Qaeda terrorists.

And even before Christmas Day, we had seen the results. Training camps have been struck; leaders eliminated; plots disrupted. And all those involved in the attempted act of terrorism on Christmas must know—you too will be held to account.

Remarks of President Barack Obama Weekly Address, January 2, 2010 http://www.whitehouse.gov/the-press-office/weekly-address-president-obama-outlines-steps-taken-protect-safety-and-security-ame.

But these efforts are only part of a wider cause. It's been nearly a year since I stood on the steps of the U.S. Capitol and took the oath of office as your President. And with that oath came the solemn responsibility that I carry with me every moment of every day—the responsibility to protect the safety and security of the American people.

On that day I also made it very clear—our nation is at war against a far-reaching network of violence and hatred, and that we will do whatever it takes to defeat them and defend our country, even as we uphold the values that have always distinguished America among nations.

And make no mistake, that's exactly what we've been doing. It's why I refocused the fight—bringing to a responsible end the war in Iraq, which had nothing to do with the 9/11 attacks, and dramatically increasing our resources in the region where al Qaeda is actually based, in Afghanistan and Pakistan. It's why I've set a clear and achievable mission—to disrupt, dismantle and defeat al Qaeda and its extremist allies and prevent their return to either country.

And it's why we've forged new partnerships, as in Yemen, and put unrelenting pressure on these extremists wherever they plot and train—from East Africa to Southeast Asia, from Europe to the Persian Gulf. And though often out of sight, our progress has been unmistakable. Along with our partners, we've disrupted terrorist financing, cut off recruiting chains, inflicted major losses on al Qaeda's leadership, thwarted plots here in the United States, and saved countless American lives.

Yet as the Christmas Day attempt illustrates, and as we were reminded this week by the sacrifices of more brave Americans in Afghanistan—including those seven dedicated men and women of the CIA—the hard work of protecting our nation is never done. So as our reviews continue, let us ask the questions that need to be asked. Let us make the changes that need to be made. Let us debate the best way to protect the country we all love. That is the right and responsibility of every American and every elected official.

But as we go forward, let us remember this—our adversaries are those who would attack our country, not our fellow Americans, not each other. Let's never forget what has always carried us through times of trial, including those attacks eight Septembers ago.

Instead of giving in to fear and cynicism, let's renew that timeless American spirit of resolve and confidence and optimism. Instead of succumbing to partisanship and division, let's summon the unity that this moment demands. Let's work together, with a seriousness of purpose, to do what must be done to keep our country safe. As we

Statement by the President on the Afghanistan-Pakistan Annual Review, James S. Brady Press Briefing Room, The White House, Office of the Press Secretary, For Immediate Release, December 16, 2010. http://www.whitehouse.gov/the-press-office/2010/12/16/statement-president-afghanistan-pakistan-annual-review.

begin this New Year, I cannot imagine a more fitting resolution to guide us—as a people and as a nation.

THE PRESIDENT: Good morning, everybody. When I announced our new strategy for Afghanistan and Pakistan last December, I directed my national security team to regularly assess our efforts and to review our progress after one year. That's what we've done consistently over the course of the past 12 months—in weekly updates from the field, in monthly meetings with my national security team, and in my frequent consultations with our Afghan, Pakistani and coalition partners. And that's what we've done as part of our annual review, which is now complete.

I want to thank Secretary Clinton and Secretary Gates for their leadership. Since Joint Chief of Staff Chairman, Admiral Mullen, is in Afghanistan, I'm pleased that we're joined by Vice Chairman, General Cartwright.

Our efforts also reflect the dedication of Ambassador Richard Holbrooke, whose memory we honor and whose work we'll continue. Indeed, the tributes to Richard that have poured in from around the globe speak to both the enormous impact of his life and to the broad international commitment to our shared efforts in this critical region.

I have spoken with President Karzai of Afghanistan as well as President Zardari of Pakistan and discussed our findings and the way forward together. Today, I want to update the American people on our review—our assessment of where we stand and areas where we need to do better. I want to be clear. This continues to be a very difficult endeavor. But I can report that thanks to the extraordinary service of our troops and civilians on the ground, we are on track to achieve our goals.

It's important to remember why we remain in Afghanistan. It was Afghanistan where al Qaeda plotted the 9/11 attacks that murdered 3,000 innocent people. It is the tribal regions along the Afghan-Pakistan border from which terrorists have launched more attacks against our homeland and our allies. And if an even wider insurgency were to engulf Afghanistan, that would give al Qaeda even more space to plan these attacks.

And that's why, from the start, I've been very clear about our core goal. It's not to defeat every last threat to the security of Afghanistan, because, ultimately, it is Afghans who must secure their country. And it's not nation-building, because it is Afghans who must build their nation. Rather, we are focused on disrupting, dismantling and defeating al Qaeda in Afghanistan and Pakistan, and preventing its capacity to threaten America and our allies in the future.

In pursuit of our core goal we are seeing significant progress. Today, al Qaeda's senior leadership in the border region of Afghanistan and Pakistan is under more pressure than at any point since they fled Afghanistan nine years ago. Senior leaders have been killed. It's harder for them to recruit; it's harder for them to travel; it's harder for them to train; it's harder for them to plot and launch attacks. In short, al Qaeda is hunkered down. It will take time to ultimately defeat al Qaeda, and it remains a ruthless and resilient enemy bent on attacking our country. But make no mistake—we are going to remain relentless in disrupting and dismantling that terrorist organization.

In Afghanistan, we remain focused on the three areas of our strategy: our military effort to break the Taliban's momentum and train Afghan forces so they can take the lead; our civilian effort to promote effective governance and development; and regional cooperation, especially with Pakistan, because our strategy has to succeed on both sides of the border.

Indeed, for the first time in years, we've put in place the strategy and the resources that our efforts in Afghanistan demand. And because we've ended our combat mission in Iraq, and brought home nearly 100,000 of our troops from Iraq, we're in a better position to give our forces in Afghanistan the support and equipment they need to achieve their missions. And our drawdown in Iraq also means that today there are tens of thousands fewer Americans deployed in harm's way than when I took office.

With those additional forces in Afghanistan, we are making considerable gains toward our military objectives. The additional military and civilian personnel that I ordered in Afghanistan are now in place, along with additional forces from our coalition, which has grown to 49 nations. Along with our Afghan partners, we've gone on the offensive, targeting the Taliban and its leaders and pushing them out of their strongholds.

As I said when I visited our troops in Afghanistan earlier this month, progress comes slowly and at a very high price in the lives of our men and women in uniform. In many places, the gains we've made are still fragile and reversible. But there is no question we are clearing more areas from Taliban control and more Afghans are reclaiming their communities.

To ensure Afghans can take responsibility, we continue to focus on training. Targets for the growth of Afghan security forces are being met. And because of the contributions of additional trainers from our coalition partners, I'm confident we will continue to meet our goals.

I would add that much of this progress—the speed with which our troops deployed this year, the increase in recruits—in recruiting and training of Afghan forces, and the additional troops and trainers from other nations—much of this is the result of us having sent a clear signal that we will begin the transition of responsibility to Afghans and start reducing American forces next July.

This sense of urgency also helped galvanize the coalition around the goals that we agreed to at the recent NATO summit in Lisbon—that we are moving toward a new phase in Afghanistan, a transition to full Afghan lead for security that will begin early next year and will conclude in 2014, even as NATO maintains a long-term commitment to training and advising Afghan forces. Now, our review confirms, however, that for these security gains to be sustained over time, there is an urgent need for political and economic progress in Afghanistan.

Over the past year, we've dramatically increased our civilian presence, with more diplomats and development experts working alongside our troops, risking their lives and partnering with Afghans. Going forward, there must be a continued focus on the delivery of basic services, as well as transparency and accountability. We will also fully support an Afghan political process that includes reconciliation with those Taliban who break ties with al Qaeda, renounce violence and accept the Afghan constitution. And we will forge a new strategic partnership with Afghanistan next year, so that we make it clear that the United States is committed to the long-term security and development of the Afghan people.

Finally, we will continue to focus on our relationship with Pakistan. Increasingly, the Pakistani government recognizes that terrorist networks in its border regions are a threat to all our countries, especially Pakistan. We've welcomed major Pakistani offensives in the tribal regions. We will continue to help strengthen Pakistanis' capacity to root out terrorists. Nevertheless, progress has not come fast enough. So we will continue to insist to Pakistani leaders that terrorist safe havens within their borders must be dealt with.

At the same time, we need to support the economic and political development that is critical to Pakistan's future. As part of our strategic dialogue with Pakistan, we will work to deepen trust and cooperation. We'll speed up our investment in civilian institutions and projects that improve the lives of Pakistanis. We'll intensify our efforts to encourage closer cooperation between Pakistan and Afghanistan.

And, next year, I look forward to an exchange of visits, including my visit to Pakistan, because the United States is committed to an enduring partnership that helps deliver improved security, development, and justice for the Pakistani people. Again, none of these challenges that I've outlined will be easy. There are more difficult days ahead. But as a nation, we can draw strength from the service of our fellow Americans.

On my recent visit to Afghanistan, I visited a medical unit and pinned Purple Hearts on some of our wounded warriors. I met with a platoon that had just lost six of their teammates. Despite the tough fight, despite all their sacrifice, they continue to stand up for our security and for our values that we hold so dear.

We're going to have to continue to stand up. We'll continue to give our brave troops and civilians the strategy and resources they need to succeed. We will never waver from our goal of disrupting, dismantling, and ultimately defeating al Qaeda. We will forge enduring partnerships with people who are committed to progress and to peace. And we will continue to do everything in our power to ensure the security and the safety of the American people.

So, with that, Vice President Biden and myself will depart, and I'm going to turn it over to Secretaries Clinton, Gates, as well as Vice Chairman Cartwright, and they will be able to answer your questions and give you a more detailed briefing. Thank you very much.

One year ago today, at a remote outpost at Khost, Afghanistan, seven American patriots showed us the true meaning of honor, integrity, and selfless sacrifice. For their colleagues and friends at the CIA, it was a heartbreaking loss of experienced veterans and young officers who served on the front lines in the fight to keep our nation safe.

For Americans to whom the work of our intelligence community is largely unknown, it was a rare glimpse into the risks that our intelligence professionals accept in defense of the security and freedoms that we cherish. And for those of us who gathered at Langley last February to pay tribute to these seven heroes and to comfort their families, it was an occasion to rededicate ourselves to their work and to the ideals for which they died.

In the year since, that is what we have done. As President, I rely on our intelligence, military, and civilian personnel every day, and I know that our country is more secure, and the American people are safer, because of their extraordinary service. Today, al Qaeda's senior leadership is under more pressure than ever before and is hunkered down in the border region of Afghanistan and Pakistan. We are relentlessly pursuing our mission to disrupt, dismantle, and ultimately defeat that terrorist organization. In the United States and around the world, plots have been thwarted, attacks have been disrupted, and the lives of Americans have been saved.

This is the legacy of the courageous Americans who gave their lives one year ago and whose stars now grace the Memorial Wall at Langley, just as it is the legacy of our troops who have given their lives in Afghanistan and Iraq. As we mark the first anniversary of their sacrifice at Khost, this is the work to which we recommit ourselves today. We will ensure that our dedicated intelligence professionals have the training and tools they need to meet the missions we ask of them. We will do everything in our power to ensure the safety and security of the American people. And like our seven patriots at Khost, we will never waver in defense of the security and liberties that keep America strong and free.

Statement by the President on the One-Year Anniversary of the Attack on CIA Personnel, The White House, Office of the Press Secretary. For Immediate Release, December 30, 2010. http://www.white-house.gov/the-press-office/2010/12/30/statement-president-one-year-anniversary-attack-cia-personnel.

Chapter 12

Barack Obama: The Wartime President

G ood afternoon. Let me begin by saying that although this has been billed as an anti-war rally, I stand before you as someone who is not opposed to war in all circumstances. The Civil War was one of the bloodiest in history, and yet it was only through the crucible of the sword, the sacrifice of multitudes, that we could begin to perfect this union, and drive the scourge of slavery from our soil. I don't oppose all wars.

My grandfather signed up for a war the day after Pearl Harbor was bombed, fought in Patton's army. He saw the dead and dying across the fields of Europe; he heard the stories of fellow troops who first entered Auschwitz and Treblinka. He fought in the name of a larger freedom, part of that arsenal of democracy that triumphed over evil, and he did not fight in vain.

I don't oppose all wars.

After September 11th, after witnessing the carnage and destruction, the dust and the tears, I supported this Administration's pledge to hunt down and root out those who would slaughter innocents in the name of intolerance, and I would willingly take up arms myself to prevent such a tragedy from happening again.

I don't oppose all wars. And I know that in this crowd today, there is no shortage of patriots, or of patriotism. What I am opposed to is a dumb war. What I am opposed to is a rash war. What I am opposed to is the cynical attempt by Richard Perle and Paul Wolfowitz and other arm-chair, weekend warriors in this Administration to shove their own ideological agendas down our throats, irrespective of the costs in lives lost and in hardships borne.

Against Going to War with Iraq, Senator Barack Obama, Delivered on Wednesday, October 2, 2002 by Barack Obama, Illinois State Senator, at the first high-profile Chicago anti-Iraq war rally (organized by Chicagoans Against War in Iraq) at noon in Federal Plaza in Chicago, Illinois. At the same day and hour that President Bush and Congress announced their agreement on the joint resolution authorizing the Iraq War, but over a week before it was passed by either body of Congress.

What I am opposed to is the attempt by political hacks like Karl Rove to distract us from a rise in the uninsured, a rise in the poverty rate, a drop in the median income—to distract us from corporate scandals and a stock market that has just gone through the worst month since the Great Depression.

That's what I'm opposed to. A dumb war. A rash war. A war based not on reason but on passion, not on principle but on politics. Now let me be clear—I suffer no illusions about Saddam Hussein. He is a brutal man. A ruthless man. A man who butchers his own people to secure his own power. He has repeatedly defied UN resolutions, thwarted UN inspection teams, developed chemical and biological weapons, and coveted nuclear capacity.

He's a bad guy. The world, and the Iraqi people, would be better off without him. But I also know that Saddam poses no imminent and direct threat to the United States, or to his neighbors, that the Iraqi economy is in shambles, that the Iraqi military a fraction of its former strength, and that in concert with the international community he can be contained until, in the way of all petty dictators, he falls away into the dustbin of history.

I know that even a successful war against Iraq will require a US occupation of undetermined length, at undetermined cost, with undetermined consequences. I know that an invasion of Iraq without a clear rationale and without strong international support will only fan the flames of the Middle East, and encourage the worst, rather than best, impulses of the Arab world, and strengthen the recruitment arm of al-Qaeda. I am not opposed to all wars. I'm opposed to dumb wars.

So for those of us who seek a more just and secure world for our children, let us send a clear message to the president today. You want a fight, President Bush? Let's finish the fight with Bin Laden and al-Qaeda, through effective, coordinated intelligence, and a shutting down of the financial networks that support terrorism, and a homeland security program that involves more than color-coded warnings.

You want a fight, President Bush? Let's fight to make sure that the UN inspectors can do their work, and that we vigorously enforce a non-proliferation treaty, and that former enemies and current allies like Russia safeguard and ultimately eliminate their stores of nuclear material, and that nations like Pakistan and India never use the terrible weapons already in their possession, and that the arms merchants in our own country stop feeding the countless wars that rage across the globe.

You want a fight, President Bush? Let's fight to make sure our so-called allies in the Middle East, the Saudis and the Egyptians, stop oppressing their own people, and suppressing dissent, and tolerating corruption and inequality, and mismanaging their economies so that their youth grow up without education, without prospects, without hope, the ready recruits of terrorist cells.

You want a fight, President Bush? Let's fight to wean ourselves off Middle East oil, through an energy policy that doesn't simply serve the interests of Exxon and Mobil.

Those are the battles that we need to fight. Those are the battles that we willingly join. The battles against ignorance and intolerance, corruption and greed, poverty and despair.

The consequences of war are dire, the sacrifices immeasurable. We may have occasion in our lifetime to once again rise up in defense of our freedom, and pay the wages of war. But we ought not—we will not—travel down that hellish path blindly. Nor should we allow those who would march off and pay the ultimate sacrifice, who would prove the full measure of devotion with their blood, to make such an awful sacrifice in vain.

Good morning Marines. Good morning Camp Lejeune. Good morning Jacksonville. Thank you for that outstanding welcome. I want to thank Lieutenant General Hejlik for hosting me here today. I also want to acknowledge all of our soldiers, sailors, airmen and Marines serving in Iraq and Afghanistan. That includes the Camp Lejeune Marines now serving with—or soon joining—the Second Marine Expeditionary Force in Iraq; those with Special Purpose Marine Air Ground Task Force in Afghanistan; and those among the 8,000 Marines who are preparing to deploy to Afghanistan. We have you in our prayers. We pay tribute to your service. We thank you and your families for all that you do for America. And I want all of you to know that there is no higher honor or greater responsibility than serving as your Commander-in-Chief.

I also want to take this opportunity to acknowledge Ryan Crocker, who recently completed his service as our Ambassador to Iraq. Throughout his career, Ryan always took on the toughest assignments. He is an example of the very best that this nation has to offer, and we owe him a great debt of gratitude. He carried on his work with an extraordinary degree of cooperation with two of our finest Generals—General David Petraeus, and General Ray Odierno—who will be critical in carrying forward the strategy that I will outline today.

Next month will mark the sixth anniversary of the war in Iraq. By any measure, this has already been a long war. For the men and women of America's armed forces—and for your families—this war has been one of the most extraordinary chapters of service in the history of our nation. You have endured tour after tour after tour of duty. You have known the dangers of combat and the lonely distance of loved ones. You have fought against tyranny and disorder. You have bled for your best friends and for unknown Iraqis. And you have borne an enormous burden for your fellow citizens, while extending a precious opportunity to the people of Iraq. Under tough circumstances,

Remarks of President Barack Obama, As Prepared for Delivery, "Responsibly Ending the War in Iraq," Camp Lejeune, North Carolina, February 27, 2009. http://www.whitehouse.gov/the_press_office/Remarks-of-President-Barack-Obama-Responsibly-Ending-the-War-in-Iraq/

the men and women of the United States military have served with honor, and succeeded beyond any expectation.

Today, I have come to speak to you about how the war in Iraq will end. To understand where we need to go in Iraq, it is important for the American people to understand where we now stand. Thanks in great measure to your service, the situation in Iraq has improved. Violence has been reduced substantially from the horrific sectarian killing of 2006 and 2007. Al Qaeda in Iraq has been dealt a serious blow by our troops and Iraq's Security Forces, and through our partnership with Sunni Arabs. The capacity of Iraq's Security Forces has improved, and Iraq's leaders have taken steps toward political accommodation. The relative peace and strong participation in January's provincial elections sent a powerful message to the world about how far Iraqis have come in pursuing their aspirations through a peaceful political process.

But let there be no doubt: Iraq is not yet secure, and there will be difficult days ahead. Violence will continue to be a part of life in Iraq. Too many fundamental political questions about Iraq's future remain unresolved. Too many Iraqis are still displaced or destitute. Declining oil revenues will put an added strain on a government that has had difficulty delivering basic services. Not all of Iraq's neighbors are contributing to its security. Some are working at times to undermine it. And even as Iraq's government is on a surer footing, it is not yet a full partner—politically and economically—in the region, or with the international community. In short, today there is a renewed cause for hope in Iraq, but that hope rests upon an emerging foundation.

On my first full day in office, I directed my national security team to undertake a comprehensive review of our strategy in Iraq to determine the best way to strengthen that foundation, while strengthening American national security. I have listened to my Secretary of Defense, the Joint Chiefs of Staff, and commanders on the ground. We have acted with careful consideration of events on the ground; with respect for the security agreements between the United States and Iraq; and with a critical recognition that the long-term solution in Iraq must be political—not military. Because the most important decisions that have to be made about Iraq's future must now be made by Iraqis.

We have also taken into account the simple reality that America can no longer afford to see Iraq in isolation from other priorities: we face the challenge of refocusing on Afghanistan and Pakistan; of relieving the burden on our military; and of rebuilding our struggling economy—and these are challenges that we will meet.

Today, I can announce that our review is complete, and that the United States will pursue a new strategy to end the war in Iraq through a transition to full Iraqi responsibility. This strategy is grounded in a clear and achievable goal shared by the Iraqi people and the American people: an Iraq that is sovereign, stable, and self-reliant. To achieve that goal, we will work to promote an Iraqi government that is just, representative, and accountable, and that provides neither support nor safe-haven to terrorists.

We will help Iraq build new ties of trade and commerce with the world. And we will forge a partnership with the people and government of Iraq that contributes to the peace and security of the region.

What we will not do is let the pursuit of the perfect stand in the way of achievable goals. We cannot rid Iraq of all who oppose America or sympathize with our adversaries. We cannot police Iraq's streets until they are completely safe, nor stay until Iraq's union is perfected. We cannot sustain indefinitely a commitment that has put a strain on our military, and will cost the American people nearly a trillion dollars. America's men and women in uniform have fought block by block, province by province, year after year, to give the Iraqis this chance to choose a better future. Now, we must ask the Iraqi people to seize it. The first part of this strategy is therefore the responsible removal of our combat brigades from Iraq.

As a candidate for President, I made clear my support for a timeline of 16 months to carry out this drawdown, while pledging to consult closely with our military commanders upon taking office to ensure that we preserve the gains we've made and protect our troops. Those consultations are now complete, and I have chosen a timeline that will remove our combat brigades over the next 18 months.

Let me say this as plainly as I can: by August 31, 2010, our combat mission in Iraq will end. As we carry out this drawdown, my highest priority will be the safety and security of our troops and civilians in Iraq. We will proceed carefully, and I will consult closely with my military commanders on the ground and with the Iraqi government. There will surely be difficult periods and tactical adjustments. But our enemies should be left with no doubt: this plan gives our military the forces and the flexibility they need to support our Iraqi partners, and to succeed. After we remove our combat brigades, our mission will change from combat to supporting the Iraqi government and its Security Forces as they take the absolute lead in securing their country.

As I have long said, we will retain a transitional force to carry out three distinct functions: training, equipping, and advising Iraqi Security Forces as long as they remain non-sectarian; conducting targeted counter-terrorism missions; and protecting our ongoing civilian and military efforts within Iraq. Initially, this force will likely be made up of 35–50,000 U.S. troops.

Through this period of transition, we will carry out further redeployments. And under the Status of Forces Agreement with the Iraqi government, I intend to remove all U.S. troops from Iraq by the end of 2011. We will complete this transition to Iraqi responsibility, and we will bring our troops home with the honor that they have earned.

As we responsibly remove our combat brigades, we will pursue the second part of our strategy: sustained diplomacy on behalf of a more peaceful and prosperous Iraq. The drawdown of our military should send a clear signal that Iraq's future is now its own responsibility. The long-term success of the Iraqi nation will depend upon decisions made by Iraq's leaders and the fortitude of the Iraqi people. Iraq is a sovereign country with legitimate institutions; America cannot—and should not—take their place. However, a strong political, diplomatic, and civilian effort on our part can advance progress and help lay a foundation for lasting peace and security.

This effort will be led by our new Ambassador to Iraq—Chris Hill. From his time in the Peace Corps, to his work in Kosovo and Korea, Ambassador Hill has been tested, and he has shown the pragmatism and skill that we need right now. He will be supported by the courageous and capable work of so many American diplomats and aid workers who are serving in Iraq.

Going forward, we can make a difference on several fronts. We will work with the United Nations to support national elections, while helping Iraqis improve local government. We can serve as an honest broker in pursuit of fair and durable agreements on issues that have divided Iraq's leaders. And just as we will support Iraq's Security Forces, we will help Iraqi institutions strengthen their capacity to protect the rule of law, confront corruption, and deliver basic services.

Diplomacy and assistance is also required to help the millions of displaced Iraqis. These men, women and children are a living consequence of this war and a challenge to stability in the region, and they must become a part of Iraq's reconciliation and recovery. America has a strategic interest—and a moral responsibility—to act. In the coming months, my administration will provide more assistance and take steps to increase international support for countries already hosting refugees; we'll cooperate with others to resettle Iraqis facing great personal risk; and we will work with the Iraqi government over time to resettle refugees and displaced Iraqis within Iraq—because there are few more powerful indicators of lasting peace than displaced citizens returning home.

Now, before I go any further, I want to take a moment to speak directly to the people of Iraq. You are a great nation, rooted in the cradle of civilization. You are joined together by enduring accomplishments, and a history that connects you as surely as the two rivers carved into your land. In years past, you have persevered through tyranny and terror; through personal insecurity and sectarian violence. And instead of giving in to the forces of disunion, you stepped back from a descent into civil war, and showed a proud resilience that deserves respect.

Our nations have known difficult times together. But ours is a bond forged by shared bloodshed, and countless friendships among our people. We Americans have offered our most precious resource—our young men and women—to work with you to rebuild what was destroyed by despotism; to root out our common enemies; and to seek peace and prosperity for our children and grandchildren, and for yours.

There are those who will try to prevent that future for Iraq—who will insist that Iraq's differences cannot be reconciled without more killing. They represent the forces that destroy nations and lead only to despair, and they will test our will in the months and years to come. America, too, has known these forces. We endured the pain of Civil War, and bitter divisions of region and race. But hostility and hatred are no match for justice; they offer no pathway to peace; and they must not stand between the people of Iraq and a future of reconciliation and hope.

So to the Iraqi people, let me be clear about America's intentions. The United States pursues no claim on your territory or your resources. We respect your sovereignty and the tremendous sacrifices you have made for your country. We seek a full transition to Iraqi responsibility for the security of your country. And going forward, we can build a lasting relationship founded upon mutual interests and mutual respect as Iraq takes its rightful place in the community of nations. That leads me to the third part of our strategy—comprehensive American engagement across the region.

The future of Iraq is inseparable from the future of the broader Middle East, so we must work with our friends and partners to establish a new framework that advances Iraq's security and the region's. It is time for Iraq to be a full partner in a regional dialogue, and for Iraq's neighbors to establish productive and normalized relations with Iraq. And going forward, the United States will pursue principled and sustained engagement with all of the nations in the region, and that will include Iran and Syria.

This reflects a fundamental truth: we can no longer deal with regional challenges in isolation—we need a smarter, more sustainable and comprehensive approach. That is why we are renewing our diplomacy, while relieving the burden on our military. That is why we are refocusing on al Qaeda in Afghanistan and Pakistan; developing a strategy to use all elements of American power to prevent Iran from developing a nuclear weapon; and actively seeking a lasting peace between Israel and the Arab world. And that is why we have named three of America's most accomplished diplomats—George Mitchell, Dennis Ross and Richard Holbrooke—to support Secretary Clinton and me as we carry forward this agenda.

Every nation and every group must know—whether you wish America good or ill—that the end of the war in Iraq will enable a new era of American leadership and engagement in the Middle East. And that era has just begun.

Finally, I want to be very clear that my strategy for ending the war in Iraq does not end with military plans or diplomatic agendas—it endures through our commitment to uphold our sacred trust with every man and woman who has served in Iraq. You make up a fraction of the American population, but in an age when so many people and institutions have acted irresponsibly, you did the opposite—you volunteered to bear the heaviest burden. And for you and for your families, the war does not end when you come home. It lives on in memories of your fellow soldiers, sailors, airmen and Marines who gave their lives. It endures in the wound that is slow to heal, the disability that isn't going away, the dream that wakes you at night, or the stiffening in your spine when a car backfires down the street.

You and your families have done your duty—now a grateful nation must do ours. That is why I am increasing the number of soldiers and Marines, so that we lessen the burden on those who are serving. And that is why I have committed to expanding our system of veterans health care to serve more patients, and to provide better care in more places. We will continue building new wounded warrior facilities across America, and invest in new ways of identifying and treating the signature wounds of this war: Post-Traumatic Stress Disorder and Traumatic Brain Injury, as well as other combat injuries.

We also know that service does not end with the person wearing the uniform. In her visits with military families across the country, my wife Michelle has learned firsthand about the unique burden that your families endure every day. I want you to know this: military families are a top priority for Michelle and me, and they will be a top priority for my administration. We'll raise military pay, and continue providing quality child-care, job-training for spouses, and expanded counseling and outreach to families that have known the separation and stress of war. We will also heed the lesson of history—that those who fight in battle can form the backbone of our middle class—by implementing a 21st century GI Bill to help our veterans live their dreams.

As a nation, we have had our share of debates about the war in Iraq. It has, at times, divided us as a people. To this very day, there are some Americans who want to stay in Iraq longer, and some who want to leave faster. But there should be no disagreement on what the men and women of our military have achieved.

And so I want to be very clear: We sent our troops to Iraq to do away with Saddam Hussein's regime—and you got the job done. We kept our troops in Iraq to help establish a sovereign government—and you got the job done. And we will leave the Iraqi people with a hard-earned opportunity to live a better life—that is your achievement; that is the prospect that you have made possible.

There are many lessons to be learned from what we've experienced. We have learned that America must go to war with clearly defined goals, which is why I've ordered a review of our policy in Afghanistan. We have learned that we must always weigh the costs of action, and communicate those costs candidly to the American people, which is why I've put Iraq and Afghanistan into my budget. We have learned that in the 21st century, we must use all elements of American power to achieve our objectives, which is why I am committed to building our civilian national security capacity so that the burden is not continually pushed on to our military.

We have learned that our political leaders must pursue the broad and bipartisan support that our national security policies depend upon, which is why I will consult with Congress and in carrying out my plans. And we have learned the importance of working closely with friends and allies, which is why we are launching a new era of engagement in the world.

The starting point for our policies must always be the safety of the American people. I know that you—the men and women of the finest fighting force in the history of the world—can meet any challenge, and defeat any foe. And as long as I am your Commander-in-Chief, I promise you that I will only send you into harm's way when it is absolutely necessary, and provide you with the equipment and support you need to get the job done. That is the most important lesson of all—for the consequences of war are dire, the sacrifices immeasurable.

You know because you have seen those sacrifices. You have lived them. And we all honor them. "Semper Fidelis"—it means always being faithful to Corps, and to country, and to the memory of fallen comrades like Corporal Jonathan Yale and Lance Corporal Jordan Haerter. These young men enlisted in a time of war, knowing they would face great danger. They came here, to Camp Lejeune, as they trained for their mission. And last April, they were standing guard in Anbar. In an age when suicide is a weapon, they were suddenly faced with an oncoming truck filled with explosives. These two Marines stood their ground. These two Marines opened fire. And these two Marines stopped that truck. When the thousands of pounds of explosives detonated, they had saved fifty Marines and Iraqi police who would have been in the truck's path, but Corporal Yale and Lance Corporal Haerter lost their own lives. Jonathan was 21. Jordan was 19.

In the town where Jordan Haerter was from, a bridge was dedicated in his name. One Marine who traveled to the ceremony said: "We flew here from all over the country to pay tribute to our friend Jordan, who risked his life to save us. We wouldn't be here without him."

America's time in Iraq is filled with stories of men and women like this. Their names are written into bridges and town squares. They are etched into stones at Arlington, and in quiet places of rest across our land. They are spoken in schools and on city blocks. They live on in the memories of those who wear your uniform, in the hearts of those they loved, and in the freedom of the nation they served.

Each American who has served in Iraq has their own story. Each of you has your own story. And that story is now a part of the history of the United States of America—a nation that exists only because free men and women have bled for it from the beaches of Normandy to the deserts of Anbar; from the mountains of Korea to the streets of Kandahar. You teach us that the price of freedom is great. Your sacrifice should challenge all of us—every single American—to ask what we can do to be better citizens.

There will be more danger in the months ahead. We will face new tests and unforeseen trials. But thanks to the sacrifices of those who have served, we have forged hard-earned progress, we are leaving Iraq to its people, and we have begun the work of ending this war.

Thank you, God Bless you, and God Bless the United States of America. Semper Fi.

THE PRESIDENT: Good morning. Before I begin today, let me acknowledge, first of all, Your Excellencies, all the ambassadors who are in attendance. I also want to acknowledge both the civilians and our military personnel that are about to be deployed to the region. And I am very grateful to all of you for your extraordinary work.

I want to acknowledge General David Petraeus, who's here, and has been doing an outstanding job at CENTCOM, and we appreciate him. I want to thank Bruce Reidel—Bruce is down at the end here—who has worked extensively on our strategic review. I want to acknowledge Karl Eikenberry, who's here, and is our Ambassador-designate to Afghanistan. And to my national security team, thanks for their outstanding work.

Today, I'm announcing a comprehensive, new strategy for Afghanistan and Pakistan. And this marks the conclusion of a careful policy review, led by Bruce, that I ordered as soon as I took office. My administration has heard from our military commanders, as well as our diplomats. We've consulted with the Afghan and Pakistani governments, with our partners and our NATO allies, and with other donors and international organizations. We've also worked closely with members of Congress here at home. And now I'd like to speak clearly and candidly to the American people.

The situation is increasingly perilous. It's been more than seven years since the Taliban was removed from power, yet war rages on, and insurgents control parts of Afghanistan and Pakistan. Attacks against our troops, our NATO allies, and the Afghan government have risen steadily. And most painfully, 2008 was the deadliest year of the war for American forces.

Many people in the United States—and many in partner countries that have sacrificed so much—have a simple question: What is our purpose in Afghanistan? After so many years, they ask, why do our men and women still fight and die there? And they deserve a straightforward answer.

So let me be clear: Al Qaeda and its allies—the terrorists who planned and supported the 9/11 attacks—are in Pakistan and Afghanistan. Multiple intelligence estimates have warned that al Qaeda is actively planning attacks on the United States homeland from its safe haven in Pakistan. And if the Afghan government falls to the Taliban—or allows al Qaeda to go unchallenged—that country will again be a base for terrorists who want to kill as many of our people as they possibly can.

The future of Afghanistan is inextricably linked to the future of its neighbor, Pakistan. In the nearly eight years since 9/11, al Qaeda and its extremist allies have moved across the border to the remote areas of the Pakistani frontier. This almost certainly includes al Qaeda's leadership: Osama bin Laden and Ayman al-Zawahiri.

Remarks by the President on a New Strategy for Afghanistan, Dwight D. Eisenhower Executive Office Building, The White House, Office of the Press Secretary, For Immediate Release March 27, 2009. http://www.whitehouse.gov/the_press_office/Remarks-by-the-President-on-a-New-Strategy-for-Afghanistan-and-Pakistan/.

They have used this mountainous terrain as a safe haven to hide, to train terrorists, to communicate with followers, to plot attacks, and to send fighters to support the insurgency in Afghanistan. For the American people, this border region has become the most dangerous place in the world.

But this is not simply an American problem—far from it. It is, instead, an international security challenge of the highest order. Terrorist attacks in London and Bali were tied to al Qaeda and its allies in Pakistan, as were attacks in North Africa and the Middle East, in Islamabad and in Kabul. If there is a major attack on an Asian, European, or African city, it, too, is likely to have ties to al Qaeda's leadership in Pakistan. The safety of people around the world is at stake.

For the Afghan people, a return to Taliban rule would condemn their country to brutal governance, international isolation, a paralyzed economy, and the denial of basic human rights to the Afghan people—especially women and girls. The return in force of al Qaeda terrorists who would accompany the core Taliban leadership would cast Afghanistan under the shadow of perpetual violence.

As President, my greatest responsibility is to protect the American people. We are not in Afghanistan to control that country or to dictate its future. We are in Afghanistan to confront a common enemy that threatens the United States, our friends and our allies, and the people of Afghanistan and Pakistan who have suffered the most at the hands of violent extremists.

So I want the American people to understand that we have a clear and focused goal: to disrupt, dismantle and defeat al Qaeda in Pakistan and Afghanistan, and to prevent their return to either country in the future. That's the goal that must be achieved. That is a cause that could not be more just. And to the terrorists who oppose us, my message is the same: We will defeat you.

To achieve our goals, we need a stronger, smarter and comprehensive strategy. To focus on the greatest threat to our people, America must no longer deny resources to Afghanistan because of the war in Iraq. To enhance the military, governance and economic capacity of Afghanistan and Pakistan, we have to marshal international support. And to defeat an enemy that heeds no borders or laws of war, we must recognize the fundamental connection between the future of Afghanistan and Pakistan—which is why I've appointed Ambassador Richard Holbrooke, who is here, to serve as Special Representative for both countries, and to work closely with General Petraeus to integrate our civilian and military efforts.

Let me start by addressing the way forward in Pakistan. The United States has great respect for the Pakistani people. They have a rich history and have struggled against long odds to sustain their democracy. The people of Pakistan want the same things that we want: an end to terror, access to basic services, the opportunity to live their dreams, and the security that can only come with the rule of law. The single greatest threat to that future comes from al Qaeda and their extremist allies, and that is why we must stand together.

The terrorists within Pakistan's borders are not simply enemies of America or Afghanistan—they are a grave and urgent danger to the people of Pakistan. Al Qaeda and other violent extremists have killed several thousand Pakistanis since 9/11. They've killed many Pakistani soldiers and police. They assassinated Benazir Bhutto. They've blown up buildings, derailed foreign investment, and threatened the stability of the state. So make no mistake: al Qaeda and its extremist allies are a cancer that risks killing Pakistan from within.

It's important for the American people to understand that Pakistan needs our help in going after al Qaeda. This is no simple task. The tribal regions are vast, they are rugged, and they are often ungoverned. And that's why we must focus our military assistance on the tools, training and support that Pakistan needs to root out the terrorists. And after years of mixed results, we will not, and cannot, provide a blank check.

Pakistan must demonstrate its commitment to rooting out al Qaeda and the violent extremists within its borders. And we will insist that action be taken—one way or another—when we have intelligence about high-level terrorist targets.

The government's ability to destroy these safe havens is tied to its own strength and security. To help Pakistan weather the economic crisis, we must continue to work with the IMF, the World Bank and other international partners. To lessen tensions between two nuclear-armed nations that too often teeter on the edge of escalation and confrontation, we must pursue constructive diplomacy with both India and Pakistan. To avoid the mistakes of the past, we must make clear that our relationship with Pakistan is grounded in support for Pakistan's democratic institutions and the Pakistani people. And to demonstrate through deeds as well as words a commitment that is enduring, we must stand for lasting opportunity.

A campaign against extremism will not succeed with bullets or bombs alone. Al Qaeda's offers the people of Pakistan nothing but destruction. We stand for something different. So today, I am calling upon Congress to pass a bipartisan bill co-sponsored by John Kerry and Richard Lugar that authorizes $1.5 billion in direct support to the Pakistani people every year over the next five years—resources that will build schools and roads and hospitals, and strengthen Pakistan's democracy. I'm also calling on Congress to pass a bipartisan bill co-sponsored by Maria Cantwell, Chris Van Hollen and Peter Hoekstra that creates opportunity zones in the border regions to develop the economy and bring hope to places plagued with violence. And we will ask our friends and allies to do their part—including at the donors conference in Tokyo next month.

I don't ask for this support lightly. These are challenging times. Resources are stretched. But the American people must understand that this is a down payment on our own future—because the security of America and Pakistan is shared. Pakistan's government must be a stronger partner in destroying these safe havens, and we must isolate al Qaeda from the Pakistani people. And these steps in Pakistan are also indispensable to our efforts in Afghanistan, which will see no end to violence if insurgents move freely back and forth across the border.

Security demands a new sense of shared responsibility. And that's why we will launch a standing, trilateral dialogue among the United States, Afghanistan and Pakistan. Our nations will meet regularly, with Secretaries Clinton and Secretary Gates leading our effort. Together, we must enhance intelligence sharing and military cooperation along the border, while addressing issues of common concern like trade, energy, and economic development.

This is just one part of a comprehensive strategy to prevent Afghanistan from becoming the al Qaeda safe haven that it was before 9/11. To succeed, we and our friends and allies must reverse the Taliban's gains, and promote a more capable and accountable Afghan government.

Our troops have fought bravely against a ruthless enemy. Our civilians have made great sacrifices. Our allies have borne a heavy burden. Afghans have suffered and sacrificed for their future. But for six years, Afghanistan has been denied the resources that it demands because of the war in Iraq. Now, we must make a commitment that can accomplish our goals.

I've already ordered the deployment of 17,000 troops that had been requested by General McKiernan for many months. These soldiers and Marines will take the fight to the Taliban in the south and the east, and give us a greater capacity to partner with Afghan security forces and to go after insurgents along the border. This push will also help provide security in advance of the important presidential elections in Afghanistan in August.

At the same time, we will shift the emphasis of our mission to training and increasing the size of Afghan security forces, so that they can eventually take the lead in securing their country. That's how we will prepare Afghans to take responsibility for their security, and how we will ultimately be able to bring our own troops home.

For three years, our commanders have been clear about the resources they need for training. And those resources have been denied because of the war in Iraq. Now, that will change. The additional troops that we deployed have already increased our training capacity. And later this spring we will deploy approximately 4,000 U.S. troops to train Afghan security forces. For the first time, this will truly resource our effort to train and support the Afghan army and police. Every American unit in Afghanistan will be partnered with an Afghan unit, and we will seek additional trainers from our NATO allies to ensure that every Afghan unit has a coalition partner. We will accelerate our efforts to build an Afghan army of 134,000 and a police force of 82,000 so that we can meet these goals by 2011—and increases in Afghan forces may very well be needed as our plans to turn over security responsibility to the Afghans go forward.

This push must be joined by a dramatic increase in our civilian effort. Afghanistan has an elected government, but it is undermined by corruption and has difficulty delivering basic services to its people. The economy is undercut by a booming narcotics trade that encourages criminality and funds the insurgency. The people of Afghanistan seek the promise of a better future. Yet once again, we've seen the hope of a new day darkened by violence and uncertainty.

So to advance security, opportunity and justice—not just in Kabul, but from the bottom up in the provinces—we need agricultural specialists and educators, engineers and lawyers. That's how we can help the Afghan government serve its people and develop an economy that isn't dominated by illicit drugs. And that's why I'm ordering a substantial increase in our civilians on the ground. That's also why we must seek civilian support from our partners and allies, from the United Nations and international aid organizations—an effort that Secretary Clinton will carry forward next week in The Hague.

At a time of economic crisis, it's tempting to believe that we can shortchange this civilian effort. But make no mistake: Our efforts will fail in Afghanistan and Pakistan if we don't invest in their future. And that's why my budget includes indispensable investments in our State Department and foreign assistance programs. These investments relieve the burden on our troops. They contribute directly to security. They make the American people safer. And they save us an enormous amount of money in the long run—because it's far cheaper to train a policeman to secure his or her own village than to help a farmer seed a crop—or to help a farmer seed a crop than it is to send our troops to fight tour after tour of duty with no transition to Afghan responsibility.

As we provide these resources, the days of unaccountable spending, no-bid contracts, and wasteful reconstruction must end. So my budget will increase funding for a strong Inspector General at both the State Department and USAID, and include robust funding for the special inspector generals for Afghan Reconstruction.

And I want to be clear: We cannot turn a blind eye to the corruption that causes Afghans to lose faith in their own leaders. Instead, we will seek a new compact with the Afghan government that cracks down on corrupt behavior, and sets clear benchmarks, clear metrics for international assistance so that it is used to provide for the needs of the Afghan people.

In a country with extreme poverty that's been at war for decades, there will also be no peace without reconciliation among former enemies. Now, I have no illusion that this will be easy. In Iraq, we had success in reaching out to former adversaries to isolate and target al Qaeda in Iraq. We must pursue a similar process in Afghanistan, while understanding that it is a very different country.

There is an uncompromising core of the Taliban. They must be met with force, and they must be defeated. But there are also those who've taken up arms because of coercion, or simply for a price. These Afghans must have the option to choose a different course. And that's why we will work with local leaders, the Afghan government, and international partners to have a reconciliation process in every province. As their ranks dwindle, an enemy that has nothing to offer the Afghan people but terror and repression must be further isolated. And we will continue to support the basic human rights of all Afghans—including women and girls.

Going forward, we will not blindly stay the course. Instead, we will set clear metrics to measure progress and hold ourselves accountable. We'll consistently assess our efforts to train Afghan security forces and our progress in combating insurgents. We will measure the growth of Afghanistan's economy, and its illicit narcotics production. And we will review whether we are using the right tools and tactics to make progress towards accomplishing our goals.

None of the steps that I've outlined will be easy; none should be taken by America alone. The world cannot afford the price that will come due if Afghanistan slides back into chaos or al Qaeda operates unchecked. We have a shared responsibility to act—not because we seek to project power for its own sake, but because our own peace and security depends on it. And what's at stake at this time is not just our own security—it's the very idea that free nations can come together on behalf of our common security. That was the founding cause of NATO six decades ago, and that must be our common purpose today.

My administration is committed to strengthening international organizations and collective action, and that will be my message next week in Europe. As America does more, we will ask others to join us in doing their part. From our partners and NATO allies, we will seek not simply troops, but rather clearly defined capabilities: supporting the Afghan elections, training Afghan security forces, a greater civilian commitment to the Afghan people. For the United Nations, we seek greater progress for its mandate to coordinate international action and assistance, and to strengthen Afghan institutions.

And finally, together with the United Nations, we will forge a new Contact Group for Afghanistan and Pakistan that brings together all who should have a stake in the security of the region—our NATO allies and other partners, but also the Central Asian states, the Gulf nations and Iran; Russia, India and China. None of these nations benefit from a base for al Qaeda terrorists, and a region that descends into chaos. All have a stake in the promise of lasting peace and security and development.

That is true, above all, for the coalition that has fought together in Afghanistan, side by side with Afghans. The sacrifices have been enormous. Nearly 700 Americans have lost their lives. Troops from over 20 countries have also paid the ultimate price. All Americans honor the service and cherish the friendship of those who have fought, and worked, and bled by our side. And all Americans are awed by the service of our own men and women in uniform, who've borne a burden as great as any other generation's. They and their families embody the example of selfless sacrifice.

I remind everybody, the United States of America did not choose to fight a war in Afghanistan. Nearly 3,000 of our people were killed on September 11, 2001, for doing nothing more than going about their daily lives. Al Qaeda and its allies have since killed thousands of people in many countries. Most of the blood on their hands is the blood of Muslims, who al Qaeda has killed and maimed in far greater number than any other people. That is the future that al Qaeda is offering to the people of Pakistan and Afghanistan—a future without hope or opportunity; a future without justice or peace.

So understand, the road ahead will be long and there will be difficult days ahead. But we will seek lasting partnerships with Afghanistan and Pakistan that promise a new day for their people. And we will use all elements of our national power to defeat al Qaeda, and to defend America, our allies, and all who seek a better future. Because the United States of America stands for peace and security, justice and opportunity. That is who we are, and that is what history calls on us to do once more. Thank you. God bless you, and God bless the United States of America.

THE PRESIDENT: Good evening. To the United States Corps of Cadets, to the men and women of our Armed Services, and to my fellow Americans: I want to speak to you tonight about our effort in Afghanistan—the nature of our commitment there, the scope of our interests, and the strategy that my administration will pursue to bring this war to a successful conclusion. It's an extraordinary honor for me to do so here at West Point where so many men and women have prepared to stand up for our security, and to represent what is finest about our country.

To address these important issues, it's important to recall why America and our allies were compelled to fight a war in Afghanistan in the first place. We did not ask for this fight. On September 11, 2001, 19 men hijacked four airplanes and used them to murder nearly 3,000 people. They struck at our military and economic nerve centers. They took the lives of innocent men, women, and children without regard to their faith or race or station. Were it not for the heroic actions of passengers onboard one of those flights, they could have also struck at one of the great symbols of our democracy in Washington, and killed many more.

As we know, these men belonged to al Qaeda—a group of extremists who have distorted and defiled Islam, one of the world's great religions, to justify the slaughter of innocents. Al Qaeda's base of operations was in Afghanistan, where they were harbored by the Taliban—a ruthless, repressive and radical movement that seized control of that

Remarks by the President in Address to the Nation on the Way Forward in Afghanistan and Pakistan, Eisenhower Hall Theatre, United States Military Academy at West Point, West Point, New York, The White House, Office of the Press Secretary, For Immediate Release, December 1, 2009. http://www.white-house.gov/the-press-office/remarks-president-address-nation-way-forward-afghanistan-and-pakistan.

country after it was ravaged by years of Soviet occupation and civil war, and after the attention of America and our friends had turned elsewhere.

Just days after 9/11, Congress authorized the use of force against al Qaeda and those who harbored them—an authorization that continues to this day. The vote in the Senate was 98 to nothing. The vote in the House was 420 to 1. For the first time in its history, the North Atlantic Treaty Organization invoked Article 5—the commitment that says an attack on one member nation is an attack on all. And the United Nations Security Council endorsed the use of all necessary steps to respond to the 9/11 attacks. America, our allies and the world were acting as one to destroy al Qaeda's terrorist network and to protect our common security.

Under the banner of this domestic unity and international legitimacy—and only after the Taliban refused to turn over Osama bin Laden—we sent our troops into Afghanistan. Within a matter of months, al Qaeda was scattered and many of its operatives were killed. The Taliban was driven from power and pushed back on its heels. A place that had known decades of fear now had reason to hope. At a conference convened by the U.N., a provisional government was established under President Hamid Karzai. And an International Security Assistance Force was established to help bring a lasting peace to a war-torn country.

Then, in early 2003, the decision was made to wage a second war, in Iraq. The wrenching debate over the Iraq war is well-known and need not be repeated here. It's enough to say that for the next six years, the Iraq war drew the dominant share of our troops, our resources, our diplomacy, and our national attention—and that the decision to go into Iraq caused substantial rifts between America and much of the world.

Today, after extraordinary costs, we are bringing the Iraq war to a responsible end. We will remove our combat brigades from Iraq by the end of next summer, and all of our troops by the end of 2011. That we are doing so is a testament to the character of the men and women in uniform. Thanks to their courage, grit and perseverance, we have given Iraqis a chance to shape their future, and we are successfully leaving Iraq to its people.

But while we've achieved hard-earned milestones in Iraq, the situation in Afghanistan has deteriorated. After escaping across the border into Pakistan in 2001 and 2002, al Qaeda's leadership established a safe haven there. Although a legitimate government was elected by the Afghan people, it's been hampered by corruption, the drug trade, an under-developed economy, and insufficient security forces.

Over the last several years, the Taliban has maintained common cause with al Qaeda, as they both seek an overthrow of the Afghan government. Gradually, the Taliban has begun to control additional swaths of territory in Afghanistan, while engaging in increasingly brazen and devastating attacks of terrorism against the Pakistani people.

Now, throughout this period, our troop levels in Afghanistan remained a fraction of what they were in Iraq. When I took office, we had just over 32,000 Americans serving in Afghanistan, compared to 160,000 in Iraq at the peak of the war. Commanders in Afghanistan repeatedly asked for support to deal with the reemergence of the Taliban, but these reinforcements did not arrive. And that's why, shortly after taking office, I approved a longstanding request for more troops. After consultations with our allies, I then announced a strategy recognizing the fundamental connection between our war effort in Afghanistan and the extremist safe havens in Pakistan. I set a goal that was narrowly defined as disrupting, dismantling, and defeating al Qaeda and its extremist allies, and pledged to better coordinate our military and civilian efforts.

Since then, we've made progress on some important objectives. High-ranking al Qaeda and Taliban leaders have been killed, and we've stepped up the pressure on al Qaeda worldwide. In Pakistan, that nation's army has gone on its largest offensive in years. In Afghanistan, we and our allies prevented the Taliban from stopping a presidential election, and—although it was marred by fraud—that election produced a government that is consistent with Afghanistan's laws and constitution.

Yet huge challenges remain. Afghanistan is not lost, but for several years it has moved backwards. There's no imminent threat of the government being overthrown, but the Taliban has gained momentum. Al Qaeda has not reemerged in Afghanistan in the same numbers as before 9/11, but they retain their safe havens along the border. And our forces lack the full support they need to effectively train and partner with Afghan security forces and better secure the population. Our new commander in Afghanistan—General McChrystal—has reported that the security situation is more serious than he anticipated. In short: The status quo is not sustainable.

As cadets, you volunteered for service during this time of danger. Some of you fought in Afghanistan. Some of you will deploy there. As your Commander-in-Chief, I owe you a mission that is clearly defined, and worthy of your service. And that's why, after the Afghan voting was completed, I insisted on a thorough review of our strategy. Now, let me be clear: There has never been an option before me that called for troop deployments before 2010, so there has been no delay or denial of resources necessary for the conduct of the war during this review period. Instead, the review has allowed me to ask the hard questions, and to explore all the different options, along with my national security team, our military and civilian leadership in Afghanistan, and our key partners. And given the stakes involved, I owed the American people—and our troops—no less.

This review is now complete. And as Commander-in-Chief, I have determined that it is in our vital national interest to send an additional 30,000 U.S. troops to Afghanistan. After 18 months, our troops will begin to come home. These are the resources that we need to seize the initiative, while building the Afghan capacity that can allow for a responsible transition of our forces out of Afghanistan.

I do not make this decision lightly. I opposed the war in Iraq precisely because I believe that we must exercise restraint in the use of military force, and always consider the long-term consequences of our actions. We have been at war now for eight years, at enormous cost in lives and resources. Years of debate over Iraq and terrorism have left our unity on national security issues in tatters, and created a highly polarized and partisan backdrop for this effort. And having just experienced the worst economic crisis since the Great Depression, the American people are understandably focused on rebuilding our economy and putting people to work here at home.

Most of all, I know that this decision asks even more of you—a military that, along with your families, has already borne the heaviest of all burdens. As President, I have signed a letter of condolence to the family of each American who gives their life in these wars. I have read the letters from the parents and spouses of those who deployed. I visited our courageous wounded warriors at Walter Reed. I've traveled to Dover to meet the flag-draped caskets of 18 Americans returning home to their final resting place. I see firsthand the terrible wages of war. If I did not think that the security of the United States and the safety of the American people were at stake in Afghanistan, I would gladly order every single one of our troops home tomorrow.

So, no, I do not make this decision lightly. I make this decision because I am convinced that our security is at stake in Afghanistan and Pakistan. This is the epicenter of violent extremism practiced by al Qaeda. It is from here that we were attacked on 9/11, and it is from here that new attacks are being plotted as I speak. This is no idle danger; no hypothetical threat. In the last few months alone, we have apprehended extremists within our borders who were sent here from the border region of Afghanistan and Pakistan to commit new acts of terror. And this danger will only grow if the region slides backwards, and al Qaeda can operate with impunity. We must keep the pressure on al Qaeda, and to do that, we must increase the stability and capacity of our partners in the region.

Of course, this burden is not ours alone to bear. This is not just America's war. Since 9/11, al Qaeda's safe havens have been the source of attacks against London and Amman and Bali. The people and governments of both Afghanistan and Pakistan are endangered. And the stakes are even higher within a nuclear-armed Pakistan, because we know that al Qaeda and other extremists seek nuclear weapons, and we have every reason to believe that they would use them.

These facts compel us to act along with our friends and allies. Our overarching goal remains the same: to disrupt, dismantle, and defeat al Qaeda in Afghanistan and Pakistan, and to prevent its capacity to threaten America and our allies in the future. To meet that goal, we will pursue the following objectives within Afghanistan. We must deny al Qaeda a safe haven. We must reverse the Taliban's momentum and deny it the ability to overthrow the government. And we must strengthen the capacity of Afghanistan's security forces and government so that they can take lead responsibility for Afghanistan's future.

We will meet these objectives in three ways. First, we will pursue a military strategy that will break the Taliban's momentum and increase Afghanistan's capacity over the next 18 months.

The 30,000 additional troops that I'm announcing tonight will deploy in the first part of 2010—the fastest possible pace—so that they can target the insurgency and secure key population centers. They'll increase our ability to train competent Afghan security forces, and to partner with them so that more Afghans can get into the fight. And they will help create the conditions for the United States to transfer responsibility to the Afghans.

Because this is an international effort, I've asked that our commitment be joined by contributions from our allies. Some have already provided additional troops, and we're confident that there will be further contributions in the days and weeks ahead. Our friends have fought and bled and died alongside us in Afghanistan. And now, we must come together to end this war successfully. For what's at stake is not simply a test of NATO's credibility—what's at stake is the security of our allies, and the common security of the world.

But taken together, these additional American and international troops will allow us to accelerate handing over responsibility to Afghan forces, and allow us to begin the transfer of our forces out of Afghanistan in July of 2011. Just as we have done in Iraq, we will execute this transition responsibly, taking into account conditions on the ground. We'll continue to advise and assist Afghanistan's security forces to ensure that they can succeed over the long haul. But it will be clear to the Afghan government—and, more importantly, to the Afghan people—that they will ultimately be responsible for their own country.

Second, we will work with our partners, the United Nations, and the Afghan people to pursue a more effective civilian strategy, so that the government can take advantage of improved security. This effort must be based on performance. The days of providing a blank check are over. President Karzai's inauguration speech sent the right message about moving in a new direction. And going forward, we will be clear about what we expect from those who receive our assistance. We'll support Afghan ministries, governors, and local leaders that combat corruption and deliver for the people. We expect those who are ineffective or corrupt to be held accountable. And we will also focus our assistance in areas—such as agriculture—that can make an immediate impact in the lives of the Afghan people.

The people of Afghanistan have endured violence for decades. They've been confronted with occupation—by the Soviet Union, and then by foreign al Qaeda fighters who used Afghan land for their own purposes. So tonight, I want the Afghan people to understand—America seeks an end to this era of war and suffering. We have no interest in occupying your country. We will support efforts by the Afghan government to open the door to those Taliban who abandon violence and respect the human rights of their fellow citizens. And we will seek a partnership with Afghanistan grounded in mutual respect—to isolate those who destroy; to strengthen those who build; to hasten the day when our troops will leave; and to forge a lasting friendship in which America is your partner, and never your patron.

Third, we will act with the full recognition that our success in Afghanistan is inextricably linked to our partnership with Pakistan. We're in Afghanistan to prevent a cancer from once again spreading through that country. But this same cancer has also taken root in the border region of Pakistan. That's why we need a strategy that works on both sides of the border.

In the past, there have been those in Pakistan who've argued that the struggle against extremism is not their fight, and that Pakistan is better off doing little or seeking accommodation with those who use violence. But in recent years, as innocents have been killed from Karachi to Islamabad, it has become clear that it is the Pakistani people who are the most endangered by extremism. Public opinion has turned. The Pakistani army has waged an offensive in Swat and South Waziristan. And there is no doubt that the United States and Pakistan share a common enemy.

In the past, we too often defined our relationship with Pakistan narrowly. Those days are over. Moving forward, we are committed to a partnership with Pakistan that is built on a foundation of mutual interest, mutual respect, and mutual trust. We will strengthen Pakistan's capacity to target those groups that threaten our countries, and have made it clear that we cannot tolerate a safe haven for terrorists whose location is known and whose intentions are clear. America is also providing substantial resources to support Pakistan's democracy and development. We are the largest international supporter for those Pakistanis displaced by the fighting. And going forward, the Pakistan people must know America will remain a strong supporter of Pakistan's security and prosperity long after the guns have fallen silent, so that the great potential of its people can be unleashed.

These are the three core elements of our strategy: a military effort to create the conditions for a transition; a civilian surge that reinforces positive action; and an effective partnership with Pakistan.

I recognize there are a range of concerns about our approach. So let me briefly address a few of the more prominent arguments that I've heard, and which I take very seriously. First, there are those who suggest that Afghanistan is another Vietnam. They argue that it cannot be stabilized, and we're better off cutting our losses and rapidly withdrawing. I believe this argument depends on a false reading of history. Unlike Vietnam, we are joined by a broad coalition of 43 nations that recognizes the legitimacy of our action. Unlike Vietnam, we are not facing a broad-based popular insurgency. And most importantly, unlike Vietnam, the American people were viciously attacked from Afghanistan, and remain a target for those same extremists who are plotting along its border. To abandon this area now—and to rely only on efforts against al Qaeda from a distance—would significantly hamper our ability to keep the pressure on al Qaeda, and create an unacceptable risk of additional attacks on our homeland and our allies.

Second, there are those who acknowledge that we can't leave Afghanistan in its current state, but suggest that we go forward with the troops that we already have. But this would simply maintain a status quo in which we muddle through, and permit a slow deterioration of conditions there. It would ultimately prove more costly and prolong our stay in Afghanistan, because we would never be able to generate the conditions needed to train Afghan security forces and give them the space to take over.

Finally, there are those who oppose identifying a time frame for our transition to Afghan responsibility. Indeed, some call for a more dramatic and open-ended escalation of our war effort—one that would commit us to a nation-building project of up to a decade. I reject this course because it sets goals that are beyond what can be achieved at a reasonable cost, and what we need to achieve to secure our interests. Furthermore, the absence of a time frame for transition would deny us any sense of urgency in working with the Afghan government. It must be clear that Afghans will have to take responsibility for their security, and that America has no interest in fighting an endless war in Afghanistan.

As President, I refuse to set goals that go beyond our responsibility, our means, or our interests. And I must weigh all of the challenges that our nation faces. I don't have the luxury of committing to just one. Indeed, I'm mindful of the words of President Eisenhower, who—in discussing our national security—said, "Each proposal must be weighed in the light of a broader consideration: the need to maintain balance in and among national programs."

Over the past several years, we have lost that balance. We've failed to appreciate the connection between our national security and our economy. In the wake of an economic crisis, too many of our neighbors and friends are out of work and struggle to pay the bills. Too many Americans are worried about the future facing our children. Meanwhile, competition within the global economy has grown more fierce. So we can't simply afford to ignore the price of these wars.

All told, by the time I took office the cost of the wars in Iraq and Afghanistan approached a trillion dollars. Going forward, I am committed to addressing these costs openly and honestly. Our new approach in Afghanistan is likely to cost us roughly $30 billion for the military this year, and I'll work closely with Congress to address these costs as we work to bring down our deficit.

But as we end the war in Iraq and transition to Afghan responsibility, we must rebuild our strength here at home. Our prosperity provides a foundation for our power. It pays for our military. It underwrites our diplomacy. It taps the potential of our people, and allows investment in new industry. And it will allow us to compete in this century as successfully as we did in the last. That's why our troop commitment in

Afghanistan cannot be open-ended—because the nation that I'm most interested in building is our own.

Now, let me be clear: None of this will be easy. The struggle against violent extremism will not be finished quickly, and it extends well beyond Afghanistan and Pakistan. It will be an enduring test of our free society, and our leadership in the world. And unlike the great power conflicts and clear lines of division that defined the 20th century, our effort will involve disorderly regions, failed states, diffuse enemies.

So as a result, America will have to show our strength in the way that we end wars and prevent conflict—not just how we wage wars. We'll have to be nimble and precise in our use of military power. Where al Qaeda and its allies attempt to establish a foothold—whether in Somalia or Yemen or elsewhere—they must be confronted by growing pressure and strong partnerships.

And we can't count on military might alone. We have to invest in our homeland security, because we can't capture or kill every violent extremist abroad. We have to improve and better coordinate our intelligence, so that we stay one step ahead of shadowy networks.

We will have to take away the tools of mass destruction. And that's why I've made it a central pillar of my foreign policy to secure loose nuclear materials from terrorists, to stop the spread of nuclear weapons, and to pursue the goal of a world without them—because every nation must understand that true security will never come from an endless race for ever more destructive weapons; true security will come for those who reject them.

We'll have to use diplomacy, because no one nation can meet the challenges of an interconnected world acting alone. I've spent this year renewing our alliances and forging new partnerships. And we have forged a new beginning between America and the Muslim world—one that recognizes our mutual interest in breaking a cycle of conflict, and that promises a future in which those who kill innocents are isolated by those who stand up for peace and prosperity and human dignity.

And finally, we must draw on the strength of our values—for the challenges that we face may have changed, but the things that we believe in must not. That's why we must promote our values by living them at home—which is why I have prohibited torture and will close the prison at Guantanamo Bay. And we must make it clear to every man, woman and child around the world who lives under the dark cloud of tyranny that America will speak out on behalf of their human rights, and tend to the light of freedom and justice and opportunity and respect for the dignity of all peoples. That is who we are. That is the source, the moral source, of America's authority.

Since the days of Franklin Roosevelt, and the service and sacrifice of our grandparents and great-grandparents, our country has borne a special burden in global affairs. We have spilled American blood in many countries on multiple continents. We have spent our revenue to help others rebuild from rubble and develop their own economies. We have joined with others to develop an architecture of institutions—from the United Nations to NATO to the World Bank—that provide for the common security and prosperity of human beings.

We have not always been thanked for these efforts, and we have at times made mistakes. But more than any other nation, the United States of America has underwritten global security for over six decades—a time that, for all its problems, has seen walls come down, and markets open, and billions lifted from poverty, unparalleled scientific progress and advancing frontiers of human liberty.

For unlike the great powers of old, we have not sought world domination. Our union was founded in resistance to oppression. We do not seek to occupy other nations. We will not claim another nation's resources or target other peoples because their faith or ethnicity is different from ours. What we have fought for—what we continue to fight for—is a better future for our children and grandchildren. And we believe that their lives will be better if other peoples' children and grandchildren can live in freedom and access opportunity.

As a country, we're not as young—and perhaps not as innocent—as we were when Roosevelt was President. Yet we are still heirs to a noble struggle for freedom. And now we must summon all of our might and moral suasion to meet the challenges of a new age.

In the end, our security and leadership does not come solely from the strength of our arms. It derives from our people—from the workers and businesses who will rebuild our economy; from the entrepreneurs and researchers who will pioneer new industries; from the teachers that will educate our children, and the service of those who work in our communities at home; from the diplomats and Peace Corps volunteers who spread hope abroad; and from the men and women in uniform who are part of an unbroken line of sacrifice that has made government of the people, by the people, and for the people a reality on this Earth.

This vast and diverse citizenry will not always agree on every issue—nor should we. But I also know that we, as a country, cannot sustain our leadership, nor navigate the momentous challenges of our time, if we allow ourselves to be split asunder by the same rancor and cynicism and partisanship that has in recent times poisoned our national discourse.

It's easy to forget that when this war began, we were united—bound together by the fresh memory of a horrific attack, and by the determination to defend our homeland and the values we hold dear. I refuse to accept the notion that we cannot summon that unity again. I believe with every fiber of my being that we—as Americans—can still come together behind a common purpose. For our values are not simply words written into parchment—they are a creed that calls us together, and that has carried us through the darkest of storms as one nation, as one people.

America—we are passing through a time of great trial. And the message that we send in the midst of these storms must be clear: that our cause is just, our resolve unwavering. We will go forward with the confidence that right makes might, and with the commitment to forge an America that is safer, a world that is more secure, and a future that represents not the deepest of fears but the highest of hopes. Thank you. God bless you. May God bless the United States of America.

Barack Obama: Success In Iraq and Afghanistan

THE PRESIDENT: Good morning. It is wonderful to be back at the United States Military Academy—the oldest continuously occupied military post in America—as we commission the newest officers in the United States Army.

Thank you, General Hagenbeck, for your introduction, on a day that holds special meaning for you and the Dean, General Finnegan. Both of you first came to West Point in the Class of 1971 and went on to inspire soldiers under your command. You've led this Academy to a well-deserved recognition: best college in America. And today, you're both looking forward to a well-deserved retirement from the Army. General Hagenbeck and Judy, General Finnegan and Joan, we thank you for 39 years of remarkable service to the Army and to America.

To the Commandant, General Rapp, the Academy staff and faculty, most of whom are veterans, thank you for your service and for inspiring these cadets to become the "leaders of character" they are today. Let me also acknowledge the presence of General Shinseki, Secretary McHugh, the members of Congress who are with us here today, including two former soldiers this Academy knows well, Senator Jack Reed and Congressman Patrick Murphy.

To all the families here—especially all the moms and dads—this day is a tribute to you as well. The decision to come to West Point was made by your sons and daughters, but it was you who instilled in them a spirit of service that has led them to this hallowed place in a time of war. So on behalf of the American people, thank you for your example and thank you for your patriotism.

To the United States Corps of Cadets, and most of all, the Class of 2010—it is a singular honor to serve as your Commander-in-Chief. As your Superintendent indicated, under our constitutional system my power as President is wisely limited. But there are some areas where my power is absolute. And so, as your Commander-in-Chief, I

Remarks by the President at United States Military Academy at West Point Commencement at Michie Stadium, West Point, New York, The White House, Office of the Press Secretary, For Immediate Release, May 22, 2010. http://www.whitehouse.gov/the-press-office/remarks-president-united-states-military-academy-west-point-commencement.

hereby absolve all cadets who are on restriction for minor conduct offenses. I will leave the definition of "minor" to those who know better.

Class of 2010, today is your day—a day to celebrate all that you've achieved, in the finest tradition of the soldier-scholar, and to look forward to the important service that lies ahead.

You have pushed yourself through the agony of Beast Barracks, the weeks of training in rain and mud, and, I'm told, more inspections and drills than perhaps any class before you. Along the way, I'm sure you faced a few moments when you asked yourself: "What am I doing here?" I have those moments sometimes.

You've trained for the complexities of today's missions, knowing that success will be measured not merely by performance on the battlefield, but also by your understanding of the cultures and traditions and languages in the place where you serve.

You've reached out across borders, with more international experience than any class in Academy history. You've not only attended foreign academies to forge new friendships, you've welcomed into your ranks cadets from nearly a dozen countries.

You've challenged yourself intellectually in the sciences and the humanities, in history and technology. You've achieved a standard of academic excellence that is without question, tying the record for the most post-graduate scholarships of any class in West Point history. This includes your number one overall cadet and your valedictorian—Liz Betterbed and Alex Rosenberg. And by the way, this is the first time in Academy history where your two top awards have been earned by female candidates.

This underscores a fact that I've seen in the faces of our troops from Baghdad to Bagram—in the 21st century, our women in uniform play an indispensable role in our national defense. And time and again, they have proven themselves to be role models for our daughters and our sons—as students and as soldiers and as leaders in the United States armed forces.

And the faces in this stadium show a simple truth: America's Army represents the full breadth of America's experience. You come from every corner of our country—from privilege and from poverty, from cities and small towns. You worship all of the great religions that enrich the life of our people. You include the vast diversity of race and ethnicity that is fundamental to our nation's strength.

There is, however, one thing that sets you apart. Here in these quiet hills, you've come together to prepare for the most difficult test of our time. You signed up knowing your service would send you into harm's way, and you did so long after the first drums of war were sounded. In you we see the commitment of our country, and timeless virtues that have served our nation well.

We see your sense of duty—including those who have earned their right shoulder patch—their right shoulder combat patches, like the soldier who suffered a grenade wound in Iraq, yet still helped his fellow soldiers to evacuate—your First Captain of the Corps of Cadets, Tyler Gordy. We see your sense of honor—in your respect for tradition, knowing that you join a Long Grey Line that stretches through the centuries; and in your reverence for each other, as when the Corps stands in silence every time a former cadet makes the ultimate sacrifice for our nation. Indeed, today we honor the 78 graduates of this Academy who have given their lives for our freedom and our security in Iraq and Afghanistan.

And we see your love of country—in a devotion to America captured in the motto you chose as a class, a motto which will guide your lives of service: "Loyal 'Til the End." Duty. Honor. Love of country. Everything you have learned here, all that you've achieved here, has prepared you for today—when you raise your right hand; when you take that oath; when your loved one or mentor pins those gold bars on your shoulders; when you become, at long last, commissioned officers in the United States Army.

This is the ninth consecutive commencement that has taken place at West Point with our nation at war. This time of war began in Afghanistan—a place that may seem as far away from this peaceful bend in the Hudson River as anywhere on Earth. The war began only because our own cities and civilians were attacked by violent extremists who plotted from a distant place, and it continues only because that plotting persists to this day.

For many years, our focus was on Iraq. And year after year, our troops faced a set of challenges there that were as daunting as they were complex. A lesser Army might have seen its spirit broken. But the American military is more resilient than that. Our troops adapted, they persisted, they partnered with coalition and Iraqi counterparts, and through their competence and creativity and courage, we are poised to end our combat mission in Iraq this summer.

Even as we transition to an Iraqi lead and bring our troops home, our commitment to the Iraqi people endures. We will continue to advise and assist Iraqi security forces, who are already responsible for security in most of the country. And a strong American civilian presence will help Iraqis forge political and economic progress. This will not be a simple task, but this is what success looks like: an Iraq that provides no haven to terrorists; a democratic Iraq that is sovereign and stable and self-reliant.

And as we end the war in Iraq, though, we are pressing forward in Afghanistan. Six months ago, I came to West Point to announce a new strategy for Afghanistan and Pakistan. And I stand here humbled by the knowledge that many of you will soon be serving in harm's way. I assure you, you will go with the full support of a proud and grateful nation.

We face a tough fight in Afghanistan. Any insurgency that is confronted with a direct challenge will turn to new tactics. And from Marja to Kandahar, that is what the Taliban has done through assassination and indiscriminate killing and intimidation. Moreover, any country that has known decades of war will be tested in finding political solutions to its problems, and providing governance that can sustain progress and serve the needs of its people.

So this war has changed over the last nine years, but it's no less important than it was in those days after 9/11. We toppled the Taliban regime—now we must break the momentum of a Taliban insurgency and train Afghan security forces. We have supported the election of a sovereign government—now we must strengthen its capacities. We've brought hope to the Afghan people—now we must see that their country does not fall prey to our common enemies. Cadets, there will be difficult days ahead. We will adapt, we will persist, and I have no doubt that together with our Afghan and international partners, we will succeed in Afghanistan.

Now even as we fight the wars in front of us, we also have to see the horizon beyond these wars—because unlike a terrorist whose goal is to destroy, our future will be defined by what we build. We have to see that horizon, and to get there we must pursue a strategy of national renewal and global leadership. We have to build the sources of America's strength and influence, and shape a world that's more peaceful and more prosperous.

Time and again, Americans have risen to meet and to shape moments of change. This is one of those moments—an era of economic transformation and individual empowerment; of ancient hatreds and new dangers; of emerging powers and new global challenges. And we're going to need all of you to help meet these challenges. You've answered the call. You, and all who wear America's uniform, remain the cornerstone of our national defense, the anchor of global security. And through a period when too many of our institutions have acted irresponsibly, the American military has set a standard of service and sacrifice that is as great as any in this nation's history.

Now the rest of us—the rest of us must do our part. And to do so, we must first recognize that our strength and influence abroad begins with steps we take at home. We must educate our children to compete in an age where knowledge is capital, and the marketplace is global. We must develop clean energy that can power new industry and unbound us from foreign oil and preserve our planet. We have to pursue science and research that unlocks wonders as unforeseen to us today as the microchip and the surface of the moon were a century ago.

Simply put, American innovation must be the foundation of American power—because at no time in human history has a nation of diminished economic vitality maintained its military and political primacy. And so that means that the civilians among us, as parents and community leaders, elected officials, business leaders, we have a role to play. We cannot leave it to those in uniform to defend this country—we have to make sure that America is building on its strengths.

As we build these economic sources of our strength, the second thing we must do is build and integrate the capabilities that can advance our interests, and the common interests of human beings around the world. America's armed forces are adapting to changing times, but your efforts have to be complemented. We will need the renewed engagement of our diplomats, from grand capitals to dangerous outposts. We need development experts who can support Afghan agriculture and help Africans build the capacity to feed themselves. We need intelligence agencies that work seamlessly with their counterparts to unravel plots that run from the mountains of Pakistan to the streets of our cities. We need law enforcement that can strengthen judicial systems abroad, and protect us here at home. And we need first responders who can act swiftly in the event of earthquakes and storms and disease.

The burdens of this century cannot fall on our soldiers alone. It also cannot fall on American shoulders alone. Our adversaries would like to see America sap its strength by overextending our power. And in the past, we've always had the foresight to avoid acting alone. We were part of the most powerful wartime coalition in human history through World War II. We stitched together a community of free nations and institutions to endure and ultimately prevail during a Cold War.

Yes, we are clear-eyed about the shortfalls of our international system. But America has not succeeded by stepping out of the currents of cooperation—we have succeeded by steering those currents in the direction of liberty and justice, so nations thrive by meeting their responsibilities and face consequences when they don't.

So we have to shape an international order that can meet the challenges of our generation. We will be steadfast in strengthening those old alliances that have served us so well, including those who will serve by your side in Afghanistan and around the globe. As influence extends to more countries and capitals, we also have to build new partnerships, and shape stronger international standards and institutions.

This engagement is not an end in itself. The international order we seek is one that can resolve the challenges of our times—countering violent extremism and insurgency; stopping the spread of nuclear weapons and securing nuclear materials; combating a changing climate and sustaining global growth; helping countries feed themselves and care for their sick; preventing conflict and healing wounds. If we are successful in these tasks, that will lessen conflicts around the world. It will be supportive of our efforts by our military to secure our country.

More than anything else, though, our success will be claimed by who we are as a country. This is more important than ever, given the nature of the challenges that we face. Our campaign to disrupt, dismantle, and to defeat al Qaeda is part of an international effort that is necessary and just.

But this is a different kind of war. There will be no simple moment of surrender to mark the journey's end—no armistice, no banner headline. Though we have had more success in eliminating al Qaeda leaders in recent months than in recent years, they will continue to recruit, and plot, and exploit our open society. We see that in bombs that go off in Kabul and Karachi. We see it in attempts to blow up an airliner over Detroit or an SUV in Times Square, even as these failed attacks show that pressure on networks like al Qaeda is forcing them to rely on terrorists with less time and space to train. We see the potential duration of this struggle in al Qaeda's gross distortions of

Islam, their disrespect for human life, and their attempt to prey upon fear and hatred and prejudice.

So the threat will not go away soon, but let's be clear: Al Qaeda and its affiliates are small men on the wrong side of history. They lead no nation. They lead no religion. We need not give in to fear every time a terrorist tries to scare us. We should not discard our freedoms because extremists try to exploit them. We cannot succumb to division because others try to drive us apart. We are the United States of America. We are the United States of America, and we have repaired our union, and faced down fascism, and outlasted communism. We've gone through turmoil, we've gone through Civil War, and we have come out stronger—and we will do so once more.

And I know this to be true because I see the strength and resilience of the American people. Terrorists want to scare us. New Yorkers just go about their lives unafraid. Extremists want a war between America and Islam, but Muslims are part of our national life, including those who serve in our United States Army. Adversaries want to divide us, but we are united by our support for you—soldiers who send a clear message that this country is both the land of the free and the home of the brave.

You know, in an age of instant access to information, a lot of cynicism in the news, it's easy to lose perspective in a flood of pictures and the swirl of political debate. Power and influence can seem to ebb and flow. Wars and grand plans can be deemed won or lost day to day, even hour to hour. As we experience the immediacy of the image of a suffering child or the boasts of a prideful dictator, it's easy to give in to the belief sometimes that human progress has stalled—that events are beyond our control, that change is not possible.

But this nation was founded upon a different notion. We believe, "that all men are created equal, that they are endowed by their Creator with certain unalienable rights that among these are life, liberty and the pursuit of happiness." And that truth has bound us together, a nation populated by people from around the globe, enduring hardship and achieving greatness as one people. And that belief is as true today as it was 200 years ago. It is a belief that has been claimed by people of every race and religion in every region of the world. Can anybody doubt that this belief will be any less true—any less powerful—two years, two decades, or even two centuries from now?

And so a fundamental part of our strategy for our security has to be America's support for those universal rights that formed the creed of our founding. And we will promote these values above all by living them—through our fidelity to the rule of law and our Constitution, even when it's hard; even when we're being attacked; even when we're in the midst of war.

And we will commit ourselves to forever pursuing a more perfect union. Together with our friends and allies, America will always seek a world that extends these rights so that when an individual is being silenced, we aim to be her voice. Where ideas are suppressed, we provide space for open debate. Where democratic institutions take hold, we add a wind at their back.

When humanitarian disaster strikes, we extend a hand. Where human dignity is denied, America opposes poverty and is a source of opportunity. That is who we are. That is what we do. We do so with no illusions. We understand change doesn't come quick. We understand that neither America nor any nation can dictate every outcome beyond its borders. We know that a world of mortal men and women will never be rid of oppression or evil. What we can do, what we must do, is work and reach and fight for the world that we seek—all of us, those in uniform and those who are not.

And in preparing for today, I turned to the world—to the words of Oliver Wendell Holmes. And reflecting on his Civil War experience, he said, and I quote, "To fight out a war you must believe in something and want something with all your might. So must you do to carry anything else to an end worth reaching." Holmes went on, "More than that, you must be willing to commit yourself to a course, perhaps a long and hard one, without being able to foresee exactly where you will come out."

America does not fight for the sake of fighting. We abhor war. As one who has never experienced the field of battle—and I say that with humility, knowing, as General MacArthur said, "the soldier above all others prays for peace"—we fight because we must. We fight to keep our families and communities safe. We fight for the security of our allies and partners, because America believes that we will be safer when our friends are safer; that we will be stronger when the world is more just.

So cadets, a long and hard road awaits you. You go abroad because your service is fundamental to our security back home. You go abroad as representatives of the values that this country was founded upon. And when you inevitably face setbacks—when the fighting is fierce or a village elder is fearful; when the end that you are seeking seems uncertain—think back to West Point.

Here, in this peaceful part of the world, you have drilled and you have studied and come of age in the footsteps of great men and women—Americans who faced times of trial, and who even in victory could not have foreseen the America they helped to build, the world they helped to shape. George Washington was able to free a band of patriots from the rule of an empire, but he could not have foreseen his country growing to include 50 states connecting two oceans.

Grant was able to save a union and see the slaves freed, but he could not have foreseen just how much his country would extend full rights and opportunities to citizens of every color.

Eisenhower was able to see Germany surrender and a former enemy grow into an ally, but he could not have foreseen the Berlin Wall coming down without a shot being fired. Today it is your generation that has borne a heavy burden—soldiers, graduates of this Academy like John Meyer and Greg Ambrosia who have braved enemy fire, protected their units, carried out their missions, earned the commendation of this Army, and of a grateful nation.

From the birth of our existence, America has had a faith in the future—a belief that where we're going is better than where we've been, even when the path ahead is uncertain. To fulfill that promise, generations of Americans have built upon the foundation of our forefathers—finding opportunity, fighting injustice, forging a more perfect union. Our achievement would not be possible without the Long Grey Line that has sacrificed for duty, for honor, for country.

And years from now when you return here, when for you the shadows have grown longer, I have no doubt that you will have added your name to the book of history. I have no doubt that we will have prevailed in the struggles of our times. I have no doubt that your legacy will be an America that has emerged stronger, and a world that is more just, because we are Americans, and our destiny is never written for us, it is written by us, and we are ready to lead once more. Thank you. May God bless you. And may God bless the United States of America.

THE PRESIDENT: Good afternoon, everybody. I want to take this opportunity to update the American people about the situation in Libya. Over the last several weeks, the world has watched events unfold in Libya with hope and alarm. Last month, protesters took to the streets across the country to demand their universal rights, and a government that is accountable to them and responsive to their aspirations. But they were met with an iron fist.

Within days, whole parts of the country declared their independence from a brutal regime, and members of the government serving in Libya and abroad chose to align themselves with the forces of change. Moammar Qaddafi clearly lost the confidence of his own people and the legitimacy to lead.

Instead of respecting the rights of his own people, Qaddafi chose the path of brutal suppression. Innocent civilians were beaten, imprisoned, and in some cases killed. Peaceful protests were forcefully put down. Hospitals were attacked and patients disappeared. A campaign of intimidation and repression began.

In the face of this injustice, the United States and the international community moved swiftly. Sanctions were put in place by the United States and our allies and partners. The U.N. Security Council imposed further sanctions, an arms embargo, and the specter of international accountability for Qaddafi and those around him. Humanitarian assistance was positioned on Libya's borders, and those displaced by the violence received our help. Ample warning was given that Qaddafi needed to stop his

Remarks by the President on the Situation in Libya, The White House, Office of the Press Secretary, February 18, 2011. http://www.whitehouse.gov/the-press-office/2011/03/18/remarks-president-situation-libya.

campaign of repression, or be held accountable. The Arab League and the European Union joined us in calling for an end to violence.

Once again, Qaddafi chose to ignore the will of his people and the international community. Instead, he launched a military campaign against his own people. And there should be no doubt about his intentions, because he himself has made them clear.

For decades, he has demonstrated a willingness to use brute force through his sponsorship of terrorism against the American people as well as others, and through the killings that he has carried out within his own borders. And just yesterday, speaking of the city of Benghazi—a city of roughly 700,000 people—he threatened, and I quote: "We will have no mercy and no pity"—no mercy on his own citizens.

Now, here is why this matters to us. Left unchecked, we have every reason to believe that Qaddafi would commit atrocities against his people. Many thousands could die. A humanitarian crisis would ensue. The entire region could be destabilized, endangering many of our allies and partners. The calls of the Libyan people for help would go unanswered. The democratic values that we stand for would be overrun. Moreover, the words of the international community would be rendered hollow.

And that's why the United States has worked with our allies and partners to shape a strong international response at the United Nations. Our focus has been clear: protecting innocent civilians within Libya, and holding the Qaddafi regime accountable.

Yesterday, in response to a call for action by the Libyan people and the Arab League, the U.N. Security Council passed a strong resolution that demands an end to the violence against citizens. It authorizes the use of force with an explicit commitment to pursue all necessary measures to stop the killing, to include the enforcement of a no-fly zone over Libya. It also strengthens our sanctions and the enforcement of an arms embargo against the Qaddafi regime.

Now, once more, Moammar Qaddafi has a choice. The resolution that passed lays out very clear conditions that must be met. The United States, the United Kingdom, France, and Arab states agree that a cease-fire must be implemented immediately. That means all attacks against civilians must stop. Qaddafi must stop his troops from advancing on Benghazi, pull them back from Ajdabiya, Misrata, and Zawiya, and establish water, electricity and gas supplies to all areas. Humanitarian assistance must be allowed to reach the people of Libya.

Let me be clear, these terms are not negotiable. These terms are not subject to negotiation. If Qaddafi does not comply with the resolution, the international community will impose consequences, and the resolution will be enforced through military action.

In this effort, the United States is prepared to act as part of an international coalition. American leadership is essential, but that does not mean acting alone—it means shaping the conditions for the international community to act together. That's why I have directed Secretary Gates and our military to coordinate their planning, and tomorrow Secretary Clinton will travel to Paris for a meeting with our European allies and Arab partners about the enforcement of Resolution 1973.

We will provide the unique capabilities that we can bring to bear to stop the violence against civilians, including enabling our European allies and Arab partners to effectively enforce a no fly zone. I have no doubt that the men and women of our military are capable of carrying out this mission. Once more, they have the thanks of a grateful nation and the admiration of the world.

I also want to be clear about what we will not be doing. The United States is not going to deploy ground troops into Libya. And we are not going to use force to go beyond a well-defined goal—specifically, the protection of civilians in Libya. In the coming weeks, we will continue to help the Libyan people with humanitarian and economic assistance so that they can fulfill their aspirations peacefully.

Now, the United States did not seek this outcome. Our decisions have been driven by Qaddafi's refusal to respect the rights of his people, and the potential for mass murder of innocent civilians. It is not an action that we will pursue alone. Indeed, our British and French allies, and members of the Arab League, have already committed to take a leadership role in the enforcement of this resolution, just as they were instrumental in pursuing it. We are coordinating closely with them. And this is precisely how the international community should work, as more nations bear both the responsibility and the cost of enforcing international law.

This is just one more chapter in the change that is unfolding across the Middle East and North Africa. From the beginning of these protests, we have made it clear that we are opposed to violence. We have made clear our support for a set of universal values, and our support for the political and economic change that the people of the region deserve. But I want to be clear: the change in the region will not and cannot be imposed by the United States or any foreign power; ultimately, it will be driven by the people of the Arab World. It is their right and their responsibility to determine their own destiny.

Let me close by saying that there is no decision I face as your Commander in Chief that I consider as carefully as the decision to ask our men and women to use military force. Particularly at a time when our military is fighting in Afghanistan and winding down our activities in Iraq, that decision is only made more difficult. But the United States of America will not stand idly by in the face of actions that undermine global peace and security. So I have taken this decision with the confidence that action is necessary, and that we will not be acting alone. Our goal is focused, our cause is just, and our coalition is strong. Thank you very much.

THE PRESIDENT: Good evening. Tonight, I can report to the American people and to the world that the United States has conducted an operation that killed Osama bin Laden, the leader of al Qaeda, and a terrorist who's responsible for the murder of thousands of innocent men, women, and children.

It was nearly ten years ago that a bright September day was darkened by the worst attack on the American people in our history. The images of 9/11 are seared into our national memory—hijacked planes cutting through a cloudless September sky; the twin towers collapsing to the ground; black smoke billowing up from the Pentagon; the wreckage of Flight 93 in Shanksville, Pennsylvania, where the actions of heroic citizens saved even more heartbreak and destruction.

And yet we know that the worst images are those that were unseen to the world. The empty seat at the dinner table. Children who were forced to grow up without their mother or their father. Parents who would never know the feeling of their child's embrace. Nearly 3,000 citizens taken from us, leaving a gaping hole in our hearts.

On September 11, 2001, in our time of grief, the American people came together. We offered our neighbors a hand, and we offered the wounded our blood. We reaffirmed our ties to each other, and our love of community and country. On that day, no matter where we came from, what God we prayed to, or what race or ethnicity we were, we were united as one American family.

We were also united in our resolve to protect our nation and to bring those who committed this vicious attack to justice. We quickly learned that the 9/11 attacks were carried out by al Qaeda—an organization headed by Osama bin Laden, which had openly declared war on the United States and was committed to killing innocents in our country and around the globe. And so we went to war against al Qaeda to protect our citizens, our friends, and our allies. Over the last 10 years, thanks to the tireless and heroic work of our military and our counterterrorism professionals, we've made great strides in that effort. We've disrupted terrorist attacks and strengthened our homeland defense. In Afghanistan, we removed the Taliban government, which had given bin Laden and al Qaeda safe haven and support. And around the globe, we worked with our friends and allies to capture or kill scores of al Qaeda terrorists, including several who were a part of the 9/11 plot.

Yet Osama bin Laden avoided capture and escaped across the Afghan border into Pakistan. Meanwhile, al Qaeda continued to operate from along that border and operate through its affiliates across the world. And so shortly after taking office, I directed Leon Panetta, the director of the CIA, to make the killing or capture of bin Laden the top priority of our war against al Qaeda, even as we continued our broader efforts to disrupt, dismantle, and defeat his network.

Remarks by the President on the Death of Osama bin Laden, White House, Office of the Press Secretary, May 2, 2011. http://www.whitehouse.gov/the-press-office/2011/05/02/remarks-president-osama-bin-laden.

Then, last August, after years of painstaking work by our intelligence community, I was briefed on a possible lead to bin Laden. It was far from certain, and it took many months to run this thread to ground. I met repeatedly with my national security team as we developed more information about the possibility that we had located bin Laden hiding within a compound deep inside of Pakistan. And finally, last week, I determined that we had enough intelligence to take action, and authorized an operation to get Osama bin Laden and bring him to justice.

Today, at my direction, the United States launched a targeted operation against that compound in Abbottabad, Pakistan. A small team of Americans carried out the operation with extraordinary courage and capability. No Americans were harmed. They took care to avoid civilian casualties. After a firefight, they killed Osama bin Laden and took custody of his body.

For over two decades, bin Laden has been al Qaeda's leader and symbol, and has continued to plot attacks against our country and our friends and allies. The death of bin Laden marks the most significant achievement to date in our nation's effort to defeat al Qaeda.

Yet his death does not mark the end of our effort. There's no doubt that al Qaeda will continue to pursue attacks against us. We must—and we will—remain vigilant at home and abroad. As we do, we must also reaffirm that the United States is not—and never will be—at war with Islam. I've made clear, just as President Bush did shortly after 9/11 that our war is not against Islam. Bin Laden was not a Muslim leader; he was a mass murderer of Muslims. Indeed, al Qaeda has slaughtered scores of Muslims in many countries, including our own. So his demise should be welcomed by all who believe in peace and human dignity.

Over the years, I've repeatedly made clear that we would take action within Pakistan if we knew where bin Laden was. That is what we've done. But it's important to note that our counterterrorism cooperation with Pakistan helped lead us to bin Laden and the compound where he was hiding. Indeed, bin Laden had declared war against Pakistan as well, and ordered attacks against the Pakistani people.

Tonight, I called President Zardari, and my team has also spoken with their Pakistani counterparts. They agree that this is a good and historic day for both of our nations. And going forward, it is essential that Pakistan continue to join us in the fight against al Qaeda and its affiliates.

The American people did not choose this fight. It came to our shores, and started with the senseless slaughter of our citizens. After nearly ten years of service, struggle, and sacrifice, we know well the costs of war. These efforts weigh on me every time I, as Commander-in-Chief, have to sign a letter to a family that has lost a loved one, or look into the eyes of a service member who's been gravely wounded.

So Americans understand the costs of war. Yet as a country, we will never tolerate our security being threatened, nor stand idly by when our people have been killed. We will be relentless in defense of our citizens and our friends and allies. We will be true to the values that make us who we are. And on nights like this one, we can say to those families who have lost loved ones to al Qaeda's terror: Justice has been done.

Tonight, we give thanks to the countless intelligence and counterterrorism professionals who've worked tirelessly to achieve this outcome. The American people do not see their work, nor know their names. But tonight, they feel the satisfaction of their work and the result of their pursuit of justice.

We give thanks for the men who carried out this operation, for they exemplify the professionalism, patriotism, and unparalleled courage of those who serve our country. And they are part of a generation that has borne the heaviest share of the burden since that September day.

Finally, let me say to the families who lost loved ones on 9/11 that we have never forgotten your loss, nor wavered in our commitment to see that we do whatever it takes to prevent another attack on our shores.

And tonight, let us think back to the sense of unity that prevailed on 9/11. I know that it has, at times, frayed. Yet today's achievement is a testament to the greatness of our country and the determination of the American people.

The cause of securing our country is not complete. But tonight, we are once again reminded that America can do whatever we set our mind to. That is the story of our history, whether it's the pursuit of prosperity for our people, or the struggle for equality for all our citizens; our commitment to stand up for our values abroad, and our sacrifices to make the world a safer place. Let us remember that we can do these things not just because of wealth or power, but because of who we are: one nation, under God, indivisible, with liberty and justice for all. Thank you. May God bless you. And may God bless the United States of America.